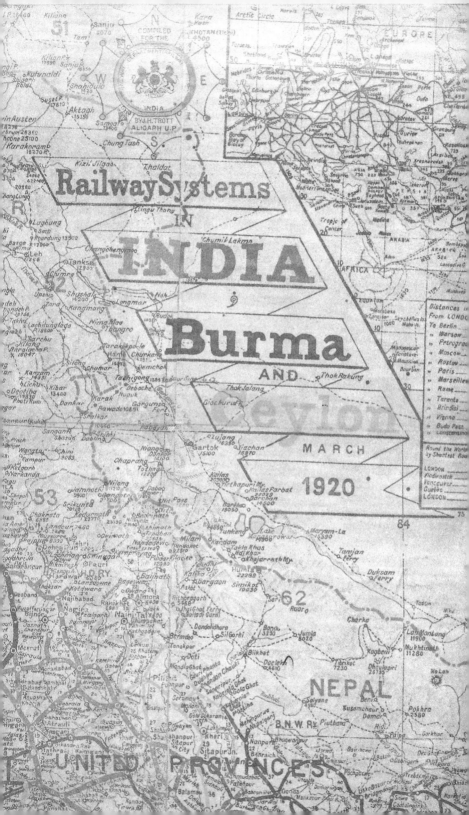

Exploring Indian Railways

Exploring Indian Railways

Bill Aitken

DELHI
OXFORD UNIVERSITY PRESS
BOMBAY CALCUTTA MADRAS
≈≈ 1995 ≈≈

Oxford University Press, Walton Street, Oxford OX2 6DP

Oxford New York
Athens Auckland Bangkok Bombay
Calcutta Cape Town Dar es Salaam Delhi
Florence Hong Kong Istanbul Karachi
Kuala Lumpur Madras Madrid Melbourne
Mexico City Nairobi Paris Singapore
Taipei Tokyo Toronto

and associates in
Berlin Ibadan

ISBN 0 19 563761 5

Printed at A. P. Offset, Delhi 110032
and published by Neil O'Brien, Oxford University Press
YMCA Library Building, Jai Singh Road, New Delhi 110001

To
those who run
Indian Railways

Contents

List of Illustrations

(between pages 164 and 165)

Once the pride of India's steam fleet, this WP–class locomotive, seen at Kazipet, looks distinguished even in its cannibalized state.

Tweed is believed to be the oldest locomotive in the world still at work. It performs seasonal duties at a sugar factory near Gorakhpur in Uttar Pradesh.

CC 682, a North British narrow gauge locomotive, having served faithfully for eighty years, lined up for scrap at Baripada in Orissa.

ZE 95 from the Nainpur shed in Madhya Pradesh collects a pointsman at Mandla Fort before reversing.

Sporting the Bengal Nagpur jubilee crest on its boiler front, this narrow gauge Bagnall tank engine (manufactured *c.* 1920) awaits repairs at Bankura shed. BDR refers to the former Bankura–Damodar River Railway run by McLeod.

The metre gauge YG-class locomotive used for working the Khamblighat gradient edges onto the turntable at Phulad, Rajasthan.

Grandiose but deserted–the southernmost station in India, Kanyakumari in Tamil Nadu.

Cast iron manufacturers' plate acquired from the Delhi Rail Museum by the author.

Two views of the princely family in the Maharaja of Jind's saloon, constructed *c.* 1932.

Bearers wearing traditional Rajasthani turbans standing outside the 'Palace on Wheels' luxury tourist train.

A fireman stoking his metre gauge YG-class locomotive on the western zone.

Northern Railway fitters from Amritsar work on the boiler of Delhi] Museum's most remarkable exhibit, the German locomotive of the forn. Patiala State's monorail system.

ZB 58, a British built locomotive of 1983 vintage rumbles over Karzan bridge into Rajpipla, a former princely state now part of Gujarat.

Thanks partly to a diet of shale, white smoke belches from the chimney of a YG-class locomotive as it eases its rake of seven coaches down the side of the Aravalli Hills in Rajasthan.

Two locally built (and badly sprung) diesel railcars cross at Chintamani on the former Kolar Gold Fields line.

A kilometre post on the narrow gauge Satpura line indicating the distance from the former headquarters of the Bengal Nagpur Railway company in Calcutta.

A selection of tickets from Indian Railways narrow gauge and metre gauge lines.

Preface

These amateur researches amount to a lilliputian exercise when viewed against the enormity of the subject. The many pleasures (and a few pains) recorded suffer from the added disadvantage of stemming from one who neither has any railway background nor any family interest in India. Accustomed to travel first as a student of subcontinental religion and then as a lover of Indian ways, one could not help but feel indignant at hearing regular complaints about the inefficiency of *all* government concerns. I felt strongly that some justice was due to the biggest exception, Indian Railways. Not being a very efficient person myself I could easily identify with the challenges faced by a vast collective of outflung parts and rather than write off India's biggest employer as an amorphous monster of faceless anonymity I preferred to see it as a rugged, faithful vehicle with undeniable and visible virtues daily on display.

Government-run railways do not live by revenue alone and I find a remarkably widespread if unarticulated public affection for the distinctive music of Indian Railways. These casual (but honestly-won) findings are presented in the hope they will encourage other lovers of the iron horse to share their stimulating encounters with India's endlessly fascinating permanent way.

A layman interested in railway matters sometimes has his breath taken away at the sudden veering in policy and my observations were made when fiscal realties deemed it wiser to upgrade the metre gauge rather than divert scarce resources to the costly work of conversion to the broad. Now out of the blue Indian Railways has done a U-turn in its thinking and a flurry of 'unigauge' foundation stones have been laid under the aegis of a railway minister who hails—like the prime minister who blessed the ceremonies—from the metric south. This overnight switch reflects India's readiness to ditch the Nehruvian socialist model of dismal creeping gains for the heady prospect of the fast track opened up by a new market economy. It seems that the end of the steam age in India will coincide with a creative spurt to acquire the latest technology.

These explorations of soon obsolete tracks and traction (that have served the nation well for more than a century) are offered in the hope that the sturdy distinctiveness of India's rail heritage will fire more passengers to enjoy the exciting stretch of undiscovered line that lies beyond the next signal.

New Delhi 1993   Bill Aitken

CHAPTER ONE

Iron Virtues

My first encounter with India-made railway engineering occurred
thirty years ago when hitch-hiking overland I saw a plume of black
smoke suspended in the early morning desert air above Zahidan. It
was a case of premature birth since the smoking engine stood on
Iranian soil. After a hellish non-stop day and night ride in the cab of a
fuel tanker from Kerman, we sped clear of the crazy undulating dunes
and in a roseate dawn bore down on something familiarly British
after weeks of exotic exile. To add to the hysteria of the overnight
desert passage, where we were bullied out to push the truck when-
ever it got bogged down in the sand, were the animal screams of the
driver's mate. He was a deaf mute and now, as the old steam engine
hoved into sight, he gargled with pleasure at having outwitted the
desert.

That evening the Pakistan Western Railways train trundled us
gingerly across the khaki wastes as green-belted waiters served trays
of hot, sweet, milky tea and tiny slices of buttered toast to the party of
Persian language students whose reserved compartment I shared.
They were returning to their homes in Quetta (Pakistan) and assured
me that the hospitality of the desert would extend to waiving the fare
of a foreign guest (in return I was asked to conceal a bolt of smuggled
cloth in my rucksack).

After the hardship of the desert passage I was too far gone to appreciate the engineering achievement that got the connecting train
from Quetta across the Bolan Pass. But I will always remember the
crawl over the Indus at Sukkur the following evening through a foot
of water. The river in benign flood was as broad-bosomed as the milk

of subcontinental kindness was constant in supply. It was too big to comprehend and would need several draughts of Alice's magical enlarger to enable me to outgrow the smug, small certainties of an insular upbringing. After thirty years of travelling by rail I still retain the original conviction that for all its faults, Indian Railways (IR) is a marvel of continuing human enterprise. It is a parable—an expression of hope whose virtues I have long wanted to record.

Efficiency is a cold subject, but warmed by subcontinental currents we find that by and large the railways of India do the job for which they were intended. Of few government enterprises can this be said and of such a mammoth undertaking as IR only chaos could be presumed. In a nation beset by teeming problems and averse to growing up to face her challenges, the economic underpinning against sure disaster derives from the unsung movement on the rails. The discipline of a massive labour force organized on bloated outdated socialist theory ought to resemble an army doing its best to prevent retreat turning into rout. But rarely does the vast system suffer from slipping wheels. As a student and regular user of the iron network, I find the criticism of railway functioning grandiloquently outweighed by the pleasures of the permanent way.

It is of the delights and virtues that one sets out to record, and in doing so to suggest that as a modern foreign body appropriated to India's 3000 million year old peninsular granite, there is scope for satisfaction that railway performance guarantees a better chance of her nearly 900 million citizens arriving at their goal. There is no question of viewing the subject merely as a rail enthusiast unconcerned for the human dimension or, worse, as a tourist, who invariably as the privileged guest of a government which dreads a bad press, gets taken for a ride—sometimes palatially. We travel as an ordinary fare-paying passenger, availing of concessions only when and where in force. The danger of accepting official benison is that the subcontinental conventions of loyalty will only allow nice things to be said of one's sponsors and though we will be at pains to show the strengths of Indian Railways, the best way to insure against further excellence would be to downpeddle the deficiencies. Not only does the free air-conditioned class ticket mitigate against the blast of personal expression but the immured passenger is cut off from the passing scene by the dark and double glazing.

As a parable of India and her ability to accommodate new ideas, the railways might be looked upon in the light of a mildly religious intrusion, a small dose of practical alchemy. Certainly, in the life of the subcontinent the railways are much more evident than in most cultures. Not a day passes without a series of railway references in the newspapers. There are tender notices for urgent technological assistance in carriage works, diesel loco factories or axle plants. Recently the position of train reservations has been introduced to tell you the waiting list position for main line trains 'it does not necessarily mean that reservation is available on all subsequent dates'. Often, in an age where India's masses are agitating for or against various causes, the railway stock takes the brunt of public fury as the undisputed symbol of central power. What the metropolitan bus fleets are to frustrated middle-class students, who torch them in protest against inadequate transport facilities, the railway carriage is to the lumpen rural citizen—a rust-coloured rag to destructive frenzy. The news regularly reads of *rail roko* (stop the trains) agitations and in reply the railway minister inserts advertisements appealing to those 'better instincts' that, by definition, a mob is not presumed to possess.

Occasionally crime creeps into the railway column, and vigilant spotters of moral decay give us the headline—'corrupt officials nabbed'—in this case a senior divisional engineer in league with a senior divisional accounts officer who were alleged to have defrauded the exchequer of 70 lakh rupees through the innocent sounding 'painting of rails'. Violent crime is not unknown either and the Kalka Mail not long ago was witness to a murder, or at least a body in a trunk, which was found in a detached coach sent to the 'washing line' at New Delhi station. The railway police summoned a tailor from his *Star and Style* shack in Purulia in outback Bengal on the strength of a label found on the dead man's trousers. This led to the culprits being tracked down. One of them turned out to be an engine driver. It was his idea to avail of the passing mail train in order to dispose of the evidence.

The Daily Impact of Railway Matters

In a single day there can be a dozen references to railway happenings in a Delhi newspaper. You may spot an essay competition on the theme 'Discovery of India by Rail' inserted by the Institute of Rail Transport, followed by a news item deploring the fact that the findings of a commission of enquiry to look into the police firing at Silchar (Assam) railway station in 1961 have still not been made public. Another indignant opinion is expressed in the Letters to the Editor column, where a non-resident Indian deplores the primitive discharge of toilets on moving trains and demands septic tanks instead, so as to produce manure and biogas at the end of the line. On the 'Op-ed' page is found a question in Parliament concerning terrorist attacks on railway assets which vie with legal agitations in the scope of their damage. On the back page the Railways are sure to feature in some sporting success, maybe a marathon runner first home, or a victorious hockey team. From sprinting queens to weightlifting vassals, sport is an activity railwaymen enthusiastically respond to.

For the historically inclined, the small section on '100 years ago' will yield valuable pickings. Of and for the great age of steam the notices range from the mofussil (upcountry) letter of October 1886 announcing the arrival of Kathgodam on the railway map to the 1888 mention of a plan to carry the Darjeeling line west from Bengal into neighbouring Nepal. Kathgodam marked the end of the Rohilkhand and Kumaon Railway and is famous for a wind that 'rushes down the hill with great force'. The correspondent, apparently carried away by the metaphor, continues, 'There is now a dak bungalow for the convenience of passengers breaking ... journey.'

The Darjeeling enthusiasm captures the optimism of Victorian engineers who seriously did not see the great mountain chain as an obstacle which could prevent them running a line from Jodhpur in Rajasthan (on the proposed London-Calcutta alignment) to link up with the Trans-Siberian traverse via a proposed Gilgit Junction in the heart of the Karakorams. 'Let the Government spend any money it may ... it will meet with no opposition from ourselves', wrote the editor grandly. He then went on to expound a familiar axiom: 'The railway is the great civilising agency of our time.'

A more lurid news item of September 1885 originating from the holy cave of Amarnath in Kashmir illustrates our belief in the alchemical nature of railways in Hindustan. The story is told of Lt.-Col. Cuppage, who visited the cave as a tourist and 'thought it no desecretion to chip off some bits (of the sacred *lingam*) to cool our brandy and water at luncheon.' Within a few years the rash presumption of the insensitive white officer was visited with terrible retribution. 'In a fit of insanity he placed his head on the lines of the Ulster Railway and a passing train severed his soul to be dealt with by the outraged deity.'

A Theological Enquiry into Railways

So pervasive in fact is railway lore in the everyday life of India that a theologian cannot be blamed for invoking comparisons with that rare entity of the highest Hindu speculation, the *atman*. The Victorians were not averse to co-opting God into their schemes for the mechanical evangelization of the globe. The Eiffel Tower, that vulgar stanchion in the arch of heaven, inevitably had been designed by a railway engineer. The early accusation of godlessness to the iron charger was dropped after Queen Victoria rode to Windsor on the Great Western. Several tombstones bear witness to the Christian pursuit inherent in the straight way. In the cloister of Ely Cathedral is a typical example of the railway faith worked into Anglican theology (admittedly of a Low Church type). Captioned 'The Spiritual Railway' (1845) it wins no prizes for ease of scanning: 'God's Word is the first Engineer/God's Love the Fire, his Truth the Steam/In First and Second and Third Class/Come then poor Sinners, now's the time/At any station on the line.' Another Midlands grave mourned more mechanically: 'My valves are now thrown open wide/My flanges all refuse to guide/My steam is now condensed in death.'

Virtue soon clouded the brows of our civilizing agent and the Victoria Terminus at Bombay is the splendid culmination of the canonization of steam. Every inch a cathedral, the VT is in fact the biggest nine-teenth century structure in Asia. Inevitably its very nobleness irritated one vicereine who felt it was 'too good for the natives.'

The *atman* by definition is beyond structure and some would claim it is so elusive that nebulousness is nearer to the grasp than the tediously infinite denials of the *neti neti* ('not this') school. But then breath itself is a pretty elusive matter though each of us depend on it by the moment. To define a reality is only to declare we have no part in it. According to the Upanishadic notions the *atman* shines eternally. Immediately our comparison with the railway falls back, mocked by the worn out flanges of a decidedly impermanent way. However, in the sense of an underlying benevolent force all the time at work to further the destiny of men, there is a sympathetic rail relationship with the rare and undying Soul of the universe. For example, to climb down from the heights of theoretical Hinduism to its daily applications, we find that Indian Railways is one of the very few organizations free of obvious caste. Like the Realized Consciousness, its motion is beyond the limitations of social station and the stultifying accidence of birth. On the other hand, many of the complaints against the Railways for their procrastinating rigmarole derive from the inbred handlessness of caste superstitions. It is easier to avoid a decision and pass the problem to another department rather than risk appearing assertive and upset the ordained stacking of the apple cart.

Our analogy breaks down over hierarchy since the *atman* soars free of all divisions and railway working depends on a division of roles. Nevertheless, as a working proposition—and there is nothing in the inherent perfection of the *atman* that could lend support to the doctrinally convenient contempt of manual activity that the brahmanical order has foisted on society in the name of Hinduism—we can detect in the nation's greatest machine echoes of an underlying spirit that performs its duty selflessly, its parts reflecting the order and purposefulness of a conscious whole. A literal rendering of classical Hinduism's *Sanatana Dharma* could be 'the permanent way'.

Some might argue that the more cut and dried dogma of the monotheistic faiths are apter symbols of a railway creed where destiny is viewed in predetermined grooves. God as an active intervener in human affairs shows his hand in the mechanical improvement of his creation. The fact remains that in the Indian setting the efficiency of the railway system is as unlikely as it is inscrutable and all the feel of a numinous force that operates in defiance of the expected result suggests something more than a mere hidden hand behind the controls. It has to be more than a lurking genius to oversee the expansiveness of such an infinite exercise, and for this reason the all-enveloping nature of the *atman* seems to fit our study more nearly than the exclusive norms of the Palestinian divine experience which forever tends to narrow down rather than sublimate the human urge to share space with the central power from which all derives.

The Railways as Social Reformer

The sociological impact of an unswerving metalled track on our subconscious has hardly been inquired into, let alone the theological implications of making straight the way—a favourite prophetical allusion to the sort of approach that leads to the Kingdom of God. Come to think of it, it is odd that the stagnant combination of cabined mortals confined to a fixed gauge and limited gait should have heralded a revolution that hastened the unshackling of human bonds. By all mechanical laws the result of railways should have been to speed up the intercourse of commerce but leave untouched the feudal equation whereby the mine owners, now able to dig deeper thanks to steam pumps, would continue to pay the labour at the old rates since the miners no longer got their feet wet.

But from the mere laying of parallel rods arose the genie of Democracy uncorked by the liberating pulse of steam locomotion. Saturated steam expands a miraculous thousandfold and instead of the piston of medieval conduct returning the connecting rod to a passive equilibrium, the escaping hiss of vapour signified a means of escape from the drudgery of the slow past. Conditioned to the draught exertions of the ox and horse at four miles per hour, all sedate notions of time and transport were scrambled when Trevithick got up steam and Stephenson senior fired the *Rocket* to bowl along effortlessly at a near miraculous speed—knocking on to thirty miles an hour. The implications for a stuffy agrarian society beset by brutal inequality were explosive. Cheap transport enabled the yokels to take a day trip to London and see for themselves how their political masters worked. The first Reform Bill happened to follow the Rainhill Trials (where the *Rocket* showed her paces) by two years. 'If this sort of thing is permitted to go on, the nobility will be destroyed' fumed one land-owning Tory, and his apprehension was echoed by Wordsworth's sonnet decrying the 'rash assault' on England's green and privileged land with the coming of the Kendal and Windermere Railway. *John Bull*, with the characteristic forthrightness of insular certainty that history delights to plough under in the scythe of progress, railed against the 'unnatural impetus' of these 'odious deformities' and 'disfiguring abominations'. Ruskin, the aesthetic guru of Mahatma Gandhi, summed up the cheapening of transport with the contemptuous reference that every fool in Buxton could now be in Bakewell in half an hour and every fool in Bakewell at Buxton. This was echoed by the Duke of Wellington's anxiety at the prospect of the lower orders becoming mobile. The cautious revising of opinion by the Establishment was seen in the turnaround of Eton attitudes when the headmaster Dr John Keate had ferociously resisted a station at Windsor. But he was soon vociferously clamouring for Mr Gladstone to lay on a special train from Slough to take loyal pupils to the Queen's coronation. Amusingly, amongst the misplaced apprehensions of savage conservatism, a scientific case was made out that the reason passengers dozed off in trains was due to incipient concussion caused by the motion of the wheels. Tunnels came in for grave and dramatic speculation on their malevolent properties and later the London Underground would be opposed by clergymen on the grounds that it would release the brimstone and fire stoked by the adherents of Old Nick.

A Rail Excursion with Dr Lardner

The most delightful reprover of newfangledism was Dr Dionysius Lardner, D. C. L. etc., who in 1850 published a treatise on the new art of transport called *Railway Economy*. This work, 'intended to fill a void in our industrial literature', does it most entertainingly and manages to fill a void in our psychological understanding too, with some original prescriptions against the disasters imagined to be soon unleashed by the coming of the railroad. Of these, the most minor must refer to the lost property department. Dr Lardner is astonished at the spectacle of red cloaks, shawls, scarves and tartan plaids and marvels that 'surely English ladies of all ages who wear red shawls cloaks &c. must in some mysterious way or other be powerfully affected by the whine of compressed air, by the sudden ringing of a bell, by the various conflicting emotions that disturb the human heart on arriving at Euston station, for how else we gravely asked ourselves, could we possibly account for the extraordinary red mass before us?' But what astonished him above all was 'that some honest Scotsman probably in the ecstasy of seeing among the crowd the face of his faithful Jeanie had actually left behind him the best portion of his bagpipes.'

The good doctor of transport, still in the area of lesser miseries, details under the heading 'Railway Refreshment Rooms' the 'squabbles about the bill, the wretchedness of the fare and the indefinite craving of the waiters.' These however he assures us were the scourges of the stage-coach age and 'are now consigned to the novelist and the historian'. (Dickens had described prototype British Rail fare as 'composed of glutinous lumps of gristle of unknown animals within'.)

Moving on to more disaster-prone areas our precise and observant guide sets out some 'Plain Rules for Railway Travellers'. Majestically logical, they combine in upper case the utmost caution with the minimum degree of inconvenience: 'EXPRESS TRAINS ARE ATTENDED WITH MORE DANGER THAN ORDINARY TRAINS. THOSE WHO DESIRE THE GREATEST DEGREE OF SECURITY SHOULD USE THEM ONLY WHEN GREAT SPEED IS REQUIRED'. In another equally reasoned equation of balanced risk the travelling public is advised to 'BEWARE OF YIELDING TO THE SUDDEN IMPULSE TO SPRING FROM THE CARRIAGE TO RECOVER YOUR HAT WHICH HAS BLOWN OFF'. To hammer home the danger the doctor enlarges and provides examples. 'It would appear that there is an instinctive impulse, which in some individuals is almost irresistible, to leap from a train to recover their hats when blown off or accidentally dropped'.

Almost as bad is the urge of hatless lineside residents to respond to the railway mania of the age they lived in: 'persons on or near railways appear to be seized with a delirium or fascination which determines their will by an irresistible impulse to throw themselves under an approaching train. Cases of this kind occur so frequently as cannot be adequately explained by predisposition to suicide'. The implied sinister, maddening effect of the railways continued at least up to 1908 when Mahatma Gandhi denounced in *Hind Swaraj* the collective culpability of these inhuman inventions that conveyed evil to the remotest hamlet. 'Railways accentuate the evil nature of man. Bad men fulfil their evil designs with greater rapidity. It may be a debatable matter whether railways spread famine but it is beyond dispute that they propagate evil'. If it is any comfort to lovers of the iron horse, the Mahatma was equally severe on the contribution of lawyers and doctors to the prompt degradation of society. 'It is machinery that has impoverished India' continued the Mahatma, 'It is necessary to realise that machinery is bad'.

Mahatma Gandhi's Bad Trip

When a revised edition of this, his core teaching, was issued in 1938 the author made no attempt to tone down his denunciation of modern civilization, diseased by its mechanical addictions. When it was pointed out that the spinning wheel was a machine—as was the human form that propelled it—the wily lawyer adopted the extreme mystical posture of Hinduism and couched it typically so that the reply sounded spiritually profound without actually saying anything: 'Ideally I would rule out all machinery even as I would reject this very body, which is not helpful to salvation'. So much for Gandhian theory. His nationalist movement that bred independence was in large measure furthered through whistle-stop tours by Congress leaders. The base at Sevagram from where his philosophy radiated was conveniently sited near India's most centrally placed railway junction. For one who declared that, 'We cannot tolerate the idea of spending money on railways', the greater part of his political mileage derived from clever exploitation of the system that got both him and his message to the common man at stations along the whole length of the country. Perhaps the most contradictory position of all lay in the fact that Gandhiji had penned his diatribe against steam locomotion on his return voyage from London to South Africa. The latest edition of *Hind Swaraj* shows an idealized portrait of the Mahatma writing the book cross-legged in the heart of rural *Bharat* but it was actually written to the throb of pounding pistons on board a steam-driven ship.

As it happened, Gandhiji's quest for national self-respect was launched by a railway incident in South Africa. A week after arriving in Durban from India he travelled on an overnight train for Pretoria, and following his *baniya* instincts, dispensed with the normal custom of first class passengers to hire bedding. At Maritzburg, a white passenger complained at this departure from convention and because of his colour the non-conforming visitor found himself forcibly detrained. That cold winter night of 1893, a decision to fight back against racial injustice was taken by Gandhi as he shivered on a bleak railway station platform. It is small wonder that the railway system would earn the wrath of the Mahatma when he came to pen his cure for colonial arrogance.

It could be argued that unconscious resistance to mechanical work betrayed the Mahatma's allegiance to the traditional twice-born distaste for manual involvement. It is significant that a favourite expression still in vogue amongst those placed highly enough in Indian society to run no risk of having to do any, is the Mahatma's belief in 'the dignity of labour'. What is noticeable in the use of a word like 'dignity' is the attempt to pass off an unpleasant activity as something ennobling. Religions other than Hinduism have no need to bail out the unfortunate necessity for human sweat since they do not posit a class of pundits born to have their dirty work done for them by lower orders. Whereas both Islam and Christianity start from the imperfection of man who is born to strive towards the perfect heaven that is God, Hinduism sees life as the overflowing of perfect divine bliss, and the human quest as a pilgrimage to the source of that perfection. Both are agreed about the goal but the means to get there differ. The transcendental concerns of the monotheists see material improvements to the universe as signs of divine approval while the one-pointed disinterest of the polytheist in the ephemerality of surface illusion finds in the doctrine of transmigration enough excuse to postpone any over-energetic encounter with immediate physical reality. Putting off unto the morrow has climatic backing to add to the respectable theology of delay.

Nowhere do we find in Sanskritic culture the notion that work is enjoyable for its own sake and that inventions to save on drudgery are the mark of inspiration. The first virtue to be extracted for Indian Railways is that, in the midst of hostile theological territory that despises working parts, and beset by a society that values the mechanical eunuch, it has managed to overcome the inherent *tamas* (apathy) of disdainful twice-born attitudes.

CHAPTER TWO

Laying the Lines

In China the onset of the railway age resulted in a reaction of physical fury. Twenty years after lines were laid in India, the Chinese experiment turned sour and in 1877 the track had to be torn up to appease the opposition of superstitious elders and agitating coolies who felt their jobs were threatened. In India brahmanical opposition to Western science was based not on reaction to technological developments but to the fear that government-sponsored railways would mean the likelihood of more Christian influence at work. They did not fear so much the LMS of the London, Midland and Scottish Railway as that of the 'London Missionary Society'. In point of fact they had good reason to view the advance of steam propulsion as the turn of the evangelistic screw. The early British traders, concerned only to shake the Pagoda tree, had been content to adopt native customs and enjoy the relaxed lifestyle of India's comparatively laid-back morality. All this changed when colonial policy stiffened and religion began to be pumped in to swell the pomp of empire.

As *Every Boy's Book of Railways and Steamships,* published by the Religious Tract Society of London, puts it: 'Into whatever part of the world the white man penetrates he takes the gospel with him'. Hastened on his way to the conquest of the heathen by the agency of steam, the missionary thanks the Almighty for having 'smote for us a pathway to the ends of all the earth'. The LMS commissioned from children's donations several missionary steamboats under the name of John Williams, the pioneer proselytiser of the South Seas who was martyred in 1839. Surprisingly, no historian has seen fit to view these Victorian Protestant activities as a mild economic version of the medieval Children's Crusade.

Orthodox Hindu Attitudes to the Railways

When the Chinese authorities hastily passed on their uprooted lines to Formosa in the hope of appeasing outraged ancestral custom, how was it that the brahmanical lobby in India did not rise in wrath against the imposition of the impure railway line of the *mlecchas*—especially when it indulged in such spectacularly unholy practices as over-shadowing the waters of sacred rivers by means of base metalled girders? According to the 'discursive notes' of the Bengal Civilian William Crooke in *Things Indian*, the railways actually stimulated Hindu pilgrim traffic and it followed that the brahmins would not be averse to an increase in their takings. It might be remembered that in the building of the Ganga Canal by Colonel Cautley where the very course of India's holiest river was to be diverted, the priests of Hardwar were won over by Cautley's dynamic enthusiasm that extended to the construction of extremely aesthetic ghats alongside the new alignment. More important for the priestly caste who made their living from catering to pilgrim needs, the canal bank conveniently took off just south of the Ganga Mai temple at Har ki Pairi and being solidly *pucca* would admit of lines of admirably accessible *dharmshalas* (religious rest-houses) along the redesigned river front. This caused them to overlook the fact that Cautley's diggers belonged to the outcaste Ods—or perhaps they accepted that the iron in the girders of empire was the best evidence of *Kali Yuga* (the iron age of Hinduism) having arrived.

Railway historians point out the massive fortifications built into the ends of the Ganga bridges which came up after the Mutiny. The 1857 uprising has so far evaded adequate labelling since its motivation was prompted by deeper forces than mere insubordination and it occurred when the concept of nationalism would have been as bewildering to the feudal defenders of ancient religious tradition as the ferocity of the outraged sepoys was to the astonished officers of the East India Company. It is assumed that having overcome the setback to their civilizing mission the British forced the railways on an India unable to resist her forceful masters after the Mutiny. That this could not be the whole truth is vouched for by the fact that the railways had got off to a fairly smooth start four years before the Golden Calm was shattered. Neither is there evidence that filthy foreign (*mleccha*) technology was opposed in principle nor that the onset of railway running had triggered off the Mutiny. One is inclined to believe that the traditional openness of the Hindu mind and its willingness to experiment would have led it to assess this foreign body planted in its midst and (unlike the Chinese reaction to reject from instinct) assimilate what could be used profitably to advertise traditional *dharma*.

Undoubtedly resistance to the modernization of Indian society was the basic background factor to the outbreak of the sepoy insurrection. The sudden notions of speedier communications sprung by Dalhousie might just have escaped censure had they not coincided with the anti-Hindu inputs of evangelistic Christianity and the even more fundamental prejudices that landed with the 'fishing fleet'. This refers to the racialism the English miss-sahibs brought with them that swelled with their memsahib status. Sex is a more primal pull than religion and it is on these uncharted rocks that the armada of British self-righteousness most likely floundered. The early Company nabobs had no problem adapting to the local way of doing things, yet when Indians aped the British they could (and still can) only expect to be laughed at. Any colonizing nation operating on such 'heads I win, tails you lose' principle was headed for dangerous shoals when it insisted on raising the flag of morality.

The Incomparable Investment of Dalhousie

Dalhousie's contribution to Indian Railways probably remains the most valuable though after a century and a half Indian railwaymen are still slightly reluctant to acknowledge his genius. In the (few) railway histories put out from the subcontinent, though Dalhousie does not receive any unfavourable mention, no effort is made to stress the fortuitousness for India in having a railway expert at the helm for the crucial pioneering stages. It is both interesting and telling to compare the assessments of Dalhousie by British and Indian railwaymen. Generally the former will be of a more mechanical persuasion, concerned about heated axles and quite ready to remove their jackets to apply some grease. The latter, even if they have the knowledge to reduce the friction, will be apt from conditioning to delegate the manual solution to a menial, justifying this non-involvement as a *karmic* means to afford a humble man a job. The intrinsic self-righteousness detected in official British attitudes happens to be exactly matched by the aloof brahmanical attitudes inherent in the structure of Indian Railways. The resulting pompousness is well brought out in a popular history where a famous Indian railway administrator (perhaps to cover up for the embarrassment of India not owning any ancient railway system in Sanskrit literature) comes up with the bullock cart 'trains' used to build the Taj Mahal, as an example of local transport genius, in what he calls 'the world's first circular railway'. Patently it is not a railway since the bullock carts ran on a road—albeit grooved to guide the cart wheels. The Greeks had used this device for their roads and the world may well have derived its 'standard gauge' for railways from the width of the axle between Roman chariots. But it is extremely unlikely that any Italian rail historian would make claims for the Appian Way to have been the forerunner of the *Ferrovie dello Stato*.

What is even more intriguing about such inventive side-tracking is how short-lived a thing history can be in the fast-changing politics of the subcontinent. Today the bullock-cart trains of Shah Jahan might face the accusation of not being truly 'Indian' since the Mughal dynasty originated beyond the confines of Hindustan. The rail enthusiast will do well in the Indian setting to confine himself to the visible evidence of nuts and bolts and learn to swallow the proposition that patriotism as an inexact science can easily fill in those voids that history, stretched to its fullness, fails to bridge.

The fact remains that the blueprint for Indian Railways was drawn up by an expert. On rail matters Dalhousie was not a mere administrator but an arbitrator equipped with deep lore, having in his capacity as President of the Board of Trade in England witnessed the suicidal wranglings of competing companies and in particular the stultifying effects of the gauge war. By Dalhousie's accumulated transport wisdom, Indian Railways were saved the costly mismanagement problems that caused so many European rail investors to find themselves at the end of a shifting rainbow—without their shirts.

The First Locomotives

Though it is customary to date the beginning of Indian Railways from 15.35 hrs. on the afternoon of 16 April 1853—as three locomotives, *Sindh, Sultan* and *Sahib* hauled fourteen coaches out of Bori Bunder, the fact is that another locomotive called *Thomason* (after a dynamic administrator of the Punjab) had started work near Roorkee on 22 December 1851. Apparently she was the first example of a colonial 'lemon', having been palmed off abroad for failing to live up to her promise at home. Today in Roorkee when you escape the jam of the bazaar and find yourself outstared by Captain Cautley's rather familiar lions guarding the bridge over the Ganga Canal (they were the models for Trafalgar Square), a sharp turn north brings you to a delightful canal-side road that follows the flow for several regal miles, with further lions (more couchant than rampant) leading on to Hardwar. In the cold air of winter the blue of the canal contrasts with the gleaming array of white Himalayan peaks in the background.

This road represents the acceptable face of Victorian engineering enterprise. Cautley's ability to beat both the objections of the Company's auditors and the priestly *pandas* of the holy bathing *ghats* argues of a man of unusual vision and determination. At the very outset of this grand and aesthetic undertaking, from Roorkee you cross the Solanki Viaduct which is the canal leaping over a drop in the countryside outside the town as though imitating the flying locks of Shiva on which the Ganga fell to bless the land. Had Cautley been more conventional in his interests and preferred the fishing fleet to Shivalik fossils, this happy canal that retrieves the reputation of later colonials would have involved less labour and little of the love it now possesses. For steam historians this viaduct was the scene of India's first locomotive at work. Alas *Thomason* proved to be more of a hindrance than a help to the construction work and those who had reassembled her parts, presumably humped by camel and bullock to Roorkee from the barges by which she had been floated up from

Calcutta, were said to have rejoiced when her boiler blew up. This final outcome to white man's magic enabled everyone to get on with the job. I was told that the boiler is still preserved in the Roorkee University museum but when I went to visit the campus—a fine sight whose architecture (approved by Dalhousie) made up for any later disappointment—it happened to be a 'second Saturday'. This, translated into the work culture of Uttar Pradesh, means that everything moves even slower than usual. I ended up being shown a marble bust of Mr Thomason, the father of the PWD. Had I been a genuine gricer I might have burst my own boiler.

The Place of Chini in Rail History

A good case can be made out for the true genesis of Indian railways having been launched from Lord Dalhousie's summer retreat, where he wrote his first minute on 4 July 1850. This Scots marquess, apart from his railway knowledge, seems to have been gifted with insights into the pick of Himalayan scenery. Not content with having discovered the hill-station called after his name in the north-west of Himachal, he traversed probingly along the Indo-Tibet road in the south-east to find an even more dramatic—and temperate—solution to his hot-weather needs. Facing the sacred summit of Kinner Kailash in a jagged run of peaks guarding the Tibetan border, Dalhousie plumped for the forest bungalow at Chini, a village amidst ageless deodar trees that look out on to the snows a hand's breadth away across the booming gorge of the Sutlej.

For a Scotsman it was a bit like coming home, especially to a hunting and fishing laird. Kinnaur adds to its sensational mountain slopes and well-stocked trout rivers a kindly and independent people who wear their Himachali caps at a jaunty angle to declare themselves borderers with their own way of doing things. For example their grape brandy is renowned, although official prudish policy pretends the daily intake is an aberration. Such embarrassments are conveniently erased by the fact that Kinnaur is now a restricted area for security reasons. In 1962 after the Chinese moves into the Indian Himalaya, the village of Chini was promptly converted into Kalpa though as I found out when I visited it, the original village continues to go by its old name locally some thirty years later.

The forest bungalow has been converted into a circuit house (surely one of the smallest in India) but the visitor can still detect the original lines, for example in the planked ceiling. As expected after the stiff climb from Rekong Peo (which, downhill of Kalpa, has now become the district headquarters of Kinnaur), I found the bungalow declared itself by the sound of a gushing stream of perennial water right above its placement. On the walk up I climbed through embarrassingly prosperous orchards where the lush lifestyle of these prolific slopes, sheltered from a monsoon exhausted by the piercing ridges of the Sutlej, gave the feel of a paradise rarely found in modern India. However, I was detained an extra day in Peo owing to a strike of fruit growers. Not even the Garden of Eden, it seems, can escape the wrath of the unions. Had our first parent transgressed in these latter days and been evicted along with his wife's slim wardrobe, no doubt a tribunal would have reinstated them pending a more equitable settlement to the hash they had made of their work-load.

Queen Victoria was fully apprised of the goings on in Chini, her erstwhile lady in waiting becoming the wife of 'Clemency' Canning. Lady Canning had visited Chini after the Mutiny on hearing of its beauties from Lord Dalhousie, her husband's predecessor. In her letters and sketches to the Queen she has conveyed the impressiveness of the wild gorge country wherein Indian Railways was conceived. Now in the National Archives the beautifully written minute of Dalhousie, actually a manuscript running into more than fifty foolscap pages (penned in immaculate copper-plate handwriting) outlined both the emphasis and pitfalls that the learned governor-general felt needed urgent attention. In a later minute he was to write about the 'three great engines of social improvement—Railways, uniform Postage and the Electric Telegraph'—which he had consciously striven to borrow from a western context and apply to India in the belief that such instruments to hasten modernity were in India's best long-term interests.

The Lat-Sahib's Limitations

Dalhousie's assessment was to prove exactly as he had hoped. Few will deny his conviction that in conferring the railways on India, England had bestowed her greatest boon, albeit accidentally. (The greatest boon according to Indian reckoning lay another century ahead when independence could no longer be denied her.) The shadow side of the Lat Sahib's arrogant paternalism was clearly seen in the acquisitive Doctrine of Lapse which led to the build-up of the Mutiny. The conceit that a mix of Victorian engineering skills and white morality was just what the Great Physician Above would have prescribed for natives reeling under the debauched rule of bejewelled princes and harem-besotted nawabs clouded the governor-general's understanding of the finite resilience of Indian society. His reforms where they were practical were seized upon and ran quickly into an Indian edition. But where he misread the stretch of Indian patience in defending her cultural norms, they bounced back on British heads with interest. Both the Rani of Jhansi and Nana Sahib were aggrieved victims of Dalhousie's highhanded doctrine. To make matters worse the British always made their sleight of hand sound nobly unctuous. A colonial predator lurked in Dalhousie and part of the India of his dreams involved the picking of native pockets for the good of their own darkened souls.

Under the humbug of racial superiority lay the real twitching nerve of economic compulsion. The takeover of Avadh that effectively made the Mutiny inevitable was sparked off by Victorian horror at the extravagant lifestyle of the Lucknow king's depraved court. But the dishonouring of a standing treaty proved that when it came to political depravity the Company's court of directors were not a whit more innocent than Wajid Ali's, though they may have appeared less foppish. The storm unleashed by Dalhousie's rush to reform and turn things Western did not fall on his own head. Was this a sign that destiny judged his motives more kindly than their fallout? The common and oversimplified charge that the railways came to India not as a present from the British government but as a means to further the economic aggrandizement of the home nation though true in practice was not entirely true in theory. A man of Dalhousie's drive and devotion to what he considered to be right can only be considered a humbug in hindsight. If he could not differentiate between the altruism of his motives and the rapacity of his acts it was because of the values of his age. If *sati* and *thugee* were bad, so too was decadent rule by princes more wedded to dissipation than the dispensing of justice. Amidst the cloying self-righteous Victorian certainty of a hotline to God was a thin red line of conviction that hardly goes with cultivated humbug. Judged by his age this nobleman's heart was in the right place and the continuing success of his plans for the development of railways in India is the best testimony to his sound transport instincts.

The single greatest achievement of his plan—though it only lasted nineteen years—was to invest in one gauge for the whole country, that too broader than most railways could aspire to. Though expensive to instal, the 5 ft. 6 ins. gap between the wheels of trunk traffic in India has paid off in the heavier loads carried and moved faster and more safely than on a gauge of narrower dimensions. Almost a foot wider than what has come to be known as the (British) standard gauge of 4 ft. $8\frac{1}{2}$ ins. it was a sensible working compromise between Stephenson's conservative instincts (that failed to distance the iron horse from its wagon-way archetype) and Brunel's revolutionary 7 ft. gauge (that assumed Manchester businessmen would one day see beyond their noses).

The First Train

Sometimes the date 1832 is quoted as the take-off year for Indian Railways, especially by the Tamil lobby which rightly points out that the very first scheme originated from Madras. However, the plan remained on paper and the action might well have started in Bengal had not the locomotive intended for Dalhousie's line to Raniganj (promoted by the East Indian Railway Company) not been delayed at sea. This enabled the Great Indian Peninsular Railway Company (founded in England in 1845) to steal the thunder of first traffickings. Plans for a line out of Bombay had existed on paper since 1843 and a committee of eminent citizens put their weight behind the proposal. The GIP was incorporated by an act of Parliament in 1849 and before the end of the year a chief engineer had been appointed. Within another year the diggings had begun. By February 1852 a shunting engine *Vulcan* was at work striking wonder in the countryside and causing the early artist to get the details all wrong, a curious feature of the pre-scientific mind that continues in India to this day, drawing from instinctive recollection rather than replicate physical reality. (In this instance, the artist was British and he severed the boiler from the grate. Presumably the separation of the fire from the water symbolized an idea not yet grasped. A case could be made that in a technologically illiterate society even the motion of traditional conveyance has never been understood in purely mechanical terms. Only the other day an advertisement in the newspaper, inserted by the chief minister of Uttar Pradesh (with the indecipherable statistics of claimed peasant uplift) was illustrated by a *Bhagavadgita* vintage chariot fronted by suitably snorting horses. Unfortunately for the concept of meaningful progress the horse-power remained unharnessed. It was beyond the artist's understanding to sketch the actual working parts to link the raw energy of the prancing steeds to the motion of the turning wheels. The view remains more magical than peripatetic.

The GIP line was ready by November 1852 and a trial run of its twenty-one miles held on the 18th. When the great day arrived for the official opening five months later, the Bombay *Times* waxed lyrical on the civilizational boon promised by the railway: 'A sun is rising on the darkened land .... The spectacle of wonders manifold'. However poorly it scans the fact that the prosaic parallel laying of lines could call forth any poetry as a response, suggests that locked up in the mundane to-and-fro movement 'converted into rotary motion' lay a universal magic worth recording. Whatever the motivation of the white colonial in laying these lines, their music outran his greed and their inbuilt benevolence outlasted the modification of his imperial desires.

CHAPTER THREE

Spokes in the Wheel

Part of the curious magic of railways is their unifying force and universal appeal. Whatever the species of political ideology under which they operate, the capitalists who built them always seem to end up as out of pocket as the idealists who run them (as in India) as a social service. This even-handedness suggests that the revolutionary switch from the clover of horse-drawn transport to the tender of black gold was a cosmic idea whose time had come. It is surely not an accident that the steam engine coincided with the high noon of Empire and that the world's first steel plant arose from the railway settlement at Crewe.

The most glaring example of colonial exploitation in India was the forced building of the Nizam's Guaranteed State Railway which almost bankrupted the world's richest ruler. With a final flick of the imperial goad the Government of India insisted that the Nizam's only remunerative agrarian lands in Berar (now in Maharashtra) were to remain expropriated on the grounds of military security. The famous Salar Jung whose museum continues to delight all visitors to the Deccan fought heroically to expose the dishonesty of colonial policy, but not even his friends at Buckingham Palace could mitigate the economic grab by the brokers of British hypocrisy. When the American Civil War snuffed out supplies of raw cotton to Manchester, Hyderabad was made an economic pawn to supply the cotton mill lobby with the good quality cotton that the black soil of Berar was famous for.

Contrast in Zonal Rail Profiles

Today, to illustrate the capacity of the railway to bounce back, the

South Central (SC) zone which inherited the Nizam's forced system is one of the best run railways in India. For the overnight traveller from Delhi, who has been astounded by the rat population burrowing between the capital's saturated lines, to wake up at Secunderabad is to seem to have moved halfway to Europe. The SC stations and rolling stock are smartly turned out, its staff are polite and helpful and the sweet music of handsome profits ring down the 'earnings' column of the *Annual Report* (crossing 1000 crores in 1990). Whereas in Delhi one goes to a surly computerized booking office after a cup of tea from a seedy platform trolley of battered aluminium, in the twin cities, gleaming stainless steel canteens invite the visitor in while the reservation clerk offers constructive alternative travel plans in lieu of the north Indian penchant for telling the public to get lost.

The contrast in the level of intelligence is striking and hits you immediately in the short number of steps you take from the train to the refreshment room. The smart polished stools turn out to be inverted *thalis* (trays) put to original use, just as the cashier who has the right change ready even before you have taken the money out of your pocket declares himself to be not a thought-reader but an intelligent anticipator of the likely note to be proferred. The difference between north and south is in the gaping gulf between apathy and imagination. It is the virtue of the homogenous Dravidian sensibility contrasted with the tumbledown lifestyle of the disintegrated Aryan. India's problem is that the life-affirming passion of the south has been subordinated to the shambles that characterize the Sanskritic culture of the Gangetic majority. Zonal railway performance only indicates the state of the nation. The wide fluctuation in regional fortunes emerges from the reports of General Managers which fill the 136th anniversary issue of *Indian Railways*, the monthly magazine issued by the rail ministry. The manager of the Eastern zone finds law and order an extraneous factor affecting railway running and mentions the intimidation and assault of ticket collectors by free-loading passengers. ('One such incident resulted in the death of a TTI at Sealdah Division.') Even more harassed is the manager of the North-East Frontier Railway whose system in 1988 bore the brunt of the Assam students agitation. With 20 per cent of its time lost to blockades and an even greater percentage sacrificed to floods and other natural calamities the desperate helmsman is constrained to suggest that the famous management experts like Drucker and Iacocca 'would probably have to become students of management all over again if they are to manage the problems of the NF Railway'.

In more recent times Northern Railway has been at the receiving end of public wrath, especially over the Mandal Report that stirred up violent memories of caste prejudices assumed to have been wished away by the constitutional abolition of the practice of untouchability. Whole trains were systematically set on fire and railway property was deliberately wrecked to endorse public resentment against government policy. The frustration of a society that destroys its own assets illustrates both the miserable gap between public awareness of the socialist basis of railway ownership and the pent-up inadequacy of the higher castes unable to work with their hands and thus unwilling to let any government clerical job slip out of their grasp.

Against such an unpromising scenario, the railways in India continue to run. Under the colonial dispensation the constraints may have differed in emphasis but not in magnitude. As an instrument of imperial policy the railways were mobilized during times of war. Not for naught did the Khyber line blueprints indicate 'Combined Booking Office Window and Machine Gun Loophole'. Nehru, on taking over the railways at independence, bemoaned his chaotic inheritance. Not only had locomotives been shunted off to Mesopotamia but the track was also pulled up for export. (A portion of the Kangra Valley line was thus uprooted.) The casual way in which the damage was done, without any regard to future planning, infuriated Nehru.

The Horrors of Rail Partition

The bewildering array of problems that hit the system overnight when Radcliffe wielded his scalpel of Partition added to the post-war confusion. Rarely has our planet witnessed such demented scenes, as the *kaflas* (exodus) of opposing communities found energy in the depth of their despair to wreak retribution on one another. Passing trains were not exempt from the peculiar subcontinental madness of apportioning all of one's problems on to the doorstep of your neighbour. After the refugees on the 35 Up clashed with those on the passing of 36 Down the grisly solution of the pragmatic politicians was to send an equal amount of traffic in either direction to ensure an equitable balance of reprisals. If India prides itself as the land that produced the modern apostle of non-violence it would seem that her need was greater than that of other nations.

Even before Independence the railways were the target of popular ire as they represented the visible presence of foreign rule. Also the endemic curse of ticketless travel began with the mass attendance of farmers at Congress rallies. It continues, with Delhi regularly receiving train loads of unpaid-for political rallyists to swell party appearances. Since the railways are *sarkari* (government owned) and the *sarkar* is socialist there is the simple conviction of the son of the soil that to travel free is a foretaste of the millennium of the proletariat. Groaning from all these afflictions the railways continue to bear the load. Post-independence policy led to a political appointee at the helm of the Railway Board whose compulsions were to appear popular, no matter how whimsical were his schemes that overrode the engineering and financial objections of professional railway-men. Clearly, the next virtue of Indian Railways, having survived the stranglehold of British capitalists, was to resist the python embrace of railway ministers squeezing out a political career by distributing railway largess, especially to the voters of their home constituency. This blatant appeal to the time-honoured feudal right to dispense patronage peaked in recent years under a minister considered to be the most modern in his outlook. What is interesting is the soft line the public takes in viewing such non-professional inputs. It is a source more of amusement than scorn that an express is diverted to the home town of the new minister as a matter of prestige almost as soon as he takes over the rail portfolio.

In a rare tribute to the railways' nation-building capacity in spite of all the political hurdles thrown at it, the renowned rail historian Oswald Nock remarks of how after Independence the transfer of railway stocks amounted to one of the most phenomenal takeovers in transport history in regard to the smooth assumption of power, both administrative and technical, by Indian staff.

Real Improvements after Independence

To rail users the most spectacular change that has come about following Independence has been the improvement in lower class comfort. Anguished cries against the subhuman carriage of third class passengers marked the itinerant pens of Nehru and Gandhi, who laboured—as most of the travelling public still does—under the belief that the railways exist primarily to cater to human comforts, as opposed to the reality that they actually pay their way by the shipment of noncorporeal freight. As Vanderbilt the proprietor of the New York Central Railway succinctly put it: 'The public be damned'. Gandhiji titles a chapter of his autobiography 'Woes of Third Class Passengers' and vividly illustrated the limitations of his doctrine of nonviolence when it came to queueing up for a poor man's ticket before facing that even more daunting challenge of forcing one's way on board. Later he describes how he travelled from Saharanpur to Hardwar in a roofless goods wagon grilled by the sun above and roasted from below by the iron plates. On another occasion, travelling third from Lahore to Calcutta, the Mahatma had to pay a porter twelve annas to thrust him through the window of a compartment. Note that as early as 1917 he refused to use the word 'coolie' though it continues to be in vogue to this day. As it happens my own experience of the crowd lining Lahore's platform some forty years later exactly matched Gandhiji's description. As the Khyber Mail pulled in, there was a gleeful whoop and before the passengers could get off there was a free for all to get on. I remember making things more difficult for myself by trying to lecture the mob. Instead of appealing to their better instincts my missionary posture invited first derision and then hilarity. Looking back I can view the contemptuous laughter of the Pathans as my initiation into the mysteries of subcontinental transport imperatives at least at the second class (unreserved) level. Animal drive more than sober detachment achieves the purpose of entraining and the advantage of joining in the melee is that enjoyment of an unavoid-able collision is much less wearing than any fretting dismay at man-kind's spontaneous resort to disorderly instincts.

Nehru's aristocratic birth made the imposition of third class travel seem an unspeakable insult and he continually likened the lot of poor travellers to be less considered by the railways than cattle. He also cherished the illusion that railway revenues derived from the humble third class ticket and like a good politician never allowed his idealism to be shaken by consultation with a commercial superintendent. In spite of a background remote from the real India and his never-con-cealed distaste for the overly simple life, Nehru fought tenaciously against the feudal expectations of his class and was rigorous in setting the example of how responsibility went with ministerial privilege. At Chittoor, where he was held up at a level crossing, he preferred to walk rather than acquiesce in the traditional mode of honouring VIP's —by bullying the gate attendants.

The Boosting of Nehru

In the year of the Nehru birth centenary the Railway Board published a gushing booklet entitled *Nehru and Indian Railways*. This slight and undistinguished laudatory volume which tells us little about Nehru and less about Indian Railways would not find a place on the shelf of any self-respecting transport library were it not for the intriguing evi-dence it supplies of how the railways in India are hijacked for political purposes. The half-hearted tone and exaggerated style of the chair-man's preface (not backed by any evidence that Nehru was an out-standing railway benefactor nor even a particularly interested obser-ver), suggests that the party committee drawn up to capitalize upon the anniversary of Nehru had simply ordered Rail Bhavan to produce a book of suitably flattering status. Amusingly, while Indian railway-men are expressly forbidden by their service contract to accept com-plimentary speeches in their honour, no rule exists to prevent them from giving them!

I had already got an inkling of this process when out of curiosity as to what went on in the carpeted boardroom of Rail Bhavan I accepted an invitation to attend the release of a new and very professional history of Indian Railways by one of its former general managers, G. S. Khosla. To my astonishment, instead of the sincere labours of the author coming in for some useful comment, we were treated to a political speech on the indispensability of Pundit Nehru. Mr Khosla's real and lasting contribution to Indian Railways after a lifetime of faithful service was totally ignored in favour of bland utterances that tried manfully to hint that Nehru, amongst his myriad accomplishments, was a railway pioneer of the stature of Brunel or Chapelon. The absurdity of these proceedings, like the vulgar prostrations of the anniversary booklet, would have made Nehru's scientific blood boil, while the conspicuous waste of public funds on these crude party exercises would have offended his refined tastes. The last word perhaps lay with the electorate which, thoroughly nauseated by the naked exploitation of Nehru's name, voted his party decisively out of power at the first opportunity after his centenary.

Political Spanners in the Wheel

Unfortunately for the railways, there was no relief from injection of political ideology into the running of the nation's biggest public undertaking. After a princely incumbent, a socialist firebrand took over as minister. He had already solved the problem of thirst by banishing Coca Cola and substituting for it a government drink so dismal that thirst seemed preferable. He had risen from the ranks of the railway trade union movement and during Mrs Gandhi's hateful Emergency had resorted to the desperate expedient of dynamiting the track. Having achieved notoriety for stirring up staff resentment against perceived injustices in Railway service, one of the minister's first acts was to insert appeals in the newspapers for the public not to damage railway property in their agitations.

But to demonstrate that he was not entirely destructive the new minister took the revolutionary step of issuing a *Status Paper* on the options and issues facing Indian Railways. Unwittingly, it reveals the political compulsions that determines policies. In the foreword the minister tells of a leader who in his constituency lost the elections by failing to get an overbridge built. Every elected politician is expected to get his pound of flesh out of the Railways or risk losing his seat for making empty promises. None of these leaders work out the cost and when all the schemes are added together, the amount is far beyond the means of the nation.

As in all official publications, the reader is disappointed by the poor display of railway achievements. Instead of highlighting a few virtues to catch the public interest and fix them as a source of pride, the aim has been to cram in as much information as possible, rendering the statistics undigestible. Thus the main object of the paper—to get the layman to think seriously about the nation's lifeline—is defeated by the obese gobbledegook of the rail bureaucrats. Another example of the wasted opportunity to convey to the public succinctly the success of Indian Railways in terms that will arouse the interest of the common man is vividly revealed in the foreword and preface to the rail history just mentioned of G. S. Khosla. The foreword is by the Minister of State for Railways and ends with the commendable if hardly exciting boast that 8.5 lakh tonnes of freight are carried daily. The preface by the Chairman of the Railway Board follows immediately (after the faithfully reproduced flourishing signature of the minister) and begins with the same impressive but hardly assimilable figure of 8.5 lakh tonnes.

When one is describing a beautiful woman it is not the custom to enumerate the number of molars in her lower jaw nor are her charms enhanced by multiplying her height by her breadth to give us the sum of her mean femininity to the nearest cubic centimetre. One is always saddened when the urge to set out to record an achievement ends up in suppressing it. The reader is left with the suspicion that what is at fault is not the experts' poor sense of expression but their expertise. For the ordinary intelligent citizen to distinguish between 5 kg. and 10 kg. is hard enough but to appreciate a figure like 8.5 lakh tonnes requires imagination of an unusual order. Unless statistics are intelligible there is no point in pressing them, except in the *Annual Report* which is read by the trade.

The Impediment of Unimaginative Presentation

One gets the impression with railway statistics, where no effort is made to spell out their meaning to the public, that the metaphysics of Parkinson are at work and the real reason that their import is not immediately clear may be because there isn't any. The higher one ascends the bureaucratic slope the more insidious grow the suspicions of some inbuilt scheme to guarantee counterproductivity. For example, where emphasis is laid too stridently on proposed economy one can almost predict a policy of current waste. And so it is with statistics which, gathered to clarify a specific situation, serve instead to cloud the picture. Our list of railway virtues must also record deliverance from bureaucratic procedures and from the even more devastating potential of political advancement.

Mention has already been made of the propensity of the new ministerial incumbent to divert traffic to his local advantage and one could plot the introduction of new express trains from the regional biases of their changing masters in Rail Bhavan. Maldia, an insignificant halt across the Farakka Barrage, sprang into prominence when its MP assumed one of the most controversial of ministerships. Maldia still merits a twenty minute delay at its platforms for passengers to recall the vicissitudes of fame. When a notable leader of the Banaras brahmanical persuasion took over the portfolio suddenly those trains accustomed to travelling south of the Ganga were re-routed to have *darshan* at Kashi. What began as humorous public tolerance of this subjective manipulation of the rail system has now begun to wear thin. In 1988 more than 200 crores went to Madhya Pradesh, most of it to boost the rail dignity of the minister's home town of Gwalior which, with a modest population, overnight awoke to find its platforms hosting forty-eight trains a day. Some of the expenses were for a Railway hockey stadium and a sum of one crore went into the purchase of an astro-turf pitch. However, few would quarrel with the minister's dedication to sport and no one can deny that as a dynamic example of what youthful drive can do in a monolithic organization like Indian Railways, his heavy homeward bound funding instinct won general approval. In the case of beautifying his home platform to receive his daughter's marriage party, the outrage of a few left wing critics was swamped by the universal sympathy for a romantic occasion. If seventeen lakh rupees had been paid from the public exchequer to make a 'model station' it was worth the outlay for the brief glimpse it gave of a beautiful princess in an age overwhelmingly given over to the croaking of ugly republican frogs. Incidentally some of the platform expenses specially contrived for the big day at Gwalior were defrayed from the minister's own pocket. Sadly even after public and private fortunes had been spent the matrimonial train undershot the red carpet and to remind the princely marriage party of what age they lived in, the fairy-tale union of Kashmir and Scindia states began not with a prancing white charger but on Shanks' pony. (Such things hardly bother the Railways. In 1898 the perfectionist Lord Curzon had been carried past the red carpet.)

Managerial Style

Earlier, the breezy young minister still accustomed to the free air of private enterprise upset the public and pained the rule book by demanding an air-conditioner in his official car (for which he offered to pay). Government auditors are sticklers for the inconsequential almost as rabidly as politicians are wedded to the pursuit of non-issues. Invariably the good general managers are those who, leaning heavily on the rules, manage to stop just short of breaking them. That way the work gets done and the audit objection remains academic. Instead of clamouring for an air-conditioner in his car, which is against the rules (which had been framed before such luxuries were thought of), the minister should have broken new ground and presented his auditor and press critics with a *fait accompli*. He could have pleaded ignorance of the rules and defended his desire for comfort by arguing that the AC fitting would result in cooler decisions at a cheaper cost. Old railway administrators of Delhi recall how the local Railway stadium was built as a 'minor work' by a dynamic manager who had mastered the art of leaning heavily on the rules. The normal timid follower of the rail rubric would have sent his proposal up to Rail Bhavan from where it would have gone on a circuit of several other ministerial burrows. By showing initiative this unusual administrator proved that the Railways could respond to the brave. He happened to work under the most perceptive of all railway ministers so far—Lal Bahadur Shastri (who winked at his initiative).

CHAPTER FOUR

A Thousand Particulars

The pervasive ubiquity of railways in everyday life works on the familiar principle that everyone ignores background noises. For most of us to be aware of their existence we need to read about a crash where the mangled remains momentarily rise to menace our complacency. Were we more honest to our psychic antennae and switched to being aware of what is actually going on around us, instead of chasing abstractions, we would be astounded at the frequent impingement of the railway.

Personal Early Rail Memories

My early memories of village life in Clackmannanshire in Scotland seemed to revolve round the timings of the local train. We lived in Tullibody, two miles from Alloa and the community hardly sustained any commerce outside the village co-op. The village had its centre of gravity at the 'High Road' approach to Alloa and we lived 'doon the brae' near the less travelled 'Low Road', which followed the railway line from Cambus. No serious student of Scotland's chief export needs to be reminded that this tiny settlement, with its single street that petered out where the river Devon joined the Forth, possesses one of the biggest grain distilleries in the world. In my boyhood we entered the Cambus woods to hear our echoes bounce off the walls of the faceless warehouses where the casks of bonded whisky aged and evaporated their mystique into the cool air off the Ochil Hills. Fifty years on one is agog to find that these warehouses have now spread more than halfway along the five mile stretch of line to Stirling. The station at Cambus is no longer open to passengers, but the siding to the base of the four great white grain silos is a reminder of how the railway helped make whisky the world's most ardent tonic. The coal mines along the windings of the Forth, like the steamer service that preceded them, have all been scythed by the ruthless blade of progress. The Wallace Monument looks down on the changing transport fashions and one realizes that history is not really about those set-piece battles for Stirling Bridge or Bannockburn but the stuff of one's passing memory; the sounds and smells of our own ordinary everyday recordings that suddenly hit us by the absence of familiar landmarks or the void of missing voices.

In order to catch the Cambus train one of the family was posted on the upstairs landing at the back of the house. When the cry came 'it's drummin' ower the brig' those intent on travelling took to their heels and scorched a hundred yards to the head of the brae leading down to Cambus. A steep thirty yard descent through the Cambus woods brought one to the Low Road and another fifty yard sprint led to the clacking white wicket that opened on to the station platform. Usually the ladies took the steps down through the woods while the boys raced down a shortcut. This enabled them to beat the LNER 'Clan' engine as it panted to a halt and buy a ticket from the booking office on the further platform. The ladies avoided these extra athletics by securing a season ticket.

The sound of the train rumbling over the Devon bridge that so dramatically galvanized our daily intercourse referred only to the Stirling train, usually bound for Edinburgh where the varnished teak complement would admit of those glorious shots of steam astride the marvellous symmetry of the Forth Bridge so massy we could see it from the top of the Ochils, thirty miles away. There was a branch line from Cambus that curved away to the Hillfoots serviced in those days by steam railcars known as 'Puffers'. These single coaches were painted green and white and bore romantic names on their sides such as 'The Fair Maid'. They glided along with a whispering clack and for these to be spotted in time, resort to my grandfather's binoculars had to be made. The branch line rounded silently to bypass the rumbling brig and to catch the Puffer the ladies had to set out according to the time-table. Only the boys could match her sprint as she passed the Dookit (a castellated landmark for pigeons) where a signalman would snatch her single-line token on his outstretched arm. The lasting pleasure of these near-empty local rail cars was to run down their length slamming the seats back in readiness for the return journey from Alloa to Alva.

Residual Rail Awareness in the Most Unlikely Terrain

For many years when I lived in the Kumaon Hills, trains ceased to provide the background noise to my day. But not entirely. Naini Tal had an out-agency and at one time an enthusiastic viceregal admirer of Ranikhet had ordered a survey to be made for a line from Ramnagar. Even in the remote interior you could not escape bombardment by rail molecules as when I stood at Vriddh Jageshwar overlooking the awe-some expanse of the inmost Himalayas seen from Almora district. Below my feet the hill dropped sheer for 5000 feet to the Sarju river. Here too a modern local leader Pundit Pant had recommended a line to tap the soapstone deposits around Bageshwar, at the very feet of Nanda Devi.

The assault of rail associations that went as high as Shimla and Darjeeling could not cross the crest of the Great Himalayan range and it was with curiosity that when I arrived in Ladakh, I bought a primer in the Tibetan script in Leh bazaar to see if the '*chukk chukk ghari*' of the Indian plains had made any impact on railless Ladakh. The slim publication sold by Thupstan Shanfan, 'Shopkeeper of the New Shar, Leh' went 'modern' to the extent of illustrating a hockey stick, a tin of cooking oil (bearing a palm tree as remote to Ladakhi experience as a canopied trolley of a permanent way inspector) and a thermos flask. But he drew the line at depicting any transport more reliable than the yak. I had occasion while living in Kumaon to accompany a village girl from the remote interior to central India and was intrigued to wit-ness the reactions of this railway innocent. At Kathgodam, the Kumaon railhead, she showed no particular wonder at the increased pace of life and while changing trains at Mathura for Indore in central India expressed no concern at the delay nor at the ensuing bustle when the train eventually steamed in. It could be that her village bearings had been so shaken that she was dazed, but her composure did not allow for such reasoning. Anyone who has seen the Kumaon village woman's work-load and the cheerful energy she musters to discharge her duties will understand that the mere journeyings by a strange mode of transport are hardly likely to pose much of a challenge. I have always held that the ridiculously costly and narcissistic expeditions to wave national flags over Mount Everest are nowhere near the he-man shows they are made out to be. Train the hill ladies of Kumaon to wear climbing boots and they would ascend Everest in half the time at a fraction of the cost. After the Chinese border threat of 1962 the Kumaon villagers were given training in arms and it was found that the women made a better line of defence, being physically more tough (from their agricultural regimen) than the men.

Rail Exposure in South Delhi

Moving from the backwoods of Kumaon to the opulence of South Delhi, I found myself returned to the familiar music of the rails. Possessed of what the newspapers refer to as a 'posh colony' address, here was the best evidence that journalists rarely check their facts. One of the last of India's noble nawabs lives in a house referred to as a 'palatial mansion' but they forget to mention that it is moated on two sides by a vile open sewer, the violent colour of its grey off-scourings being fully matched by the affront of its near-combustible stench. Across the road, a senior bureaucrat who is given to lecture mountaineers on the need to keep their base camps clean, has, behind his house and between the railway line, given birth to a midden of jettisoned household refuse.

Each year the obtrusiveness of passing railway traffic shouts out the message of line saturation. There is hardly a pause between the wail of the diesel horn of a goods train held up at the outer signals to Nizamuddin and the scream of an overtaking, faster trunk express as it decelerates for the congested run in to New Delhi.

The irony of the city's mind-boggling growth ('the fastest growing city in the history of civilization' as the contractors put it, though their definition of urbanity might fall short of Socratic notions) is seen in the 'Goods Avoiding Lane' that once marked the outer limits of Lutyens imperial seat. 'Friends Colony', where I moved to after Kumaon, has nothing to do with Quaker concerns. Set beyond the Ring Road it was a spacious if not (thanks to the railway) quiet stretch with the modest bungalows of refined government servants who had made it to the top by their various talents and who were characterized by the distinction of proven merit in their senior callings. However, the presence of the policeman able to pay cash for several rambling acres might have raised the eyebrows of the Sahibs—had any chosen to stay back.

Today, in spite of the excruciating rumble of fast traffic, the extensive layout still lends greedy appeal to the very rich industrialist. Their rule-bending residences reverberate to the thunder of long-distance rakes twenty-one coaches long. Tremors are set up in what was once the sandy bed of the River Yamuna, and as I write I can catch the shuddering quiver of a cupboard door as an endless trundle of fuel tankers clacks by in a powerful statement of the economic dependence of India on her metalled way.

In season, bamboo *chiks* are raised to deprive the rustic arrivals to Delhi of any glimpse of opulent back-yards. As a club with its swimming pool and tennis courts flashes by, the comfortably ensconsced second class passenger fails to register his privilege over the more outwardly rich resident who every few minutes has to break off his business deal in order to allow the noisy traffic to flow. One's day is pleasantly punctuated by thoughts of subcontinental geography as the lines wake to the accelerating thunder of the Shatabdi Express around 6.30 a.m. The reason it takes 15 minutes for India's fastest train to cover seven kilometres from New Delhi is due to the delay caused by the confusion of buying a ticket—6.15 in the morning is not the best time to ask bleary-eyed booking clerks to get a move on. It is simpler to avoid the tension of the well-off when outraged at having to join a queue and buy a platform ticket. That way you are, according to the Railway rules, entitled to board the train and can have the ticket made out at leisure by the guard without fear of penalty.

India's Fastest Train

The Taj Express follows its more impressive supercessor but is now no longer under steam. It gets back to Delhi in the evening twenty minutes before the Shatabdi though the latter has been 705 km compared to the 199 km run to Agra. The first account I read of the Shatabdi's sensational possibilities was by a lady on whom it 'failed'. Stuck in the stalled train outside Delhi at Faridabad for more than an hour waiting for a relief engine she would have been quicker to have taken a bus. My own journey on it to Gwalior left me unsatisfied because it seemed more like an airline experience than travel by rail. The countryside was effectively blocked out and one got the uneasy feeling that as with the villages around Delhi airport where expensive stone walls came up on the orders of Sanjay Gandhi to obscure the raw reality from the disapproving gaze of the tourist, this train was more of an official exercise in demonstrating prestige than a genuine outgrowth of Indian Railways' culture.

One's lasting impression of the Shatabdi was an echo of Bishop Heber's hymn (written incidentally during a tour of Upper India). Every prospect of the sleek rolling stock pleases but the stationary arrangements are vile. Attend the New Delhi counters at 6 a.m. and you fall victim to the experience of great bureaucratic mindlessness. Nobody knows which is the proper queue and with a shortage of time, the mixture of rudeness and panic is enough to put any tourist off Indian Railways for the rest of his life. Incredibly, to buy a ticket you have to fill in a reservation slip. This means getting out your specs, digging in your pocket for a pen and then finding something to lean on. You lose your place in the line to buy a supportive timetable but find, after querying, that they only stock the Northern Railways timetable while the Shatabdi runs over the Central's lines.

A notice says 'The train superintendent will look after your comforts during the journey'. But it is already too late; for the ordinary passenger his day has been spoiled by the hassles and fatuous paperwork. On board, the comfort resembles an aircraft, with the crucial difference that there's no newspaper in the rack. The Railways in their dog in the manger attitude cannot be bothered to provide any and see to it with their bureaucratic delays that you do not get time to buy your own. To rouse a traveller early and then keep him from his morning newspaper is the most diabolical form of denial and one heartily curses the superficial priorities of Indian Railways. The motion of the train is too fluid to allow you to write straight though the actual speed of 85 m.p.h. was achieved by the steam engine 100 years ago. (Sixty years ago the Cheltenham Spa Express was averaging 66 m.p.h. on the Great Western and by 1932 the Cheltenham Flyer was averaging more than 80 m.p.h. Rail connoisseurs recall that between 1910 and 1930 the LNWR line out of Euston was the classic track for passenger comfort with a perfectly smooth ride and a rolling stock faultlessly balanced and sprung, hauled by a Claughton class locomotive at near 60 m.p.h.)

The Glory Hole That Is Agra

We are served orange juice in one of those cardboard containers with a meanly diametered straw that turns the promise of sensual intake into a pulmonary survival test. This is followed by a snappily packaged omelette which an enthusiastic travel agent sitting alongside (obviously on a free ticket) assures me is the hottest item he has ever had served for breakfast on land, sea or air. (He overlooked the fact that the texture seemed to speak of yesterday.) The compartment was too insulated from the landscape to provide a truly memorable journey and any conveyance that manages to blot out the fiery winter sun climbing above the ghostly mist of *Braj Bhumi* does India a grave disservice. The fashion for dark glass to keep out the glare is a dangerous precedent for shutting out the less pleasant reality of rural poverty. Foreign tourists come to see the real India and the attempt to raise baffle walls only makes the inevitable moment of contact worse.

Agra must be the most woeful tourist destination ever devised. It gives you the very worst of India, displaying at the heart of its disgusting civic collapse the architecture of escape. The Taj—if you spend a whole day watching its moods—can be cloying in its sugary appeal and is too mathematically masculine to leave much to the imagination. The romance may spring from its setting by the river or from being seen by moonlight. The motivation of its builder is a greater memory than the formal swank of expensive materials competently arranged, with knobs on.

I took the Taj Express back from Agra and experienced total confusion at every level. I was short-changed by the booking clerk, ripped off by the rickshaw-wallah and overcharged at the platform tea stall. It was absolute bedlam to board the train, with a shrieking mob of reserved ticket holders fighting to overcome a similarly disposed mob of 'detrainees'. Suitcases and bundles were heaved and lugged to aid the ignorant armies in their feverish struggle but since all the seats were numbered, after the momentous clamour to prise a trophy from the tumult, each had to surrender his seat to the proper claimant. Dazed infants caught up in these epic manoeuvres of their middle-class progenitors could hardly be blamed for wanting to set railway property on fire when they reached the age of incendiary intent.

Agra brings out the most venal in people, with its hordes of touts, agents, fixers, middle men, fleecers, milkers, extractors, hangers on, advisers, smooth-talkers, double-dealers, crafty artists, and seedy salesmen. A visit to the Taj will put most tourists off India for life. The Agra trip is rampantly appalling and above all—as entraining on the Taj Express will reveal—prolific in the frantic expansion of futile gestures.

But to return to our Delhi departures—thereafter at two-hourly intervals one's ears can (with practice) detect all the famous names in the book taking their leave of the Capital. The Frontier Mail, once India's fastest under steam, now blares a cautious passage through the office-going build-up before 9 a.m. to be followed by the longer alternative to Bombay, the Punjab Mail at 11 a.m. Noon hears the Kerala Mangalam scream by while its lesser half (in terms of distance covered) the Karnataka Express departs nearer midnight. That old faithful, the Grand Trunk Express sets out sedately in the early evening while an upmarket variant, the Tamilnadu Express, hurls itself Madras-wards towards the witching hour.

A dozen less familiarly labelled expresses flash by; grinding in between are those bottom-of-the-league pariahs the Shakurbasti Shuttle and the Ghaziabad Passenger. The tycoons of our colony walk abroad for their constitutional too early to be aware of the daily invasion of these slinking suburban stoppers. In order to avoid ticket checking, many early morning passengers alight at Okhla station nearby and make their way along our fashionable footpaths to the Ring Road in the hope of finding the outside of a bus to cling to for the onward journey to the heart of Delhi. Meanwhile, the owners of the mansions which back on to the track have driven away in their limousines to catch the company helicopter. For them the Shakurbasti Shuttle might as well be the latest number at a five-star disco.

Delhi's Transport Deficiencies

Though the fastest growing, Delhi must also count itself among the most clueless of cities since it has not begun to address itself to its transport deficiencies. An artificial creation that radiated out from the great dome of the King-Emperor's stand-in housed on Raisina Hill, Delhi was not designed for easy shuttling to Shakurbasti or any other *basti* for that matter. As a very rural halt for the merging of the Southern Punjab lines with their archrivals—the Great Indian Peninsular, and the Bombay, Baroda and Central India Railway, the 'New Imperial City' as it was called, made no bones about its priorities. First built were the Viceregal Lodge (now Rashtrapati Bhavan) and the Secretariat followed by the Commander-in-Chief's residence and the racecourse. Delhi took more than fifty years to come up with the semblance of a public rail service, and the Ring Railway—'*Delhi Parikrama Electrical Rail Sewa*', was but another of the white elephants spawned by the 1982 Asian Games—whereby the Nehru progeny announced to the world that if India couldn't win any gold medals at sport, at least it could lavish money on stadia to enable us to watch other nations (and in particular the Chinese) do so.

The Ring Railway was a good idea but goes in the wrong direction. Citizens want to get to the centre of Delhi while the railway is designed to circumvent it for most of its thirty-five kilometres. The trains are few and far between and terminate at Nizamuddin, itself tucked away in an inaccessible place.

Since the financial results of this service are not easily extracted from other suburban routes, it seems likely that the line is as heavy a loser as all appearances suggest. Imagining weekdays to be over-crowded, I tried out the Ring route on a Sunday.

A Ride on Delhi's Ring Railway

Nizamuddin's broad and spotless platform for the scheduled 9.35 a.m. EMU (Electric Multiple Unit) was deserted, so I was able to stroll up and down inhaling the unusually hygienic sensory perceptions of this immaculate station. The overbridge still boasted those famous symbols of Mrs Gandhi's Emergency—exhorting the common man to do the noble thing his trusted leaders fought shy of doing; '*Sarkari kam Janata ki seva*' barked out a big hoarding and one smiled as ten minutes went by as the Government kept us, in the interests of selfless service, waiting for the EMU to start. Apparently the driver was watching his favourite TV serial. One of the most amusing pastimes for the traveller accustomed to delays, whether bus, train or air, is to check out the Sanskrit count. The noble, stiff and academically resurrected tongue of the palefaced Aryans has a musical ring and rendered into English equivalents for 'Staff cloakroom' and 'Chief Accounts Executive' provides some spectacularly resonant (if unintelligible) clusters of sound. At Nizamuddin I spotted the impressive '*Pratikashalaya*' but the classical associations of 'great expectations' for a soulless slabbed waiting hall only added to the irrelevant role of Sanskrit as a channel of linguistic voodooism.

On the wall outside the staff rooms are plaques in honour of war heroes 'Honoured by Railways for their conspicuous gallantry'. At the very clean restaurant nearby a rate list displays the international flavour of the capital's tastes. A South Indian vegetarian *thali* sounds excellent value for seven rupees while a lighter bite of Britannia cake ('one piece only') comes for seventy-five paise. Flower pots distinguish Nizamuddin from the enormously scruffy competition up the line. New Delhi railway station is abysmally mucky, but then the mass of humans trampling its platforms makes it more of a wonder that it can function at all. Teeming both day and night, the litter of baggage human and otherwise makes any visitor blanch at its future prospects. Rail traffic is expected to double within a decade and if these projections hold good for the rat population living between New Delhi's lines, the pundits may soon be searching for a suitable Sanskrit equivalent for 'Godown reserved for bubonic plague victims'.

Lutyen's Failure to Integrate Pomp with Commerce

It was imperial indecision over railway prestige that led to the creation of Nizamuddin as an overflow for a poorly designed capital station. Almost all visitors to New Delhi are struck by the incomplete vision of its founders. For the world's noblest vista of Rajpath to end in the dismal shrunken nipples of a stadium instead of culminating in the upraised splendour of the Purana Qila is an anticlimax almost as stultifying as the vast vacant centre-piece of that loveliest of commercial circuses, Connaught Place. Instead of leading the railway grandly into its appointed place at the heart of the nation's economic well-being and providing it with a terminal of fitting proportions, the narrow concern of the imperial builders was simply to impress the natives by erecting the world's biggest barn atop Raisina Hill. This is why the hexagon with its surround of pathetic protein-deficient domes resembles a study in the diminishing size of brassiere cups—the descending hierarchy of emasculated princely residents. Their Highnesses were forced to build these puny outriders to today's Presidential Palace to symbolize where the real power lay. However, the lofty colonial distaste for the princely lifestyle undid them and these carefully measured mini-domes (calculated not to compete with the paternal pap of the *Lat Sahib*) were set too far back to boost the arrogant British game plan.

Today the main line steals into Delhi unregarded, hesitant to follow the traditional Barakhamba route that it briefly touches at Nizamuddin. Like a ticketless traveller it slinks by to avoid the Supreme Court and disappears behind Bengali Market and an encroaching Cola company.

It almost kisses Connaught Circus at Minto Bridge but then, realizing it is unwanted, veers away to a no-man's land between the old and new cities. The blank space in the middle of Connaught Place yearns for a centre-piece and had a worthy terminal come up here its presence might have triggered off the logical follow-up of supplementary lines radiating to Delhi's outskirts. But the new capital was conceived as a royal dismissive gesture that wanted to be free of Calcutta's commercial grip. Railways came far down the social list in the pecking order. Rajpath was designed primarily for royal elephants and the railways signified perhaps the unromantic reminder of half-caste liaisons.

The Ring Railway only magnifies the woeful neglect of the planners to design a viable city. The train crew at last turned up as the last strains of *Sri Ramchandra ki Jai* faded away from the TV screens in the railway quarters alongside the platform. For one and a half rupees you can go right round the city, stopping at twenty-two stations in a scheduled run of one-and-a-half-hours. I chose to go clockwise and saw from the timetable that this represented the Up train. The five coach unit wastes no time at the passing stations, just 30 seconds then straight off again with its alarming acceleration. When EMU no. 221 leans to the curve you lurch forward as the brakes bite, then shoot back as she whines clear of the points to power into full flow. Her sound is exactly reminiscent of the London Underground but the absence of doors and advertisements plus our echoing bolt through the red rock cuttings of the Aravalli Hills ends any further resemblance.

All the way we pass railway quarters layered like the rest of hierarchical Delhi according to the size of one's beak. Landmarks like Nirula's Restaurant, the Nehru Stadium, and the Ashoka Hotel glide by followed by the Rail Museum. You remember most the thoroughly delightful arched elegance of the Lodi and Jorbagh Colonies for senior *babus*. Beyond the Safdarjung airfield can be discerned the awkward onions of the Safdarjung tomb indicating the greener pastures of Delhi's ruling enclave, where from manicured lawns of ministerial import, the capital's cultural set droop moodily in their prescribed *kurta-pyjamas*, as some sponsored mahatma drones on about the glory that was, or should have been.

The Other Face of Delhi

The real portion of Delhi comes soon enough when the cantonment ends. Lines of bare bottoms voiding along the line declare the party cult patronizing *jhuggi* (makeshift) colonies, some of which extend on to the station platform itself. It comes as a sock on the civic jaw after cleaving through the countrified air of spread-out and laid-back South Delhi to turn into the dusty reeking sprawl of slum colonies that will continue all the way back to New Delhi. Now the tracks are lined with flapping shreds of plastic bound over flimsy roofs whose dwellers gather round noisome culverts performing chores in archetypally slimy creeks. Delhi's open sewers flow opulent and proudly defiant like a forgotten river awaiting overtures from Smetana. The oil-rich sludge has the glistening promise of all those Paracelsian virtues inherent in the stink of putrefaction. From the bowels of Shakurbasti emerges enough methane to fuel several of the festivals of culture so assiduously funded by an erstwhile ruling coterie.

As we flick through the entire gamut of the Asian Games flyovers, the clogged traffic, even on a Sunday morning, appears to defy their intention. Like the Ring Rail, these costly concrete spans were designed to solve specific transport problems, but neither scheme seems to have been far-sighted enough to have allowed reality a say. The train has been empty most of the way, occupied by a few servants with shopping bags on short hops between stations, perhaps indicating that their normal mode of conveyance—the bicycle—had got a puncture. More besetting problems for the common man than transport hassles are etched into the undersides of the flyovers.'For all kinds of sex consult Rajesh Amritsarwala'. Rajesh is eminently more a man of the people than a rival Vinod Gupta who advertises himself as 'Specialist in hopeless cases—Always flies by air'. To judge from the chief scourges posted on the wall there appears to be a sinister nexus between baldness and virility. If Rajesh and Vinod are to be believed, Ben Johnson would have done better to swallow hair restorer than steroids.

It comes as a surprise at Shakurbasti to learn that the Ring Railway is not circular after all. The driver gets out and changes places with the guard and five minutes are allowed for this reversal of roles. We backtrack to Daya Basti, swerve to miss Old Delhi ('Delhi Junction' to railwaymen) and halt before a metre gauge steam train simmering across the platform at Sadar Bazar. To avoid confusion the suburban stations have 'Delhi' affixed. Thus Delhi Sadar, Delhi Kishanganj and Delhi Safdarjung distinguish local halts from further flung sound-alikes. 'Delhi Sarai Rohilla' is a must: on the Northern Railway list there are some six other stations starting in *sarai* (which happens to be the closest working equivalent of 'station').

Be careful not to get carried away by the figures at the bottom of the yellow station name boards. Normally these refer to the height above mean sea level but to find Himalayan altitudes above 11,000 feet on Delhi's platforms only means you have to deduce that the number is the local postal pin code. The sight of steam no matter how dilapidated is sure to carry away the railway faithful and an unsched-uled halt at Sadar for ten minutes enabled me to acquaint myself with the exciting possibilities of a ride on these most menial but rug-ged of passenger trains. The blinkered loco at the head of the run-down rake was sublimely scruffy, but in spite of her sooty halo and battered smoke deflectors, she resembled to my eyes the Mona Lisa with sun-glasses on. Another YG clanked by with a goods train on a raised line making one realize that the charm of Sadar Bazar lay in its crazy paving, where both lines and platform reared if not drunkenly then in a teeter of benign disrepair.

The Impact of Saturation on Sanitation

Moving from the poor relation of steam back to the snooty glide of broad gauged electric, suddenly our carriage was full. For all of the one kilometre to New Delhi, this extravagant outlay of five EMU coaches was paying for its keep. One had thought the excremental wafts and grit-blown wastes of Kishenganj and its Dickensian Delhi Cloth Mills building were the crowning touches to our bottom-end circuit of civic balefulness and imagined that the run in to the nation's premier railway station would be nominally in keeping with its status. But this short stretch was even more luridly unkempt and its rubbish-strewn approaches raised the subject of urban refuse to a sublime intensity, with the answer indubitably blowing in the wind.

In a magnificent gesture of being above it all, the EMU pulled up right in front of the main entrance, as though ready to roll out the red carpet for the escaping passengers, most of whom furtively made for a less obvious exit. Anyone arriving by the *Parikrama Sewa* to receive the freedom of the city might tip the driver to overshoot the privilege after witnessing the outer circle of dusty decrepitude. Fortunately, the last stretch back to official visible Delhi atones for the gruesome backside exposed on the western perimeter.

The Jhelum Express (also known as the *Zulum* for its erratic behaviour) stands on the platform while behind it, having to be content with the *shehnai* music of the auspicious hautboy queues the Shalimar. Clear of the congested tracks we come full circle to the bougainvillaea and sleek avenues reserved for the policy makers. Up Tilak Marg lay the residences of Sanjay Gandhi and his bulldozing DDA minions. The erstwhile penthouse of the proclaimed modern Shankaracharya superceded the dome of the Supreme Court and the narrow gauge diesel loco parked in the Pragati Maidan siding reminds us of the disciplined days when Siberian cranes in the neighbouring zoo flapped their wings in tune to his Five Point programmes. From the Trade Fair grounds created by Mohammed Yunus, a cheer-leader of the Nehru family, to the 'Sanitary Landfill' of Jagmohan, Sanjay's anointed axeman-administrator, the final whiff of the Emergency hits you with its exhalations. Hitting top speed the EMU clocks in at 11.22 a.m. depositing us under yet another exhortation: 'Work more. Talk less'. If whoever wrote that was serious, the answer might lie in entrusting the destiny of the nation to railwaymen. They get on with the job, meet their targets, and make up for lost time.

CHAPTER FIVE

Foreign Exposure

Before examining the corridors of Delhi's railway power let us continue our plunge into the deep end—of travel by passenger train. These slow and not terribly hygienic rakes qualify for what the rail statistician terms 'inferior services'. But there is a silver lining to this cloud and the chances are your passenger will be pulled by steam. One journey by these rustic conveyances will teach you more about railway concerns than a bound volume of *Status Papers*. Unfortunately, well-known writers on railway travel rarely find their way to these poor relations of the system. Paul Theroux, it is true, found his way to Rameshwaram in a passenger but I suspect this train had started out as an express.

The chief characteristic of a truly inferior passenger train is the absence of any reserved accommodation. Usually tourists are fobbed off with more reputable fare, preferably hauled by an electric engine or at least a diesel—sometimes assuming the title of 'superfast' (to honour the illusion it is advisable not to reduce km.p.h. into miles per hour).

Indian Railways goes out of its way to facilitate the foreign tourist who enjoys perks normally reserved for senior level officers. Partly, this is racial discrimination in reverse, where the visitor is deliberately not encouraged to mesh with the local way of doing things lest he goes home with the opinion that India is nowhere near as mechanically advanced as she pretends to be. It is also sound business sense since the tourist buys his roving ticket in foreign exchange and enjoys an extraordinarily handsome travel bargain. Partly too, it is the traditional concern to treat the guest as God and provide him with the hospitality appropriate to his station. And the fact remains that ingrained in the Aryan psyche is a compelling fascination towards fair pigmentation.

Western Bias Against Hindu Instincts

Every Indian reader of best-selling travelogues grows weary of the Anglocentric view of his 'quaintness' and waxes impatient at the absurd assumption that casual Western opinions constitute the last word on an India whose paradoxes no Indian would dare to pronounce a verdict upon (except tentatively with the open-ended Rigvedic option—'Only the gods know; but who knows?'). A lot of apparently 'scientific' certainty voiced in these brief foreign encounters only adds up to a mild draught of the fault-finding missionary Katherine Mayo diluted for a more understanding age. But little has changed from the Victorian view that Hindus (in particular) are an inscrutable lot given to doubtful customs performed before unappetizing manifestations of deity. I remember my very first Durga Puja in a Calcutta *pandal*, the chief public worship of Bengal, performed before a clay likeness of the Mother Goddess. While the other foreign guests tucked in to the eatables I, as the earnest student of comparative religion, would keep strict vigil to see that no unspeakable vice would take place while the audience's back was turned. The drummer worked himself up into a frenzy and surely this betokened some heathen climax to prickle one's God-fearing scalp? Then the drum went silent, and at a signal from the officiating priest the drummer withdrew. With bated breath I waited for the denouement to this terrifying development. There wasn't any. The ceremony was over and I was resigned to discover the officiant cheerfully tucking into his fried *luchis* in a far corner of the tent. The sum of Hindu backsliding as I was to find on many other occasions only amounted to a penchant for beating a drum.

The ridiculous notions most people deprived of a healthy exposure to comparative religion hold about their neighbour's faith renders education an exercise in exaggerating the imaginary fears of our fellow men rather than encouraging the acceptance of the fact that inner convictions, like outer habiliments, differ only in constructional detail.

One of life's chief cruelties is to be brought up by parents who, ignorant of their own religion, teach their children nonsense concerning the piety of others.

It is tiresome to read the Western traveller's preoccupation with the external marks of humanity and conclude that the size of boot and thickness of fat are the sure test of advanced wisdom. By these standards, the slender physique of the East and its daintier concern to express tenderness is passed over in favour of the gross clumsiness of insensitive muscle. Railway books on the subcontinent illustrate the inevitability of British authors viewing the Indian scene as a funny imitation of their own system. Their patronizing prose invariably musters the bad English of well-meaning hosts as evidence that India is content to limp along as a second rate aper of colonial fashions. Only a moment's thought ought to explode these missionary fancies in modern dress. The size of India and the assortment of her railway problems makes any comparison with smaller countries laughable. She has come to terms with the huge rail challenges on her own, borrowing ideas from all over the world.

No doubt the early pattern was faithful to British standards and practices but the momentum of a subcontinent could not be maintained from one small source. American and Canadian models were imported, as were French ideas and Japanese ones. In furthest Assam, the metre gauge line was laid by an Italian, while the track railway to Ooty and its locos derived from Swiss technology. French, German and Japanese-built engines still chug along narrow gauge lines, while a few locos manufactured in Budapest still do service on the metre. The classic flowing lines of the WP Pacifics take among their partners for the last waltz of Indian steam some Viennese beauties, while the electric models replacing them have been brought from Sweden.

Indian Engineering Inputs

In what ought to shatter the colonial myth of overhanging dependence, Indian railwaymen are now commissioned to build and run whole new railways in developing countries like Libya, Iraq and Nigeria. No doubt their elocution remains dated and their manners old-fashioned, but professionally they are equal to the best. Such obvious facts rarely come over in the stereotyped voyages of Westerners conditioned to the outmoded assumption that anything 'Made in England' guaranteed the product. India's first locomotive for export issued from the holy city of Banaras in 1976, a metre gauge diesel for Tanzania. The contract (for fifteen engines) was secured against severe international bids and it might be noted that the factory was only in its twelfth year of production.

While the first steam loco to be manufactured on the subcontinent was built at Ajmer in 1895 (now preserved in the Delhi Rail Museum), it should not be forgotten that Indian ingenuity and the local craftsmen's marvellous gift of improvisation had earlier assembled locos from spare parts imported from Britian. The virtue of self-help and the confidence of master-builders enabled the very first planned (though second to run) Indian railway to make up for some lost ground. When the East Indian line to Raniganj faced problems because of the delayed delivery of its imported carriages, the British engineer put his Indian craftsmen to work on drawings of the originals and the missing carriages (lost at sea) were soon made up for.

In the telling of history the interpretation has always favoured those in whose language it is written. The illiterate Sherpas have had no say in how Everest was climbed, while base-camp brigadiers—with an eye to a peerage—manufacture accounts of their own indispensability—making sure to conclude their remarks on the eve of the Queen's birthday. Similarly, railway lore has been heavily romanticized in favour of the expatriate sahibs, overlooking the equally heroic labours of Indian enterprise. On the occasion of the first train from Bori Bunder, European euphoria was so high that it allowed slip the un-Victorian sentiment of praising *deshi* initiative: 'Much has been hard about the Indian dilatoriness but here was an instance of despatch and promptitude in a country in which such undertakings were entirely new.' In another significant observation, the *Overland Telegraph and Courier* remarked, 'The opening of the GIP Railway will be remembered by the natives of India when the battlefields of Plassey etc. have become the landmarks of history.'

The Sacrifice of Indian Labour

The construction of the track beyond Thane was faced with the near-impossible incline of the Western Ghats which had to be crossed before Bombay's coastal traffic could be released on to the Deccan plateau for access to the rest of Hindustan. That epic engineering struggle up and over Bhor Ghat, one of the earliest undertakings of Indian Railways, was probably one of its most daring. The cost in human lives was appalling; some ten per cent of a labour force of forty thousand are estimated to have died from the rigours of the contract. This aspect of Indians paying the price for their own railways is usually played down in favour of a colonial view that chooses to stress the paternal vision of the board of directors. In raising the line over the Sahyadris there was one genuine romantic factor that could be exploited to divert attention from the suffering of the coolies. The widow of the first British contractor, instead of retiring gracefully on her husband's premature death only a few months after his arrival in Bombay, determined to see the work completed in his memory.

Today, with all its problems ironed out, the *ghat* line down from Pune seems deceptively sleek as the Deccan Queen purrs painlessly past the agonies of its construction. The first alignment had involved reversing stations with those hardly reassuring catch sidings. The specially designed *ghat* banking engines also gave off tremors of the hysterical: a gory sketch in the *Illustrated London News* shows the remains of one of the spectacularly massive and formidable O-8-OST locomotive, whose weight had caused it to fly off the end off its tether. Perhaps the true test of quality lies in how near the mangled remains resemble the original Kitson.

To prove the zany aspects of reversing stations, Spike Milligan has attempted to explain their layout in terms of the caste system, with its complicated levels of working and the occasional resort to ritual suicide. The arch-Goon, incidentally, was born not far from Bhor Ghat.

The Contribution of the Anglo-Indian

In the equally gentle railway writings of Jim Corbett whom many forget was a railwayman when not despatching man-eaters, we are introduced to the sterling qualities of the humble gangs who form the backbone of the rail system and from whom many shining qualities emerge. In this, the least appetizing of jobs, the soul-killing hump of coal from one gauge to another, Corbett's casual labour force met all its targets, though they were underfed and unpaid. The unspoken trust between the workers and the Railways whose representative Corbett was enabled the raw materials of the system to flow smoothly. The example of Corbett himself points to a gaping void in railway history. It is now almost forgotten how the entire middle level of railway running was left in Anglo-Indian hands. Eager to prove to their aloof sahibs that their performance could always be relied on, the Anglo-Indian community monopolized the railway institutes all over India and for their brief tenure of glory they shone as some of the most professionally conscious railwaymen the world has seen. Whether as engine drivers, guards, station masters or working as supervisors or mechanics, the Anglo-Indian was gifted with a verve and loyalty to the Raj that would cost him dear. Mechanically precocious, administratively meticulous and professionally tough, they echoed faithfully those qualities their British railway masters valued most. Unwisely, they backed the wrong horse and when 'Imperial Destiny' was scratched from the Indian stakes most of them followed the Raj into exile, their numbers scattering over what was left of the empire. In the peremptory delivering up of a loyal minority into the jaws of a hostile mainstream (and many other victims continue to curse the British sell-out—including the Sikhs and Nagas) is reflected the callous face of perfidious Albion.

It is also forgotten how India came to terms with this major exodus of middle-level talent. Almost of the same order as the Anglo-Indian taste for mechanical wizardry was the Muslim *mistris*' skills. (One hundred years ago Parsis on the GIPR commanded a higher salary than Hindus or Muslims because of their driving skills.) At the time of Partition a situation arose where the Railways had the overriding problem of swapping parties of Muslim drivers bound for Pakistan in exchange for Hindu clerks bent on transfer to Hindustan. The transfer of man-power continues on a more friendly note and Indian engineers are nowadays invited to instal whole rail systems in Islamic countries. In recent years considerable acclaim has fallen to engineers on depu- tation to Rail Indian Technical and Economic Services. For example, in Iraq, where a high speed railway has been built and operated by Indian know-how, an engineer made himself especially popular when in his spare time he worked out for the host nation the secrets of a foreign electronic circuit which its European donor had refused to yield. In point of fact, India first sent locos overseas for the Abyssian expedition in 1867. In 1896 men and (metre gauge) locos were sent to help build the epic Uganda Railway. Photographs of the locomotives appear in Charles Miller's history of the project, *The Lunatic Express*. It was the Indian labour force who were the victims in J. H. Patterson's classic, *The Maneaters of Tsavo*, which describes the building of the line.

Nostalgic Imperial Hangovers

The lordly opinions of foreign writers still tend unconsciously to re- gard Indians as a client people. Just as India was a market for Man- chester goods, its exotic flavour continues to be bottled for recalling the glories of the Raj. (In the making of the film *Jewel in the Crown* for Granada TV, neither the author nor the host country got anything from the deal.) The problem is to distinguish between the insular blindness of the writer, which every visitor is burdened with, and the deliberate distortion of events which give India the blame for some subjective occurrence. While modern travellers are more open-eyed and well informed about Asia and believe themselves to be more sympathetic to different cultural patterns, the prejudices of childhood are never far from the surface and begin to peep out when any physical stress is high. It is interesting to view one recent book of railway photographs called *The Imperial Way* and note how the captions fail to be impartial in their intended objective appeal. The introduction to this book by the noted *National Geographic* photographer Steve McCurry is by

Paul Theroux, who returns to the Indian railway bazaar after ten years to find it largely unchanged. A study of a father and son in a Banaras carriage, where the old man affectionately has his arm round the child (with a goat in his lap), is captioned 'Resignation on the faces of a farmer and his son'. Composure would have been nearer the truth but this word does not lend itself to the fatalism demanded of oriental stereotypes. Another scene is captured at the waiting hall at Howrah station, where a mother crouches alongside her daughter. Rays of sunlight play on their heads while all around in the shadows groups of passengers engage in the vivacious intercourse of companionship untroubled by having to perform it squatting on the floor. 'A shaft of sunlight pierces the gloom of Calcutta's Howrah station' reads the caption, though there is no gloom—except possibly in the photographer's misplaced sympathy. In his well-fed estimation the mother probably seemed gaunt-faced and the daughter but skinnily endowed. Viewed from unconditioned eyes, however, the group catches the exact nuances of growing up, with the girl's gangly posture softened by the tender promise of her maidenhood. Rather than any embarrassing study in malnutrition it is a transfixing image of the wonder of the emerging feminine principle. Instead of the gloom of Gethsemane this scene could just as well be of a young Madonna transfigured.

Rail Sales Package Abroad

It was with disbelief that I heard from a publisher how these books of railway photographs are put together. Apparently, in order to get the cover shot of a steam engine in front of the Taj Mahal just right, the photographer received a stream of telex instructions direct from America. According to this source more than a lakh of rupees went in to arranging this single slide of steam against marble. At least the best known of international steam photographers Colin Garratt does not hide the extraordinary lengths to which his profession goes in order to get the perfect picture (or fake shot, according to your point of view). During his commendably vigorous campaign to record the last of the world's steam fleet, Garratt describes in *Around the World in Search of Steam* how he travelled to Burdwan in Bengal to photograph the XC class, the nostalgic big brothers of the 'Flying Scotsman'. The depot foreman (since this was India) treated his guest as God and catered to Garratt's every whim. Imagine any Indian photographer turning up at Crewe in England and asking the loan of an engine for a weekend, then when he had got it, insisting that it should be painted the colour of his choice. This scenario could never happen on British Railways and the Indian applicant would get no further than a stiff note of official regret. In India such miracles do happen and in 1979 while a Marxist government in West Bengal railed against bad colonial habits, down the line Garratt had his XC painted in the blue livery of the LNER—at the Indian taxpayers' expense. It seems there are no limits to British rail arrogance and after extracting all these concessions from his Bengali hosts, for the choice photograph Garratt imperiously demanded the Indian 'additions'—the cowcatcher and front lamp—be removed. In what is the most artificial touch of all—though to Garratt's credit he does not conceal the deception—he got a cowherd to sit on the banks of the river watching the train steam over. The boy is dressed up in specially purchased clothes of primary colours to contrast with the engine's livery. For half an hour the goods train (on the Bolpur pickup) shuttled back and forth across the bridge until her steam output was black and voluminous enough to satisfy the most stringent demands of this professional preserver. After all this contrived nostalgia what he did not mention was that these locomotives enjoyed a bad reputation with the drivers for their unstable motion. While one is entitled to dismay at the make-believe, there can be no doubt that Colin Garratt's sincere pursuit of the poetic pose will be of invaluable service to posterity in conveying wherein lay the intangible magic of a steam engine on the run. (And costs are relative—advertising for a few minutes TV exposure of British Airways can cost 50 crore rupees these days.)

For the ordinary spotter whose railway pleasures are confined to the odd weekend outing, the ambitious tours of subsidized correspondents need not be envied. The flavour of railways is not necessarily boosted by a privileged resort to first class. However, for the photographer undoubtedly it is common sense to get written permission from the Railway authorities at the top. While you may get away with the occasional snap in rural interiors, it is normal on main line stations for any wielder of a camera to be challenged. Many gricers from the West compare India's fear of the camera with the excessive caution displayed at Yugoslav railway stations. Was there some mystic ingredient, one wonders, in the chemistry of non-alignment that made Tito and Nehru see eye to eye on railway restrictions? The 'Railway Service Conduct Rules' (framed after Nehru's death) today sound both neurotic and xenophobic: 'Keep away from demonstrations. Don't indulge in bigamy. Don't join foreign language classes without permission.'

Solving the Matter of Non-Aligned Hysteria

For many years I accepted the Luddite notion that India reacted to cameras from feelings of inadequacy that translated into hypersensitivity. Foreigners who took photographs of WPs steaming past level crossings were up to no good. Either they were colonialists who captured our ancient technology in order to laugh at us abroad or they were terrorists who with the aid of the photograph would forward it to an enemy embassy for a bomb attack. Undoubtedly the neurosis theory has a lot going for it and the general suspicion of a camera being used for anything but a studio mugshot still excites earnest rural opposition. However, on my occasional visits to loco sheds—invariably neurotic occasions in spite of the spelled-out permission from the highest authority—I came to sense another factor. Often the reactions to a camera are physically extreme and this, I now realize, is due to their indubitable value as evidence. Slowly it dawned on me that a permit is not enough. It was one's sudden arrival out of the blue that had an unsettling effect on the workforce. While getting my permit renewed annually (since one cannot offer the slightest bait to the evasive eels who sit behind office desks waiting to pounce on any possible flaw in your credentials), I was puzzled as to why the Public Relations Officer was so keen to know my itinerary beforehand and so eager to provide me a free ticket. It seemed absurd that on top of all this he insisted on sending a man to accompany me (which I declined, as I did the ticket—there are no free lunches for the traveller who prefers to practice free speech).

The matter gelled quite dramatically when I was told that a bright young officer recruit I loved to discuss railway matters with had been shot outside the officers' club of a new posting, which happens to be one of India's biggest depots for railway stores. His family told me that on taking up his new responsibilities he had been shocked at the systematic racketeering that went on in his department and decided to put his foot down. His colleagues told him to grow up and not be foolish, that all this was normal. He should wink at the anti-Railways activity and receive a cut from the universal purloining of countless stores. When the young officer held out against the crooked culture of his seniors he was threatened. When he actually set about weeding out corrupt elements from his department he was shot at as he parked his scooter outside the club. He had become a business liability to the flourishing private enterprise that lived off a public undertaking.

Officially, the shooting was put down to regional antagonism, since he was a North Indian posted far from his home. It was the violence of the retribution that gave me the clue to my lack of welcome in government offices and workshops. The men on duty are not neurotic about national security; they are terrified you may stumble on to some departmental scam.

One of the most striking denominators of governmental activity is the public face put on any inspection activity. Days before the VIP visitor is expected, the whole place is tidied up and whitewashed so as to be unrecognizable from the usual scruffy office the public is accustomed to attend. Officers who performed this charade themselves at the junior level are hardly inclined to disturb regimental custom, and when it is their turn to inspect they know that too close an examination is against the code of received tradition.

Rather than accede to Railway pressure and land oneself with a chaperon who would make straight the way and assure the local staff that my interests were purely mechanical, I decided to go it alone.

This has resulted in a rather bare cupboard of investigations into railway nuts and bolts, but what little has emerged has been achieved honestly. And the fact is that the ordinary person is turned off by too much technical detail. The need is for the more intelligible railway virtues to be aired.

CHAPTER SIX

Passenger Delights

It took two years to get round to reacquainting myself with the grimy steam engine I had seen that Sunday morning at Sadar Bazar. The advantage of a Sunday was that the lack of wheeled traffic at any rate made some progress possible from New Delhi station, where I parked my motorbike. From there I took a cycle rickshaw which skewered its way along Qutb Road with clucks and clicks from the driver as he dodged the horse-drawn tonga traffic. The station is situated in the middle of the hump to mark the lines that branch off to Old Delhi station and might be considered one of the busiest spots on earth. On a Sunday a market for used clothes is held here and hawkers had spread themselves well into the middle of the road.

The Oldest Metre Gauge Line

I climbed down to the tottering platform to book my ticket and walked right to the end where YG 3458 was cooling her heels for an 11.00 departure. I had almost forgotten about this line and had only been reminded a few days earlier when a retired military gent I sat next to at a Jazz concert (that featured a sexy Anglo-Indian blues singer long resident in Australia but whose lingering aura had been enough to stir this elderly colonel out of his retirement) mentioned the Farukh Nagar branch as being one of the oldest on the metre gauge. Checking this up, I found that it was built in 1872, soon after Lord Mayo had made the doubtful decision to allow a second gauge on the dubious theory that more lines could then be built as they would work out cheaper. He is said to have expressed the view that the trunk gauge represented an elephant's load while the feeder lines for less populated terrain would be satisfied by the back of a donkey. Put more succinctly, the Viceroy's decision appears to have halved the price but doubled the problem.

Farukh Nagar had been blessed with a branch line to lift salt and I was curious to know what the wilds of Haryana state had in common with the punishments of Siberia. But the guard knew nothing. I pressed him to say something about the town at the end of the line of which I had read about as possessing a Nawab who had joined in the events of 1857 and had been hanged by the British for his pains. '*Kuch nahin*' said the guard with an air of finality. 'There's nothing there. You're wasting your time.' The guard, I sensed from his disparaging mannerisms, thought the 1 DF Passenger (second class only) somewhat below his dignity, and he viewed any enthusiasm for it with distaste.

Aboard a Slow Passenger Train

The passengers were mostly of that typical motley of village hangers-on to an urban economy. Daily they brought milk to the capital from the obscenely uddered buffaloes of Haryana and they were now going home with their milk churns hooked on to the outside of the carriage windows. To an outsider they would seem poorly dressed, intensely animated and unconcerned that their peanut shells or fruit peel littered the floor where they sat. To a Delhi resident they were simply *kisans* (farmers) adequately clothed for the season, uninhibited in expressing their opinions, and childlike in their concentration on the pleasures of the tongue. Only bloody fools and Englishmen would interrupt sensual appetites, especially when the Railways employed menials to do the insignificant job of sweeping up afterwards.

The train was full but by no means overcrowded. A good many of the farmers fell to their Hindi newspapers when the passenger train pulled out. From the headlines to the last page they were offered a solid diet of politics which they feasted on with the same level of enjoyment as the peanuts. Those unable to afford a newspaper or who found reading too much of a drag discussed politics instead. It makes you realize how sanitized foreign accounts of rail journeys—invariably cut off from common concerns in their upper class compartments —can be, when they miss out on what is surely a national obsession peculiar to the subcontinent.

My own obsession was the minority one of standing up front near the door recording on a pocket sized machine the exhilarating sounds of an unleashed mustang. No matter how wheezing her credentials or ancient her lines this was one goods engine who defied the song, 'the old grey mare, she ain't what she used to be'. Sprinting away to the shriek of her thrilling whistle a steady beat was soon achieved and the wheezing glands were magnified as we shot under bridges until the brakes were slammed on for the first of the eleven stations in our six rupee outing (one way) of fifty-three kilometres. The most commonly held grudge against a passenger train is that it is slow and, therefore, boring. In fact I have always found the sense of speed much higher on these rural stopping trains. I would go so far as claim that travel by the 140 km.p.h. Shatabdi Express is utterly tame in comparison to the Delhi–Farukh Nagar passenger. This is because the vestibuled comforts of the main line train insulates the traveller from the flow of celerity. To experience speed as opposed to reading of its effect on a speedometer requires an exposed relationship with the passing elements. In order to burst out in song the soul needs to be dislodged from its normal housings, and for the paltry sum of six rupees this despised and condemned passenger train exultantly performed that magic of release.

At Sarai Rohilla a countrified air has already begun to descend on the essentially rural concerns of the metre gauge. At Kishenganj the steam loco shed appeared surprisingly derelict for that of a capital city but the logic of the smaller line explains the casual air. Delhi Junction is actually at the end of the metre gauge system from western India's point of view and its sluggish tempo is quite in keeping with a dead end. A notice on the platform at Rohilla suggests that if you have a complaint you should write to Bikaner, all of 463 kilometres away. This station also is prized by railwaymen for its delightful single-storey retiring rooms which enable officers to stay quietly and cheaply almost in the heart of the city; Karolbagh, a central suburb, is only minutes away.

Here too one can see the scourge of Mayo's decision, with coal being shovelled from the big hoppers of the broad gauge on to the smaller wagons parked alongside. The drudgery described so well by Corbett in the twenties thanks to a fatal miscalculation by a non-railway administrator continues with no end in sight. What Partition did to the political life of the nation, a second gauge had done to the integrity of the system. For anyone who doubts the role of the railways in underpinning the economy, a walk across the extensive overbridge at Sarai Rohilla will reveal the capital's thesaurus of grain and petrol reserves, the long green rakes of the first vying to outdistance the tail of receding tank wagons. Without these two basic commodities the bulk of the capital would not be able to knead its *chapattis* nor cook them.

The Aesthetics of Steam on the Run

The YG engine, once clear of the clutter of the inner city, makes her own music. The fireman hangs on to the whistle chord joyously giving a few extra '*whee-whee*' flourishes while the clacking momentum slackens. Then you hear the almost human panting of a body fighting its own inertia and overcoming the drag of heavy odds. The hiss of dedicated steam slowly gets its breath and beating ever faster attains a berserk climax of hugely satisfying motion. The whistle now trills in defiant ecstasy as if to declare that nothing can beat the abandon of such exalted chase. Then to prove its human crafting, the steam is eased off and the flat-out racer gracefully responds to the tug of the bit. At the station she gasps like any sprinter after the effort. It is the affection one feels for this matching of fire and water and the engine's almost human behaviour under stress that makes the steam horse such a source of fascination.

No other machine quite appeals to our instincts as much as this heroically unpoetic assembly. Modern jet airliners have invincible aesthetic attraction, yet to travel in them is to fuel every known frustration.

Fast sports cars also possess an animal aura, while sprinty motor bikes deliver their power neat, yet none scan so easily as the railed steamer. We are forced to accept that like the tiger the steam locomotive is a one-off spark from the divine anvil; if not a portion of eternity, at least an indicator of the baffling bliss of an other-worldly mood that would need William Blake's passion to unfathom. The plain fact is that this most unlikely construct of metal, when energy is breathed into her, becomes an object of love. If the *atman* bestows equal worth on all things that shine in the heart of men, it must follow that there is a place too for the cosmic salvation of insentient machines. And if true love extends to the acceptance of moles on the backside of one's beloved, there has to be room in heaven for the steam engine.

Dubious Luxury on Wheels

At Delhi Cantonment the litter of plastic bags begins to thin out: this must have been a contributing factor for starting the Palace on Wheels luxury train from here. Positively raved about as an uniquely Indian experience, the Palace on Wheels, according to the railway buffs I have met, is higher on tourist gimmicks than on any lasting transport memory. Professional globe trotters I spoke to rated it as a railway rip-off with very little actual exposure to steam. One should have thought the blurb would have warned them: 'Members of the tour are warmly welcomed by officials and handed folders that contain information about the tour including the itinerary . . . they are garlanded by girls in colourful attire to the accompaniment of lilting melodies played on traditional instruments watched by decorative elephants and festive camels' (one of whom—and who can blame it—is espied 'gazing into nowhere'). The carriage attendants are 'magnificently clad in ethnic coats and trousers, ever-smiling and infinitely courteous'. Then, amidst clouds of 'delicately billowing smoke' (presumably slugged into the grate by a fireman wearing white gloves)—you are off. The departure recalls the setting out of the first train from Bombay in 1853: 'A band struck up a rousing tune, 21 guns boomed a salute and the crowds cheered lustily as its 14 carriages filled with 400 distinguished guests slowly receded into the distance'. The difference being that those early guests travelled spaciously on the house while you will have to pay 2000 rupees a night for a cramped bunk and take your bath with a bucket and brass *lota*. The most alarming confession of this socialist pipe-dream (the Palace on Wheels earns more than a crore of rupees each season for the government) is in the brochure's parting kick: 'Depart Agra 21.45 hrs. Arrive Delhi 07.45 hrs'. You pay 2000 rupees to cover 350 km in nine hours! I had occasion to travel on the inaugural run of the modern version of the Palace on Wheels and found it an enjoyable railway experience, if somewhat taxing gastronomically because of the five-star menu.

Now that we approach Haryana the drinking water on the station platforms comes from a handpump. The signs of conurbation are evident in the haciendas that have come up to link the villages. These are the week-end farms of Delhi's rich who use the tax-free status of agriculture to offset their business appearing too successful. A young man standing in the doorway confirms that most of the land between Delhi and Farukh Nagar has been bought up by the Delhi *seths* (merchants). We pass several townships of expansive layout and elaborately modern design. 'This is a backward area,' he adds gloomily. 'You would be better off seeing Jaipur.'

The Rural Mood of Haryana

A donkey aroused by our insistent whistle, his ears laid back, cavorts alongside the engine in unequal competition. The embankment is grazed by short-fibred sheep. Woollier by far are a pair of camels who stand out by their dark brown hue. A gypsy encampment flicks by and I raise the camera to try and catch the brilliant smiles that flash coyly behind scarlet bobbing veils. The train fairly thrashes down the line between halts, totally belying the reputation of slow passengers for cruising languidly to avoid cows on the line. Instead, the driver and his two firemen seem to delight in hitting top speed in the shortest possible stretch, and for an ear attuned to the nuances of furious connecting

rods and the stroke of frantic hissing pistons here is the ultimate ecstatic music of the mechanical spheres.

Garhi Harsaru Junction, where the branch line curves away to un-
dulate over pronounced dune country, had its moment of glory when
Richard Attenborough commandeered it for the railway scenes in his
film on Gandhi. It is a solid little wayside station with the sort of dur-
ability the permanent way once inspired. Modernization work has
extended along the main line to give this modest junction a face-lift
which includes an unnecessary but very north Indian glossy coat of
pink paint on the rugged stone exterior of the booking office. However, the architecture of one hundred years ago has triumphantly
weathered the cult of Delhi's modern paint pot. (Any traveller can tell
he is in the north from the applied philosophy of the Public Works Department spelled out on all public walls: 'When in doubt paint it pink'.)

It has taken us nearly two hours to reach the forty kilometre post
but time seemed to fly as spiritedly as the dashing train in its bursts of
flat-out felicity between stations. At every stop a few milkmen got out
and a few passengers got in. Not one of them seemed concerned to
mark the berserk joy of compressed steam nor took note of the remarkable fusion of agriculture and industry as this throbbing shuttle wove
its headlong course against the pattern of the fields. The passive lapse
to unconscious behaviour so characteristic of the poor man means
this lack of wonder at their mode of progress is shared by the passenger complement. I find that it is this that makes a passenger train
less of a memorable journey than it should be. With more articulate
company there is always the chance of igniting that rare feeling for
the miraculous leap from a harness of leather to the bolder reins of steel.

The truth of a passenger train lies in its acknowledgement of unsophisticated acquaintance with science. The newspaper so avidly
devoured, is the sign of an educational breakthrough that will surely
change the surly feelings of the *kisan* for his barely considered industrial
environment into a pride of possession. In no other nation is despair
so spontaneously flaunted as in north India. *Hindustani bemaan* ('all
Indians are crooks') is the common complaint of the man in the street
and between the lines of self-deprecatory humour one can also detect
the desperation of a born loser. Have *Bharat*'s historical defeats led to

the loss of self-respect or did a prior lack of *izzat* (honour) occasion Panipat and Plassey? Corruption, that eats into the vitals of a healthy society, undoubtedly resprouted its killer weeds once the British left India. One could almost hear the sound of its growth after Nehru took the fatal step to initiate his power-happy daughter into the political structure. Asian society's dependence on lineal continuity and the genetic deterioration implicit in nepotism only added to the terrible challenge of India having to match up to the demands of a modern scientific democracy with a politically vocal but culturally conservative population.

Traditional Constraints on Social Progress

Worse was the inability to face the constitutional paradox of a nation declared free on paper but chained by the unstated, immovable custom of the twice-born. Our train load of moody, lowly *sudras* passing through their 'backward' inheritance had no leavening of middle class presence. Apart from the guard, who had already made his preferences clear, we were a collection (to polite Delhi society) akin to unbranded Jews, a motley of poor and undesirable citizens, partly by virtue of our ignorance but primarily because of our birth. The doomed status of the passenger train, we are told, has nothing to do with caste since the poor of the higher castes are also forced to avail of this cheap transport to the capital. But ground attitudes count for more than juggled statistics and the sense of hopelessness written on one dark face tells more than all the bland reassurances of the minister responsible for social fairness.

One is almost grateful for the brutal opinion of most Railway managers that these branch line passengers are a waste of time and money and should be scrapped to allow more investment in trunk routes for richer, less-backward clients. For once, at least, the naked lust of Delhi's managerial 'haves' to have more is on the surface. The scruffy surroundings of Sadar station should be closed to give a better impression of the Railway's drive to modernization. Presumably this would envisage a powdered milk plant being set up near Farukh Nagar,

though it is more than likely the manager sahib's wife will still insist
on fresh farm milk and cause her financially squeezed husband to pay
extra for it when it comes—vibrated to a consistency approaching
butter—by bus.

For once the political veto of the Railway Minister could serve the
ends of social justice. The non-human projections of the merely mechanical rail outlook sometimes need to be overruled. While the local
MP in India is a notorious animal, often making the most ludicrous
and uneconomic demands on the railways (an example of the extra
pressures under which professional railwaymen are expected to notch
up profits), there can be no doubt that public welfare should be seen
to be a real concern for the administering rail authorities. Though it
means a loss of face to dedicated officers of the fast-forward school,
the reopening of hastily closed passenger lines shows democratic
sensitivity to public indignation—something which any worthwhile
nation ought to be generating.

The short pilgrim stretch of thirteen kilometres between Mathura
and Brindaban was closed as a loss-making line but had to be reopened
when religious feelings ran high. Note here how there has been total
acceptance of the railroad into the mystical paraphernalia of pilgrimage.
The iron way in the Kali Yuga has become a necessary part of the
ritual. In Gujarat the even less profitable branch lines of the Gaekwad's
narrow gauge, where tons of coal were shovelled to move half a dozen
passengers, had to be restored after being decimated by flood when
irate village elders objected to the closure on the important principle
of never having been consulted.

Pride Versus Cost

Almost all the narrow gauges in the country are hopelessly in the red
and must make Lord Mayo's ghost equally so. Yet there is no denying
that for their day they served the public well and have an honoured
place in IR history. Darjeeling's remarkable survival has been accepted
by the Railways, and rather than provoke the public whose streets it
is so intimately a part of, it seems likely that mechanical decrepitude

will be allowed to take its toll. Meanwhile the losses in measurable factors mount up while an immeasurable amount of goodwill towards India and her faithful railway system gets added to daily by the foreign tourists who have come from the ends of the earth to see one of the world's transport marvels, maintained by tenacious Indian workmanship that refuses to admit defeat against the forces of history and terrain. The David and Goliath battle fought daily by the tiny saddle tank charging remorselessly up a mountainside to arrive at Asia's highest station (7407 ft) is a mighty symbol for a nation accustomed to lose its battles.

The vexed question of whether the social costs should be borne by a reluctant system caught between the professional demands of commercial success and the equally onerous duty of being seen to perform the equitable deeds of its socialist inspiration, hits the traveller hardest when he sits on the wooden slatted seats of the passenger coach. At each station he notes that a goodly selection of detrainees slope off free after the manner of the workers' millennium, when rail travel will be at company expense. When you see a main line passenger pull up at a station, as at the prosperous market town of Muzaffarnagar in west U.P. and deliberately park itself before an escape wicket well beyond the ticket collector's attentions through which the entire batch of alighting passengers nimbly extricate themselves, it makes you realize that these trains are very near the millennia indeed. I do not recall ever having been accosted by a ticket examiner on a slow branch line train. In one sense the proletarian paradise has already arrived in rural areas.

In the *Indian Railways Yearbook* for 1987–8 a whole chapter is devoted to 'social costs'. In a delightful admission of the stranglehold of ideology it says, 'Being a public utility undertaking Railways do not have the freedom to strike a balance between the two conflicting objectives of earning substantial revenues and meeting social responsibilities'. This somewhat peevish tone is maintained throughout the list of liabilities detailed, in which our branch line passenger is assailed for its scandalously unremunerative profile. The state governments are taken to task for refusing to accept the Railways' recommendations to close down these services and we are back again at the resentment felt by professional transport operators for the spokes put in their wheels by populist politicians. Incidentally, a great loser of revenue are those spectacularly overcrowded suburban trains that pour in to **Howrah** and **Churchgate**, with commuting *babus* clinging on to their subsidized season tickets as grimly as their toe grips a hold on the bulging compartment threshold.

In his *Status Paper* (published in 1990) Minister George Fernandes presents both sides of the argument and reminds the public that it is also possible for loss-making lines to have a place in local affections (as with the Darjeeling train) and qualify to be 'a part of the socio-economic environment of the area they serve'. This corrective to the *Hard Times* philosophy of our utilitarian Rail Gradgrinds is not allowed to degenerate into the sentimental and the Railway Minister points out that the commuting traffic (which loses more than the small branch lines) might need to stand on its own feet. Although the minister adopts the tactfully evasive language of the *Year Book* to hint at hard options, at least he has the courage to do the democratic thing and take the public into confidence about the Railways' future course. The language of official handouts like the glossy paper they are printed on (to swell operating losses) are couched in the soothing prose of appeasement and astonish by their inability to communicate. They manage, with a reptilian double-jointedness, to wriggle together irreconcilable positions that render both meaning and intent baffling.

One interesting feature of a passenger train—perhaps the only virtue of illiteracy—is its absence of graffiti (if you discount election symbols). Primary education in the rural areas has led to a major disfiguration of public places and where there are fewer walls, the wayside milestones come in for some juvenile amendment. In the averagely unkempt toilet of our carriage there was but one bleak notice—'Do not waste water' but needless to say on this decrepit rolling stock none had been provided to waste.

End of the Line Atmosphere

The junction of Ghari Harsaru was set in the midst of marigold fields that satiated the city's call for colourful temple ceremonial. When talking to the driver about his badly leaking locomotive he invited me on to the footplate for the bucking branch section in the boondocks. The view in the shimmering noon of the wildly fluctuating track made one agape at the notion that these weaving lines could host eight trains a day. The way ahead seemed more like a roller-coaster run and to lift their salt the engineers had not bothered to leaven the intervening pitch. We passed the exceedingly rural halt called Sultanpur Kaliawas which announced the large bird sanctuary nearby at an extensive *jheel*. Another three kilometres of striving against the upheaval of the dunes brought YG 3458 and her five coaches to the ancient reversal triangle at Farukh Nagar. It was 1.30 p.m. and time for a cup of tea from a wayside stall.

The old station still possessed a semblance of past consequence and a padlocked door had stencilled over it in faded tones 'Drivers' overnight room'. Six shackled fire buckets stood forlornly abreast of the tender which, having reversed beyond the broken-down loco shed, had now backed on to the platform to take us back at 2.00. The sand in the buckets had shrunk under the grilling heat and turned into baked bricks. The locals, knowing better, aped city affectations by throwing their cigarette stubs into these surviving icons of a distant culture. The line's full 117 years were evident as we sinusoidally backtracked to Garhi Harsaru, the train bouncing gamely over the hurdles of clay. However, there was the satisfaction at having sneaked in before the sickle of history had severed this withering limb that cries out for the chop.

A wait of twenty-two minutes was timetabled at the junction, no doubt necessary in earlier years when connecting trains could transfer their stopping passengers. On that Sunday afternoon nothing stopped and at the time I was tempted to agree that the halt, once one had examined the extent of its modest presence, was excessive even for our passenger. However, on replaying the tape recorder at home I was surprised by the joy of an unexpected encounter. Pacing to ward off the boredom I was so quick to detect in others, what I had made myself oblivious to—was the ongoing wonder of rural largesse. From my machine poured forth the untroubled bird song of a hushed country station. Entranced by the purity of this uplifting background music to which I had closed my ears, it seemed only fitting that the date my Sunday choir should have raised their voices on was 1 April.

CHAPTER SEVEN

Express Lineaments

The single greatest difference the Railway Age brought to the world was the sense of clock time. One hesitates in the Indian setting to describe timefulness as a virtue, since for millennia *Bharat* has functioned successfully without it, preferring rather to emphasize the sway of eternity. Diurnity and the pressure of a lone lifetime in which to play out our journey have made the callings of the monotheistic faithful more urgent. To Hindu and Buddhist notions, borrowed from the cyclic pattern of nature, sufficient unto the next life is the *karma* thereof. The medieval plodding draught animals set the pace of society's unflurried order. The horse that beat the speed record along the Great North Road from York to London, like the first marathon runner, was prone to drop dead from the exertion. When *Mallard* came to set the world record for steam in 1936 (near the Great North Road) the effort nearly killed her and the proud streamliner one sees in York Rail Museum today might be considered a heart-transplant model since her over-running resulted in destruction of her 'middle big end'.

The Stimulus Released by Steam

The temporal round was rudely ruptured by the potential of steam to make the wheels of life turn faster. It frightened the conservative and exhilarated the visionary but having demonstrated its superior gait the iron horse never looked back. As feared, 'the number of horses in the Kingdom were severely reduced.' It made a statement about directions never before open to the common man and stimulated his enquiries about what lay over the horizon. The medieval mind conditioned to follow the sure rote of the seasons and relate to the crawling majesty of the sun was released as though from a catapult. The freedom steam brought is well caught in the remarks of the young woman who sat aboard the *Rocket*'s winning run: 'One of the most sublime spectacles of human ingenuity and human daring the world ever beheld'.

The Assertion of Time

Time, that 'unique subjective', once varied from village to village and the early Railway companies were forced to assert Railway Time as a standard which all passengers should strive to attain. From the logic of this decision, countries that the iron rails had begun to undergird now had an extra binding of national time. As early as 1840 the Board of Trade supported the notion of all railway stations in Britain conforming to the London clock which daily was checked against the Greenwich model. For Ireland the timepiece was carefully stowed aboard the mail train each day. India chose Madras Time until Standard clocks were introduced.

Railway clocks became a byword for precision and Mahatma Gandhi's favourite turnip time-piece might well have been the sort of chronometer that delighted the heart of an Anglo-Indian station master. The wall clock in the dining room at Barog on the narrow line to Shimla is marked 'Benson of London, NW Railway 1903' and its steady service is typical of the new loyalties railway culture brought into everyday focus. More often than not the present to a faithful employee after a lifetime of loyal service was a clock inscribed with touching references to daily attendance and duties diligently performed.

The consciousness of time revolutionized attitudes and enabled fatalism to be outdistanced. 'Going places', 'racing the clock' and 'full steam ahead' were not just the phrases of a new-found confidence but direct challenges thrown to the formerly invincible elements. The railways, it might be remembered, were conceived by industrialists who wanted to move heavy materials cheaply. Their takeover by the public, which happened as effectively in India as in Europe, spoke of a latent daring in the human breast that had previously no opportunity to test itself. But in India, more than any appeal to individual adventure, was the familial pull that enabled the clan to fulfil its rites jointly. What had been an unthinkable and abominable conveyance of weeks was now but a matter of hours. Time, that had been the great deceiver, was overnight converted into a prime deliverer to become the great uniter of divided families.

For most travellers their experience of Indian Railways begins and ends with the ticket marked 'mail or express'. Exaggerated praise for first class comforts and stinging criticism of second class overcrowding are staple fare unchanged for more than a hundred years. The good press far outweighs the bad and in the short four decades since Independence this traveller has been pleased to see the sort of comforts once exclusive to the upper class now standard fitting on second class carriages. It is true that speeds have not kept up with the cushioning but anyone aware of the same old tracks being made to carry twice the traffic will be sympathetic to railway constraints.

An abstract of the *Annual Report* called *Facts and Figures 1987–8* in an attractive booklet tells us that the number of conventional coaches has doubled since independence but, needless to say, so has the passenger demand. It doesn't let on about express speeds in the intervening years and you can hardly blame the Railways for not advertising the measly average of 47 km.p.h. for the broad gauge, which is what the *Rocket* could hit more than 150 years ago when travelling light. The *Rocket* indeed ran faster than our present day metre gauge expresses and this embarrassing state of affairs may have had something to do with the Railways' decision in 1988 to upgrade *chotey* line technology to make it safe for faster trains.

The most typical journey second class passengers make will be on an express or mail train. For the difference between the two, incidentally, the passenger is cautioned to enquire of the Coaching Tariff published by the formidably named 'Indian Railways Conference Association' at an equally impressive address—State Entry Road, New Delhi. One has to hand it to the Railways for the most searching of detailed rules whose legal flavour resists any dilution and thus accounts for iron way jargon becoming part of the capital's argot.

A Delve into Railway Publications

In a complimentary booklet called *Passenger Handbook* published by the Directorate of Public Relations in 1989—the year of the Nehru centenary—a creditable resume of Railway working is neatly presented, providing the public possesses the ability to understand its phraseology. It starts inevitably with an earth-shaking quotation from Nehru, whose anniversary gave the excuse for its appearance: 'The whole purpose of travel is to remove parochialism'. It tells us in a nutshell that IR is the largest railway in Asia and the fourth largest in the world. The total track length runs to some 62,000 kilometres (about 38,500 miles) the greater portion of which was laid before Independence. (The age of the lines has to be borne in mind while comparing average speeds.) Organized under the Railway Board, the system operates from nine administratively independent zones each of which is further subdivided into divisions for operational convenience. IR amounts to the second largest undertaking in the world under a single management and its workforce—in excess of one and a half million—makes it the ultimate employer. Every day eleven million passengers are transported along the three gauges that comprise the total track. If passenger traffic is thick, freight movement is fast. Unfortunately, as mentioned earlier, officialdom brought up on the need to obscure public information (lest more is demanded) gets tongue-tied when there are genuine achievements to be bruited, and lapses into the habitual mode of casting a shroud of statistical gibberish when plain speaking would have served better.

We can bypass the tables of 'Number of Originating Passengers and Average Lead' and 'Passenger Kilometres'. What they are manfully trying to dig out—but only succeed in burying—is the staggering increase of passengers since Independence (a rise of almost 200 per cent) and the even greater increase in the length of the journey they take. Because of the extent and thoroughness of railway statistics it takes a couple of years for them to find their way into print in the *Year Book*. Their sale from government book outlets guarantees another year of apathetic delay before the reading public can lay its hands on them. In 1988 there were nearly 3000 mail/express trains out of a total of some 7000 carrying passengers. The average length of a train works out to five and half carriages, which shows how absurd some of these beavering fact sheets are when we all know that the bulk of trunk express trains contains a complement of not less than 20 coaches these days. More often than not intermediate stations prove to have platforms that cannot cater to the increase in length.

The Advantages of Bland Travel

The passenger does not have to be told that 68 per cent of trains are now hauled by diesel or electric traction. Steam has been relegated to the sidelines and its absence (more on the broad gauge than the metre) makes the mail journey a distinctly less exotic rail experience. True, it is faster than the national average suggests, cleaner and more economical to run, but the price is that we lose out on that magical ingredient of flashing pistons betokening a relationship between the human rider and his willing workhorse.

In comparison to the steam-hauled passenger train, now the pariah of the tracks—the average express train on a trunk route will be a fairly bland transport experience. It will enable the foreign tourist in his upper class berth to say something nice about India in his book of instant impressions and cause the more pernickety of Indian second class passengers to write stiff letters to the editor of their national daily (under a 'redressal of grievances' column) bringing to our notice a grave deviation from standard practice—usually of a minor but disgusting nature. In short, the journey, were it not for the decency of the passengers (most of the way) would be as conspicuously smooth as it is eminently forgettable.

In booking your seat—a much more polite undertaking outside the Hindi-speaking heartland—one has been initiated to the formalities of the iron way. They originate with the reservation slip whose full blown name is 'Requisition for Reservation/Cancellation/Return or Onward Journey'. A close study of this form while waiting in the queue can prove to be an educational experience. You can learn for example that '*Kri Pri Ooh*' is the Hindi for 'P.T.O.' (instead of '*Pee Tee Oh*'). Also, you can detect that the wheel has come full circle for railway smokers. The increasing fashion for non-smoking compartments will soon take us back to the early days when smoking on the railways was taboo. It was only allowed legally in England from 1868. A famous music hall entertainer took his name from the orange prohibitory diamond on British compartments windows—'Nosmo King'.

However fashionable it is to jeer at socialist concerns, the point has to be conceded that the early private railway companies treated its poorer passengers like savages. Bundled into cattle trucks, the door was locked on them until legislation forced the companies to at least water its livestock. Compare the pre-Independence complaints of Gandhi and Nehru at the callous disregard the Railways had for its cramped and sweating legions battling to find a foothold on a rake drawn up primarily for the privileged. Their spacious coupe was in exact colonial expansive proportions to the crushed native confines.

The dictionary meaning of 'express' is 'done, made, sent' and those raved-about cross-continental mail trains of the nineteenth century with their luxurious kowtowing to the comforts of the sahibs exactly express their statement of a confident era, just as our trunk route expresses today with their reserved berths for the commonest of passengers reflect how far the currently despised principle of socialism has in fact made us more human in the extension of our care.

An Express Primer

My First Railway Journey is a child's book of pictures published by the National Book Trust (1986) and in it the artist's impression of a journey by Indian Railways is—as expected—entirely drawn from the express. The cover shows a diesel somewhat foreshortened to suggest speed (but more likely to cover up for the artist's unfamiliarity with a WAG 4.) The first picture emphasizes the point made by the then chairman of the Railway Board to Paul Theroux about the family impact of rail travel. It shows a husband and wife with their child settling down in a second class three-tier sleeper opposite their aged parents. A red-shirted coolie (officially referred to as 'porter') rams a suitcase (whose size may be in contravention of the rules) under the seat. The chances of the couple being fined 'six times the luggage booking charge' are remote since it is as unlikely the ticket collector will be able to think in terms of 'permissible centimetre capacity' as the passengers.

The next page gives us a double-spread of a platform, possibly at Banaras. The bustle of the scene is well caught and the tastiness of the hot food paraded by the smiling stall holder almost tangible. Inside the compartment again, the elderly couple are comfortably cross-legged with a shared meal between them on the seat. A ticket examiner checks to see that their child is not over five years old and, since senior citizens now can also claim a discount, he has to adjudge who is sixty-five in the tooth. The next view is bare of an obvious message as it looks out on to the passing scene, but to the rail enthusiast it imme-diately attracts attention by pointing to the crucial genius of India to adapt to its own needs the importations from another culture. This picture shows the train window pattern on express stock, which comes in three layers to enable you to survive whatever the circumstances of the way may throw at you. The inner glass pane is the obvious choice to keep out the grit, though less in demand now that steam has ceased to shovel cinders. Sometimes a gauze screen intervenes to keep out un-wanted insect life and the steel shutter that drops outside it with a clang is the effective sun-shade, which if not cool at least has slats riven along it to permit some air. Each of these three alternatives nestles into its groove cleverly and is locked by a spring and slide. Another de-fence is the outside angled bars, which permit commerce but deprive entry. A good example of appropriate technology for the wear and tear of rough and ready rural India are the crude but durable door locks at the end of the compartment. The simple double-drop bolt is a highly effective locking device.

To demonstrate how quickly technology is changing, one of the most traditional aids to the thirsty passenger is also depicted—a water bottle (usually available for sale on the platform). This is the sophisticated version of the unbeatable village *garha*, India's magical earthen water pot that keeps the water both cool and tasty. With the emphasis on second class comforts—no more elite coupes and fewer first class compartments are to be built—water coolers are soon to be standard attachments for the convenience of sometimes desperate passengers.

What comes across in this book of pictures is the generous roominess of the second class sleeper compartment. After the hectic scrum on the platform to escape to one's reserved haven is cause enough to invoke a blessing on the head of Mr Dandavate—who as minister espoused the cause of comfortable berths for the passenger of modest means. That the entire journey remains a heaven of uneventful intrusion is another matter. Let us take the trunk route eastwards to Assam and learn the hard way about those happenings which the rule book gives a wide berth to.

The Tinsukia Side-Winder

The Tinsukia Mail is no great shakes as an express and is an example of how political patronage has worked to the public advantage of stranded Assam. The minister felt this far junction needed an express so he provided one. Once established, the public could relied on not to let this prize escape them. As it happens, the Tinsukia (sometimes because of its shortcomings called the *tin dukhia*—'hat-trick of miseries') is not a through train except in title. At Guwahati you have to leave the broad gauge, cross the platform and enter a metre gauge compartment. According to the Railways, the switching of reservation is done with a minimum of fuss but this being translated into the realities of the way in a nation given to using its lungs, means a fifteen minute screaming session with a black-jacketed gentleman in a peaked cap at Guwahati, who concludes that anyone who can scream that long probably deserves an overnight onward berth.

Starting from Delhi in the evening, an electric loco contemptuously eases away our rake of twenty crammed bogies to the soulful mourn of its horn. We move on to the graceful curve leading to the great booming bridge over the Yamuna. (Note that the train starts at Old Delhi and allow an extra hour to get through the traffic.) Rail addicts will be delighted to find at the station bookshop a rich selection of railway lore in the form of abstracts on fares, commercial concessions and luggage booking rates. You can buy a handbook giving the name of every station in India and the initials under which professionals recognize them. Also given is the distance from 'DLI' (Big Apple). The book runs to 275 pages. Of less weight but containing much more intriguing rubric is the confusingly titled *Calculated Fare Table* which carries a key to the mysteries of luggage allowance. These range from the booking in the brake van of 'small calves under 0.76 metre in height at the shoulder, not exceeding three in number', to snakes with 'securely fastened and closely fitting lids' and tortoises whose baskets 'should be soaked with sufficient water before acceptance of booking and of such type that the tortoises may not be able to protrude their neck out'. Another hazard to be guarded against is the 'undetected charpoy' (string bed) in the compartment—especially 'when not in pieces'.

Tickets Please

However, with our RAC ticket ('reserved against cancellation') we are legally entitled to climb aboard and occupy at least a reserved seat, hoping to catch the ear of the conductor to allot us any cancelled berth. The conductor, with his long list of duties which include regulating passenger numbers, checking their tickets, collecting surcharges, evicting moustachioed occupants from the 'ladies only' cubicle and 'paying prompt attention to all complaints of passengers in regard to non-working of fans, lights, taps etc', is not a presence to be trifled with. One waits respectfully while he sorts out the problems of an 'RJQ' whose name is missing from the 'return journey quota'. 'Quota' is a word of pregnant significance on a government railway, since it allows room for pulling strings -- and also an escape route for anyone caught plucking them to personal advantage. One of the perks of a government job is to ride first class to the scene of one's duties.

Similarly, in socialist India the government is the biggest buyer of motor cars so that all its officers travel in style.

As the train rumbles over the grey slack of the Yamuna which looks every inch worthy of her status as step-sister of the god of death, the fascinating sight of a procession of tongas and cyclists appears below between the gaps in the girders. The railway takes precedence, but such is the cacophony of the honking road traffic that our metallic echoes are drowned in the clangour of the congestion below. This hymn of unleashed decibels is a splendid orchestration of India's ability to exult in any act of transport and lend to all movement a sense of unrestrained jubilation.

In November night falls early and by the time we near our destination in Assam it will be dark by 4.00 in the afternoon. We have 2500 kilometres to cover and will spend three nights on the train. But the metre gauge section of 561 kilometres beyond Guwahati alone gobbles up eighteen hours. The rake glides easily into Kanpur to meet the dawn. A browse through the morning *Pioneer* newspaper brings us painlessly to Allahabad, then a late breakfast of an omelette (wrapped in foil which qualifies it for the title of 'casserole') will see us to the pivotal junction of Mughal Sarai, one of the world's biggest marshalling yards. The train halts for half an hour and the curious collector of the classic age of steam furniture will find that hardly long enough to satisfy his fascination.

The Wonder That Is Bihar

We are now on the confines of Bihar and our apprehensions of this unruly state are soon justified when a crowd of short-distance government babus force their way in. Strangely, the conductor who is paid to prevent such happenings is no longer to be found at his post and does not reappear till the interlopers get off at Bhagalpur, that infamous town that has etched India's name on the map of crime committed at official behest. Discretion in these lawless parts will repay the visitor who feels called upon to stand up for justice. The problem lies in the fact that the law enforcing agencies are often on the side of the enemy and in the most embarrassing indictment of the quality of democracy, criminals pose as political leaders. At least let us be grateful that we only had to share our seat with the ticketless motley. Their confidence suggests they have a pact with the railway authorities and the convenient absence of the conductor implies he had been profitably advised to make himself scarce.

A few months after my trip I read in the newspaper of a foreign tourist who had, fearing Bihar's reputation, taken a day train along this section. Her second class air-conditioned chair car was threatened at dagger point by shoeshine boys who relieved the passengers of their luxury items and cash. They then pulled the communication chord and decamped with their loot. It is for this reason notices on Indian Railways are prominently displayed telling the public what to do when robbed in an armed dacoity. The official rigmarole tends to give the game away when it urges the victim to insist on a receipt from the Railway authority with whom the report was lodged. This amounts to a confession by the Railways that they themselves are not too happy with the security provided by the state government. A little reflection on daylight robberies ought to make it clear that dacoities can only occur with the connivance of the Railway staff. Local licensed stall-holders alone have access to the platforms and conductors are on duty at carriage doors to check who boards. As with the ticketless passengers in my reserved compartment, it is reasonable to assume that the tourist robbed of her cash and camera would have been better advised to pay the local staff some sympathy money and recover her goods rather than write to New Delhi where the official enquiry will end up with the suspects paying a pliant doctor for a certified alibi. One statistic the railway does not choose to mention is how many of these enquiries end up with the culprits being apprehended.

The reader conditioned to read between the lines will find a suspiciously worded sense of overkill in the *Annual Report* chapters on 'vigilance'. 'The Vigilance Organisation is determined to root out corruption from the Railways and will go all-out in the direction of achieving its objective.' Note that what sounds like total commitment is cleverly converted into partial response; only a hint at moving in the right direction. Unfortunately, the Rail (or any other) vigilance

organisation is held in public esteem with the sort of humour reserved
for the pious speeches made by politicians in Gandhi caps. If it wants
to be taken seriously, IR might make a start by transferring any officer
who advocates all-out crusades in general directions.

Occasionally, public resentment towards Indian Railways boils
over and the press reports will speak of irate passengers who 'discon-
nected hose to prevent the train from starting'. Only the foreign tourist
imagines that this refers to the fate of Malvolio having overtaken the
garters of the guard.

Into the Green Corridor of Assam

Clear of the crime-prone Gangetic belt the Tinsukia turns north to
cover the new line connecting West Bengal with the North East. As
one of the great engineering triumphs of the post-Independence era
this linking line was built at a phenomenal pace by a legendary IR
figure on the mechanical side, Sardar Karnail Singh. Turning east
again at New Jalpaiguri (the junction for the Darjeeling narrow gauge
branch line), the broad gauge runs parallel with the old metre track
for most of the way to Guwahati. As already advised, only the untried
traveller allows himself the luxury of losing his temper over the non-
appearance of his name on the onward list. You can recognize him by
his red face, still on the platform as part two of the Tinsukia Mail pulls
out, his name unaccountably having turned up on the next day's roster,
if the apologetic clerk's clipboard is to be believed.

As the sole rail line through the wild tangle of Upper Assam, the
metre gauge is under heavy strain and passengers may be espied
clinging to the roof as the YD diesel loco yaws into wooded curves of
the spectacularly dense jungle of the North East so reluctant to admit
an intruder. You may have glimpsed the profile of a Beyer-Garratt
lined up for scrap behind the walls of the Guwahati yard and would
certainly have responded with relish to the Yankee style of the clanking MAWD steam locos on shuttle duty. These imported MacArthur's
comprise the chorus girls of India's steam stable—you can see for yourself all you wanted to know about naked locomotive working parts.

Much awaited is the important junction of Lumding, perhaps the most isolated of railway settlements in the subcontinent but containing the biggest holding of steam on the North East Frontier Railway. It is now too dark to make out their numbers, but the sound of simmering boilers and the arthritic groans of 'Moguls' relegated to shunting duties makes it inevitable that one will have to come back. The third morning you wake to the grey smog of Tinsukia which turns out disappointingly to be a coaling junction and most untypical of the brilliant verdure that characterizes the surrounding tea garden estates. Late last night at Dimapur, the rail-head for the tribal state of Nagaland, there had been a slight altercation over the consumption of beer in our sleeping apartment. Far from the spiritual concerns of the mainstream (where the thought of anyone enjoying bottled self-transcendence arouses shrill anathema) it was not the intake of beer that worried us but the cheerful insistence of the intoxicated intruder (again with the connivance of the conductor) of his willingness to share a berth with the only lady in the compartment.

CHAPTER EIGHT

Track Records

To the early promoters of railways, Hindustan hardly seemed the promised land. An East India Company feasibility study compiled for the House of Commons in 1845 listed some very dramatic drawbacks and couched them in almost poetic terms. These included 'periodical inundations, violent winds, the influence of a vertical sun, the ravages of insects & vermin and spontaneous vegetation'. The rail historian G. S. Khosla neatly points out that the very verticality of Surya the Sun god would cancel out the ravages of insects, though he does not spot that this literary memorandum has been signed by T(homas) L(ove) Peacock who, besides being the 'Examiner of India Correspondence' for the East India Company was the author of *Nightmare Abbey* and a close friend of Mary Shelley, the creator of *Frankenstein*.

However, obsessed with the Russian Bear, Dalhousie urged a line north west. The first obstacle to be crossed was the River Sone in Bihar. This major bridge gave the builders the confidence needed to span the Ganga and Yamuna higher up and their bridges at Allahabad and Delhi, built after the sepoy insurrection—like the stations they led to—were designed to be defended in the event of further hostilities breaking out. The astounding lines that blasted their way over the Chappar Rift to the North-West Frontier or toiled up to Shimla (the summer capital of the Raj) through 103 tunnels, reflected the Victorian virtue of self-confidence and were essential proof that railways were the true religion of modern mass movement, with the mechanical engineer a kind of John the Baptist figure who went ahead and made straight the way for messianic imperialism. Some prodigious public works were accomplished by these thorough gentlemen who viewed their terrain with the eye of an artist and ran their line through it with the feel of a surgeon. Rarely does the traversing track in India offend by its alignment. It bends to the superior hand of nature and, like any sensible person would, chooses the narrowest part of a stream for its flying leap.

Indian Labour Skills

Occasionally, the humdrum driving of a level advance changes into poetry and hill lines are sure of a place in any technical rail anthology for the inspiration that got them where they are. It is in flirting with the impossible on the Darjeeling and Ooty grades that passenger affections are stimulated and the background genius of the mechanical staff comes to be fully appreciated. From the very beginning it was realized that Britain was a bad model for developments in India, since the one was on a fast track of industrial growth with a sense of disciplined despatch whereas the other was both rurally poor and scattered, with unfenced attitudes that gave right of way to the cow on the line. One early proposal to get round the overlapping instincts of India was to suggest a hanging line raised eight feet above the ground. Some of these 'desperate nostrums' as Dalhousie called them, were actually tried out since rail transport was an untested institution. (In England Dr Dionysius Lardner was given an experimental train by the GWR, but in spite of two crashes the doctor survived—to the chagrin of the donor.) It is hard to grasp the singular inventiveness of early railway engineers who had to create a working system from scratch. The fact that they hit on the basic models that have continued largely unchanged to the end of the steam age is a tribute to their enlightened grasp of what it took to run a railway. Men like Brunel of the Great Western were not mere founding fathers of the Railway Age but visionary engineers whose level of genius was comparable with that of the Renaissance giant Leonardo. It is tragic that because of the Indian milieu, unaccustomed as it is to honour manual achievements, the country's great mechanical talent has rarely been noticed and her inventors scarcely recognized, except if they win acclaim overseas.

No less worthy than the engineers outwitting the obstacles in order to give an easy run were the Indian labour forces, drawn from the lowest levels and from whom little pride in such drudgery could be expected. But it was largely due to their dogged co-operation that the trunk routes become operable when crucial sections that demanded an extra effort were tackled by bare hands and overcome at the cost of many injuries. From a colonial point of view the martyrs were the British engineers improvising with a sense of mission, but from the Indian angle the real heroes were the labour gangs toiling up against colossal odds, their casualty rate running into tens of thousands, victims of epidemics of wild animals and of their own low resistance to the agonies thrust on them by an unrelenting terrain. The early major works of engineering thrill by their directness but modern master-pieces of mechanical skill do not lack in comparison for ingenuity and resourcefulness. The modern ore lines of eastern India upraised and practically airborne around tribal Orissa, bear comparison with the poetry of the early bridges over the Ganga. A new line from the port town of Mangalore which cuts through the lush coastal Sahyadri range to make possible a metre gauge link with interior Karnataka has remarkable aesthetic potential as a tourist run but so far pas-sengers can only respond to its echoes overnight. For the traveller who delights in rare engineering craft of quality, the line from Lumding across the North Cachar Hills in Assam to Badarpur on the River Barak will revive the days of pioneering workmanship never since beaten.

It was by a fluke, or possibly divine intervention, that I realized my heart's desire to see this line, as it can only be seen from the point of view of its inspecting engineer. My progress through Assam was sluggish owing to the surly attitude deliberately shown to outsiders and made worse by unhelpful railway officers. They were rude when approached in the guise of an ordinary citizen, then turned fawning when a letter of introduction from the Rail authorities was produced. In order not to spoil my journey I kept away from the Railway estab-lishment which, at least in Tinsukia behaved as sootily as their miser-ably maintained engines.

Assam's Kaziranga Express

Things began to go my way when on a loop line to Furkating from Jorhat I was invited on to the footplate of a YP steamer hauling the most remarkable express I have ever ridden. When I quit its coaches to join the driver there was not a single paying passenger on board. The Kaziranga Express was another expression of that bitter war between the Railways urging that uneconomic traffic be closed down and the state government (through the local politicians) fighting to retain a prestigious anachronism whose only practical purpose now was to drain the nation of coal. Unfortunately, the antagonism towards the central government was so great when I made my journey through Assam, that the empty train symbolized a reality mainstream India does not want to face—that there can be two opinions about what is good for a particular region.

It was dark when the valiant Telco-built loco ended its wheezing run at Furkating Junction. Here I was to wait for a mainline train to take me to Lumding where I proposed to spend the night on the platform. The timetable showed a passenger early next morning that worked its way up to the hill-station of Halflong by midday. Changing over platforms I could catch a returning passenger and be back in Lumding for another night on the tiles. But at least I would have had some leisurely exposure to the mechanical joys of climbing slowly up this supremely aesthetic line which drives its flighted course over towering chasms and through tunnels bordering on, and sometimes fashioned by, the sprawling bamboo jungle.

At Furkating the train that pulled up to take me to Lumding was an express and none of its doors would open to admit any but a reserved ticket holder. After my Up journey with the incident of the beery intruder into our sleeping compartment, I could hardly blame the locals for keeping their doors locked at night. Eventually I entered the only open compartment I could see, knowing that when the conductor did appear I would be turfed out since this too was reserved. But at least I might be able to stand in the corridor till the next station. Just then two boys came collecting donations for Durga Puja, which was due to be celebrated next day. They asked if I had any objection to subscribing to the worship of the goddess (since in the tribal tracts we were about to enter, Christianity holds more sway). As a mountaineer whose life on several occasions had been at the mercy of the goddess, I was only too grateful to be able to express my thanks for her saving grace.

The moment the boys left the conductor arrived and when he heard my makeshift itinerary bowled me over by saying 'I can give you a sleeping berth to Halflong'. I had landed in a through-coach to Silchar (at the end of the line) that would be joined to the Barak Valley Express (from Guwahati) at 4.00 in the morning. With such astounding luck I decided to go the whole hog to Silchar and asked the conductor to book me accordingly. Later at Lumding as our carriage was being united to the BV Express there was a terrific row between the night-shift conductor and some passengers over the corrupt manner in which illiterate applicants for a berth were being made to fork out twice to two different officials. The temperature rose so much that the conductor had to leave the compartment for his own safety. Not being able to follow the arguments held in Assamese and Bengali I could only join in by glaring disapprovingly at the new conductor when the consensus seemed to demand it.

Assam's Bamboo Line

The line next morning wound up in its dappled glory and was every-thing I had been led to expect. For the railway lover this was the Engineering Book of Genesis; a Garden of Eden where the Great Architect of the Track looked upon the work he had inspired and saw that it was good. Every metre of the 116 kilometre ascent to Halflong was a gripping handshake between earth and sky. Here was a railway line worthy of the gods. The setting was unforgettably green and the plashy bamboo brushed the train as her flanges screeched round the tight curves. I was accustomed to the hill bamboo of the Himalayas which can grow monstrously obstructive in the stem as you try to hack a way through its stinging elasticity. Here, the growth hormone had all gone into the leaf and voluminous fronds a foot long cascaded in an avalanche overbowering the line. The riotous springing of this sap-happy jungle in its sombre green dignity only added to the marvel of the machinery installed by puny but determined track builders. Somehow the airy girders that reached out agonizingly over a river bed (and dispensed with railings to make the exercise seem even more desperate) were not contrasting red oxide transplants that offended the wild flow of nature. These javelin hurls of iron struts, tossed out as gregariously as the jungle gaps they bridged, sang their own song of harmony. They joined in the chorus of wayside thanksgiving to a triumphal passage, where man for once was mindful of the rule of nature. Nothing seemed to be environmentally amiss except the slash-and-burn custom of the tribals and that had long preceded the laying of the line. From the plaques outside the tunnels one could gauge the progress of the line in the early years of this century. From the solid gravestones to be found at the side of the ballast one could trace the lineage of some Cornish miners specially sent to shore up the tunnels. A remnant of an oil pipeline from Assam to Chittagong was pointed out to me: part of the pleasure of this sensuous line was to conjure up its great days under steam and in less fractious times.

By another odd trick of the goddess, a migrant Bengali reader of the Delhi *Statesman* came up with exactly the evocative statement I longed to read. In a personal communication he wrote:

Your article on the 'Bamboo Line' brings back nostalgic memories of a childhood lived in the halcyon days before Partition. This was also when dream river steamers plied with swan-like grace regularly between the unique water-front of Barisal town—held by many to be one of the loveliest and most picturesque in the world—and Dacca City on the Burhi Ganga, touching on the way the railhead at Chandpur which had its wharf and a landing pier for a jetty, apart from the large railway terminus. (All these places are in Bangladesh now.) After disembarking at Chandpur, following an overnight steamer journey from Barisal, the Barisalian cast off his lurching gait born of years of travel by water-borne vessels and suddenly turned himself into a self-assured landlubber capable of boarding trains with alacrity. By then the time would be midday. After a quick bath and a hearty meal in one of the homely hotels on the outskirts of the Chandpur railyard, one would be ferried across a strip of water to a marketing centre on a nearby island from where (as from the steamer approaching Chandpur during the day) the line dividing the turquoise blue flow of the Meghna from the vast dull grey waters of the Padma was distinctly discernible. Marketing over, one came back by the same ferry boat, securely put the purchases in the hotel and had a round of the sprawling railhead busy with shunting steam engines.

A hectic day would end with an early evening meal at the hotel, thereafter off to the station and into the waiting carriage that would take one from Chandpur to distant Tinsukia in Upper Assam. That was a cosy journey lasting more than 36 hours through hills and bamboo covered dales of unbelievable beauty by a train pulled at the front by one engine and pushed from the rear by another. Stations like Badarpur, Lumding and a host of others leap into the memory as one tries to reconstruct after half a century a childhood journey through Assam's hill section by the through train as it was called in those days, passing through some 25 tunnels on the way. Halflong station would be reached around early noon the next day and the passengers' olfactory nerves would be greeted by the soft scent of a thousand roses abloom in the station yard where the gulmohurs also ran their separate riot of golden red under the gleaming eastern sun. The train would stop here for two hours for refuelling, watering and general tidying up and allow the passengers to stretch their limbs, take a hurried bath at the water taps and then gobble a full-belly meal in the railway catering house. Those who were game for an outing could meet with the breath-taking beauty of Halflong Hill with its famous ridge known as Lovers Lip and the charming waters of the exquisite lake surrounded by flora that attracted flitting butterflies and humming bees.

Fortunate is the Delhi travel writer who has a *pravasi* readership of the likes of S. R. Ghosh-Dastidar. He conveys the touch of the heaven I felt as we climbed to Halflong. But closer acquaintance with the hill-station (on the return from Silchar) unfortunately made me want to get away as quickly as possible. For a start, the diesel that hauled us up from the entirely Bengali valley of the Barak broke down this side of Halflong and we had to wait two hours for a replacement. However, a lingering flavour of paradise did appear on the platform with freshly cut pineapple picked from the nearby slopes at giveaway prices.

The Backward Mood of Halflong Hill

When the train did get into Halflong I was brushed aside by the stampeding tribals who made off up the hill as though their lives depended on it. Clearly, since everyone, young and old, participated in the melee it had to admit of a meaningful conclusion and sticking out my elbows I joined the rush and began to give as good as I got. This brought me to the door of such a dilapidated truck-cum-bus that one might have collapsed from hysterical laughter had it not been for the manic press from behind to climb over me to get in. Once more with elbows flailing and a foothold won on the rickety step, I squeezed aboard in what looked like Noah's Ark complete with every kind of bleating animal. The 'bus' resembled an overblown station wagon and was the first country bus I have travelled in that actually boasted of a thatched roof. Incredibly, more passengers kept squeezing in until the driver's nose was flattened against the windscreen. Then in this unlikely forward position—the steering wheel obscured by the press of bodies—the ancient vehicle coughed into life and roared up from the railway station to the town. The ascent was by an emphatically spiral road, so the bus seemed to be travelling on two wheels most of the way. No wonder the original roof had fallen off.

We were deposited without ceremony in the *chowk* (mini-square) of the small unlighted township. As with the rest of agitating Assam, no one spoke to outsiders so I could find a hotel only by following reluctant signals. The hotel manager was also not into communication and demanded an extortionate amount for a very modest cubicle. He seemed disappointed when I agreed to take it. Just as Assamese students were agitating against strangers in their land the local tribals of the hills around Halflong were agitating against the Assamese. I had come to Halflong for tourist interest and hoped to see the hill opposite the town called Jatinga where the annual bird 'suicide' phenomenon takes place. When I learned that it wasn't a trick of nature so much as a contrivance of the tribals to slaughter the confused birds (drawn to their lanterns) I wasn't sorry that events the next day decided me to shake the dust of Halflong from my feet. The surly population I met in the morning in the bazaar happened to coincide with the poorest material conditions I had seen anywhere in India. As my mission was mechanical I did not see why I should get caught up in the mood of political disillusionment that so many agitators appear to actually cherish.

From such a small, jungle-bound and poorly serviced place the only bus had gone early in the morning and the train would not arrive till noon. A taxi driver took me down to Lower Halflong and whispered that if I spoke to the guard of a goods train he might let me ride the rods. This was exactly the sort of way in which to travel the most interesting section of the line as it wriggled its way back down to Lumding over the most precarious of stilted viaducts and through a series of impressive tunnels faced with grey stone. When the guard read my letter of railway recommendation he was only too happy to let me stand on the apron of his guard's van from where I could drink in the splendours of this one-off descent.

Exhilarating Travel by Trolley

Further down the line at Maibong, coming up fast behind us, was a motorized trolley bearing the inspector of the permanent way, who was performing a most demanding job to check that the mountain line was clear for traffic. Suspicious of an outsider engaged in the dangerous pastime of photographing railway property, the inspector descended on me at the next halt and demanded to know (through a menial) if I had permission to flaunt a camera. The permit worked like magic and to my utmost joy the menial was relegated to the goods train while I was invited to sit alongside the inspector on his petrol-driven trolley. No better way to experience the run of this line could be imagined. Seated almost at ground level the trolley could hit 30 km.p.h. At this speed I felt as if I were on a roller coaster, shooting out from a curve on to a singing viaduct that boomed across the void, leaving one slightly sick with apprehension at the sudden disappearance of the ground. It was a magnificent moment, an exhilarating ride that made one's heart swell with pleasure at the skill of the line builders and the precision of the maintenance crew. Before we got down the hill the cold night had closed in and with the headlight on we blared our way past all the signals pegged in our favour. At Lumding, we braked under the main platform to look up into the wondering faces of the passengers. The rush of mountain wind later gave me a bad cold but that seemed a fair price for a mechanical miracle to have arisen from the most unpromising of beginnings.

From the inspector I learned that the line had taken eleven years to build to Badarpur, a distance of 162 kilometres. There are 585 bridges and the longest tunnel is 595 metres (no. 11 out of 37). There are 600 curves and the tightest is 16 degrees. The gradient of 1 in 37 makes this the steepest metre gauge adhesion line on Indian Railways (Ooty in the south runs on a rack) and also accounts for the delightfully slow ascent to Jatinga which is prefaced by a non-stop run of nineteen kilometres at that grade. Other travel jetsam from that memorable encounter includes my hotel bill from Halflong. On the back is printed: 'Warning: Strictly prohibited in hotel premises: Sick or disabled person, gambling & drinking, interference with menial establishment of the hotel, entry of opposite sex into rooms without prior permission. Hotel gate closes at P.M.' The more auspicious receipt of the Sri Sri Santoshi Maa Puja, Children Park, Institute Colony, Badarpur says: 'We welcome your Presence at our Puja Mandap', a pleasant reminder of Assam's enduring maternal mode.

Being in one of the heavy rainfall areas, the NEF Railway in Assam has the annual task of picking up the pieces after the monsoon deluge. The Brahmaputra is a perennial source of sorrow to railway engineers, undoing their labours and reducing the track to a mangled mess. But like the recuperative jungle, the railways bounce back and traffic starts moving again in a remarkably short time. This emergency drill is done without the slipshod fatalism that could make repairs a further danger to traffic. It is this commendable professionalism at the higher levels, in league with self-imposed discipline lower down the line, that makes any closer look at the system so satisfying. For example, on the already mentioned empty express to Furkating, the driver several times applied the brakes and brought the train to a dead halt according to the rule book. This was so as to cross weak culverts newly repaired after flood damage. A man was posted at each bridge with a book which the driver had to get down from the cab and sign.

The Excellent Status of Indian Railway Morale

It is on these small but character-reflecting routines that the real safety and success of Indian Railways depends. The public, accustomed to the trumpeted triumphs of big contracts and extensive projects, overlooks that behind each and every train is the co-ordinated contribution of more than 1000 men and women. The man who waves the flag, blows his whistle or waves a lantern at a level crossing at night is but one of a whole army of background workers whose small effort goes to making the whole so profitable. These unseen workers have no occasion to be corrupt. Their unsung faces need to be remembered when we hear of uniformed staff who are amenable to a bribe.

Sometimes written on the walls of a loco shed or on the side-tank of an engine is the admonition, 'A minor omission spells a major disaster'. From these useful workshop mottoes the secret of the mechanical success of IR may be gleaned. George Birdwood of the India Office in his handbook published a century ago—*The Arts of India*—points out that, 'In every village exists a permanent endowment of artisans and the mere touch of their fingers is sufficient to transform whatever foreign work is placed for imitation before them into something rich and strange and characteristically Indian. In India everything is hand wrought and is therefore more or less a work of art.' Certainly the early lines were laid by bare hands, the rock having been prised and hewn by pickaxe. The result is that many of the Railway works we take for granted are not just solid and enduring objects but possess virtue from their artistic strength. Rather than be merely impressed by the fine record of mechanical achievements we need to be educated to look closer at these bridges and engineering works with an appreciative eye. We can find in their fashioning the same qualities of dependability and sound workmanship that qualify the Railways in the eyes of a loyal observer to be itself a work of art. In other words, we need to be alive to the beauty of the Rail fabric and responsive to the enduring texture of a remarkable public asset.

Modern Engineering Achievements

There has been a serious failure on the part of the Railways to make better known the mechanical breakthroughs that have occurred since Independence and of epic constructions like the line to Assam, the details of which have hardly been spelt out. The 230 kilometre line (originally laid for metre gauge traffic) was accomplished in two years during which time twenty crore cubic feet of earth and rock were moved, most of the work having to be done between November and April. When the line was opened—on the day India was declared a republic in 1950—the politicians basked in the glory though the actual achievement of the line lay in the tremendous contribution of the labour gangs. It is sobering to record that many of the successors to Karnail Singh (who went on to become chairman of the Railway Board) have been content to play down the role of their professional colleagues and mouth instead self-serving speeches written to boost the minister's party.

Why is that we only recall the old bridges built under the British dispensation but take no pride in the remarkable, aesthetic and soaring spans that have come up since Independence? We only hear the cynical reports of some structure that has collapsed from the poor quality of the materials or—more likely—the malfeasance of its building contractor. The apathy of government service permeates the Railway publicity departments. Wrong assumptions are allowed to flourish unchecked while exciting information that announces unique engineering feats is allowed to slumber.

The Dufferin Bridge at Kashi (Banaras) was built in 1887 and regirded in 1947 without interruption to the traffic. It is now renamed Malaviya Bridge. The cleverness by which it was modernized might have irritated Lady Dufferin, for it was she who found the Victoria Terminal in Bombay 'too good for the natives'. Mokameh, the site of Jim Corbett's transhipment labours, was rewarded with a memorable bridge in 1959 getting on for two miles long. The foundations of this project were sunk to a depth approaching 200 feet, a world record for this kind of project. When the terrible storm in south India wiped out the line to Dhanushkodi on Christmas Day 1964, the entire 107 spans of the Pamban bridge linking Rameshwaram to the mainland were crushed by tidal waves. In a matter of only nine weeks a new bridge had replaced the old and the island of Rameshwaram was again made accessible to pilgrims.

The proposed 837 kilometre Konkan line linking Bombay with Mangalore will incorporate the very latest in bridging technology and should lay at rest the idea that modern engineers lack the creativity of the old.

~~~~~ CHAPTER NINE ~~~~~

Conveyance of Merchandise

My one and only ride on a goods train has already been described but it must be remembered that in remote areas with few transport options the public is bound to display some initiative. It may not be a transport virtue in India that the rules can be so relaxed as to accommodate passengers in the most unlikely of wagons but this is nevertheless a compassionate fact of all rural lifestyles. Similarly, in the carrying of voluminous luggage the Railway authorities tend to turn a lenient eye on extra baggage since this is a cultural norm of the train traveller. Because of the family feeling generated on a long journey and the conversion of a compartment into a temporary home, it is but natural that people want to spread out their things and have at hand familiar domestic furniture. Western travellers look askance at the traditional bedding roll and heavily bound tin trunk, yet these fading symbols of the golden age of steam speak of an enduring relationship between the iron way and its homely user.

The Origins of Freight on the Penydarren Tramway

The phenomenon of freight is really what Railways are all about, though the public continues to fancy that this is a secondary activity after their own passage. The Railway arose from the need to move raw materials in bulk and it is appropriate that in the very first exercise to show what steam power could move on iron tracks, the train carried pig iron, a commodity which in its undressed state Indian Railways continues to convey on its most prestigious modern ore lines.

In 1804 the Cornishman Richard Trevithick, the real designer of the steam locomotive (whose name has been forgotten in favour of James Watt and George Stephenson) took on a wager set by some south Wales ironmasters to move ten tons of iron from Merthyr Tydvil to Abercynon almost ten miles away along a gradient of 1 in 145 and run the empties back. Horses had been used on the Merthyr tramway hauling wagons on rails made of short lengths of cast iron, which provided a flange to guide the wagon-wheel. On 21 February Trevithick was ready to collect the 500 guinea prize. With five wagons and seventy passengers the journey was made in just over four hours. On the way to Merthyr a way-side plaque commemorates the very spot where the trundling 'tramway' had seen one of the most momentous journeys after Columbus's voyage to the Indies. The Penydarren locomotive preceded Stephenson's locomotives by more than twenty years. The locomotive, or rather the replica built for the Welsh Industrial and Maritime Museum in Cardiff, looks like a giant watch mechanism.

Trevithick the Inventor of the Steam Locomotive

It needs to be questioned why the name of Trevithick is so little regarded and how it is that his historical engine finds no place in public affection? The reason seems to be that Trevithick, unlike Watt and Stephenson, spread his talents too thinly and neglected to apply commercial instincts to his pure engineering vision. James Watt, with canny Scots foresight and precision, was able to upstage both Newcomen, the inventor of the stationary steam pump and Trevithick, the first person to manufacture a steam locomotive that hauled a load on rails. Watt improved on the Newcomen pump to make it more efficient and thus commercially viable. His business partnership with Matthew Boulton at the Soho factory in Birmingham announced the arrival of the industrial era. Trevithick's bad luck was to lack a business partner who could have harnessed his genius and channeled the restless energy that was as explosive in his own inventions. To illustrate the fatal slip between cup and lip, in toasting the success of the very first full-size steam carriage for road use in Britain, Trevithick's team got out at the top of a steep hill near London to celebrate. It was Christmas Eve 1801 and the boisterous crew overlooked the fiery nature of their conveyance. 'The parties adjourned to the hotel and comforted their hearts with a Roast Goose and proper drinks, when forgetful of the Engine its Water boiled away and Iron became red hot and nothing that was combustible remained either of the Engine or the house.' Later, the barely literate inventor ruefully noted: 'I believe that Mr B. and Watt is abt. to doo mee every enjurey in their power...'

For the record, the first use of the word 'railway' occurs in 1681 and 'railroad' in 1702. It was around 1850 that the latter was adopted for American usage. 'Wagonway' was in use up to 1950 in Aloa and denoted a short cut from the station to the docks. Some would date the principle of guided transport by parallel grooves in stone blocks back to the Babylonians who, incidentally, favoured (like the Greeks after them) a gauge of over five feet. When the steam railway mania overtook polite society with the opening of the Liverpool and Manchester Railway in 1830 the poet Alfred Lord Tennyson celebrated the occasion with the lines, 'Let the great world spin forever/Down the ringing grooves of change.' Apparently he was short-sighted or not very mechanically disposed. The train had flanged wheels and hugged the lines securely without any suggestion of being groovy!

Freight Returns: The Railways' Bread and Butter

As already mentioned, however, the subject of goods trains, despite the fact that they yield 75 per cent of the revenues of Indian Railways, rarely stirs the public imagination. To watch an express train roar past a level crossing arouses some interest and occasionally passion, if the locomotive is a streamlined Pacific but the unending clack of a featureless freight rake only irritates the held-up motorist. The movement of freight like the motion of the bowels is better imagined than investigated. The more the proud *Year Book* hurls at our heads those internationally competitive statistics which show that India leads the Japanese in the 'turn-around of wagons', the less the man in the street registers the greatest background economic reality of his everyday life.

As is to be expected, Dr Dionysius Lardner has a chapter on Goods Traffic though it is only half as long as the preceding treatise on Passenger Traffic. Recommending a rational approach to the subject, he gives us a helpful breakdown of factors that will yield the most meaningful formula. '1st. The quality of goods booked—T. 2ndly. Their mileage—t. 3dly. The number and description of vehicles employed in their transport -- W. 4th. The mileage of these vehicles—w. This gives us the average distance of the goods carried—t/T and the average distance of the vehicle carrying them—w/W.' He goes on to note that in the goods trains of England in 1847, 'It is curious that pigs and calves are transported to an average distance so much greater than the cattle and sheep.' This is unlikely to have any bearing on a true incident reported by an Indian holy man who in the early years of the twentieth century was proceeding to Cambridge for his studies by a local train. At one of the stations a fully intoxicated farmer entered the compartment and to the consternation of the assorted audience of well-bred passengers sat down luxuriously and announced in a rustic voice: 'Ladies and Gentleman, Oi just vooked* a pig'.

To pursue Dr Lardner's quest for the 'average', the Indian freight train average load in 1988 was over 1000 tonnes, hauled on the broad gauge at an average speed approaching 23 km.p.h. The inadequacy of steam traction is laid bare in comparison to diesel and electric locomotive utilization which is six times better. For a goods train the key to success is an engine that gets a heavy load moving from scratch. Steam, for all its beauty and willingness, is no match for a purring dynamo and its silently flooding current.

Rail apologists tell us the iron way is six times better than road transport, then dilute their absolute claims with qualifications. Always the public is left wondering at what transporters are trying to tell us. In selling their brand they would do better to admit the shortcomings rather than hedge their boasts with footnotes about the sense in which the word 'efficiency' is used. Nothing in the Railway Year Books could be less poetic than trying to make sense of professional enthusiasm over a hat-trick in meeting freight targets. To be fair to the

---

* 'Booked'

Railways, their performance has been achieved against natural and political calamities like floods and strikes and one can sympathize with those who sincerely put their shoulder to the wheels that run India's economy only to find that others are from personal frustration ready to sabotage what little progress has been made. (A national trait discernible in the negative resort to belittle success.)

Goods Wagons: The Railways' Beasts of Burden

The pride with which we are told, 'Wagon utilization of Indian Railways compares favourably even with some advanced railway systems of the world' is unfortunately weakened by the technical jargon that shows India ahead of Japan in the league of 'net tonne kilometre moved per annum per tonne of wagon capacity'. Viewed from the angle of public interest it seems unlikely that the much vaunted reduced time lag between two successive loadings of a wagon—twelve days in 1988—is a tremendously exciting breakthrough. Yet measured against the IR holding of nearly 350,000 freight cars (most of which to the casual eye appear to be rusting away up forgotten sidings) this is a brilliant achievement of a vast undertaking clearly on the move.

One of my favourite counts while waiting on far off platforms is to tick off the number of 'foreign' goods wagons in any passing train. In the North East you will find a smattering of wagons from every zone in India. To my surprise the guard's van I boarded to travel down from Halflong Lower was of Southern Railway parentage. In Kerala and Tamil Nadu in the south, as in Rajasthan and Gujarat in the west, wagons with North East Frontier markings will be found on their lines, the metre gauge track being interlinked more extensively than the broad, though this is a comparatively recent accomplishment.

The fleet of freight cars stood at four lakhs in 1980 but has been whittled down by the drive for efficiency. In the gross traffic receipts for 1988, freight brought the Railways almost 6000 crores (compared to the revenue from passengers which raked in just over 2000 crores). Passengers and consignees will argue that with their charges forever on the increase it is hardly surprising that the Railways continue to record profits. When the average citizen is told a railway consignment awaits him, his heart sinks and he sets off for the far end of New Delhi's railway station with a prayer to St Antony (who is the patron saint of lost property) and a supplementary petition to St Jude (the saint of lost causes). Surprisingly, after you have tripped over the random heaps of gunny sacks and flourished your way-bill in front of the sole official on duty, your bundle of books forwarded from Bombay is identified from thousands of other miscellaneous objects strewn over the platform and you make off to record yet another minor miracle of the system. The odds of any order appearing out of the chaos that is a parcels office reminds one of the working rule of most Indian institutions still committed to the primitive mode of 'scatter and cover' as opposed to the shelving instinct of modern packers who believe in 'stack and forget'. The following motto I have seen, appropriately, on a Railway officer's desk: 'The impossible we do right away. Miracles take a little longer'.

Booking a Motorbike on the Dakshin Express

My experience of booking a motorbike in the luggage van is about as far as I have personally been involved in freight movement. This means turning up a couple of hours before the departure of the train, emptying the tank of petrol and 'packing' the headlight with straw and gunny sack. Particulars of the owner and his destination have to be printed on the compulsory name-plate, then one is in a position to approach the booking office. To ensure that the bike is put on the same train as yourself it is inevitable that you pay someone 'to do the needful'. In the main Delhi station the booking staff are only too eager to be of assistance and, having quoted a price, they will personally see the machine is put on and report back with a salute. At Nizamuddin (next door) on one occasion I put the bike on the quieter Dakshin Express but there were no extra hands on duty at the booking office on a Sunday night. Seeing this opening a sergeant of the Railway Police sidled up and warned me of the dire inconvenience if the train left without my bike. But how could it, I questioned, when the train appeared to be empty and the brake van vacant? Ah! but who would deliver the bike from the booking office to the relevant platform, mused the policeman when he had the means of prevention? I asked him how much it would take for him to forego his veto and we settled for ten rupees.

About an hour later when I had found my reserved seat (thanks, incidentally, to the platform coolies since the reservation lists on the notice board were hopelessly illegible) I walked to the front of the train and was surprised to see the brake van packed (including two other motorbikes) while my own vehicle—the first in the queue—had been left standing outside. 'It will go tomorrow', the two coolies loading the van told me. As the van faced the booking office two platforms distant I yelled across to my Godfather in uniform. On hearing of my letdown he waved his fist at the coolies who grinned and made room for my bike. They had not been aware that my insurance premium was paid up.

Getting one's bike off can be much more expensive, especially at an intermediary station where time is short and gangs of coolies all contribute to extricating the machine from under a pile of miscellaneous bundles, bales and baskets. After that hectic exercise you also have bills for broken gear levers or snapped cables. A vital detail is to choose a train that arrives in the morning, as evening trains, when they run late, will get you to a destination when all petrol pumps have closed and you will have to push the thirsty bike to your destination.

On returning to Nizamuddin I once had the satisfaction of beating the system (though I still ended up pushing the bike two miles home). I had gone to Macherla in Andhra Pradesh to see the metre gauge branch line (now converted to broad) and discovered the bike's fourth gear had shed a tooth. Not only would this prevent me from doing wheelies but it might snarl up the rest of the gear box. With a sense of doom I fitted a '*deshi*-duplicate' part in this one-horse town and set out hopefully to see some other lines. While returning to Hyderabad to catch an evening train about a week later the new gear wheel followed the old and jammed the bike 150 kilometres short of my target.

Excursion to the Barsi Light Railway

I had visited the fascinating Latur end of the Barsi Light Railway, a
narrow gauge line so cleverly designed that it returned the dividends
of a metre. However, the station staff had been surly and unhelpful,
one of them going to the extent of suggesting I must have stolen inside information since I knew so much about the old steam engines
on this line, some of which were aesthetic beauties of international
acclaim. As a matter of fact I had got all my information from an
Indian Railways publication *Locomotives in Steam*. In a building set
aside for the loco drivers where I was invited next, someone voiced a
fundamental shortcoming of certain members of the Barsi administrative staff. Now when anyone mentions the 'Barsi Light Railway' I
recall that driver's trenchant description—the 'Silly Buggers Railway'.
My visit all that way had been to try and find out what had justified
this line in the first place, when Barsi did not boast of any princely
connexions and its north east-south west diagonal incision across
the Deccan plateau might have seemed when viewed from outer space,
more like the scar of an appendix operation on the map of India than
a viable narrow gauge route that ran all of 327 kilometres. (According
to GIPR freight statistics 'Barsee' referred to a good variety of cotton.)
All the morose station staff could come up with was that the line's
chief source of profit had been the sending of chickens to Bombay.
(Whether they had started out as eggs I did not enquire.) Certainly
Latur station had long since stopped serving omelettes and when I
tried for a cup of tea that too was not available after the local train had
left behind its diesel shoebox. Latur town, however, was something
else, with a bustling agricultural market including modern shops and
a rare sense of zing for rustic Marathwada. For the first time in rural
India I saw a young woman dressed in a pair of trousers. I spent that
night in the town of Parbani on the Nizam's old metre gauge system.
In the hotel I got talking to some young engineers who had come to
bid for a tender at an auction next day. As they drank they boasted
that the auction was a formality since they had paid to fix the auctioneer.
When I asked which town had given rise to their entrepreneurial skills,
they answered 'Latur'.

The laugh was on me, however, when late at night I heard but ignored a sustained battering on my door. I supposed it was the engineers who after their late meal wished to tell me more of what it takes to run a light railway. Next morning I found it was the police. They had spotted my motorbike outside the hotel and concluded from the Delhi number plate that I must be a terrorist.

Shortly afterwards the bike broke down and the only way I could reach Hyderabad was in the back of a truck. As it was Sunday evening not many vehicles were operating and I ended up amongst the cases of empties in the back of the local 'country liquor' lorry. What with the full moon rising and me seated on the bike trying to keep it upright amidst the maddening reek from the cases of leftovers that was one journey to remember though with the combined effects of heavenly and earthly intoxications I hardly recall the details.

To add to the ferment of my befuddlement the bike was put on the train first and then covered up in a phalanx of grape boxes. When we got to Delhi and the door was slid open there were so many grapes you couldn't see the bike. The coolies named a hefty sum to drag the bike out at Nizamuddin but as this would mean further damage I decided to go home and come back later. After two hours, bathed and refreshed, I returned to the platform to find not a grape nor a coolie in sight. Alone and waiting in a sober state on the platform to be pushed to the nearest garage was the bike. Fortunately, it was too early for the police sergeant to be on duty.

Rail Security and Protection Forces

The problem of policing the railways has always been a vexed one since the responsibility for enforcing law and order is a state subject though the name 'Government Railway Police' sounds like the Railways have a major say in the matter. The force varies in quality from state to state, which gives the overall security network a sense of incohesiveness. To mitigate this in part, the Ministry of Railways has raised its own Railway Protection Force which in recent years, owing to heavy freight losses, has had to be armed. In 1988, for example, they had to open fire on thirty-three occasions and nearly 70,000 cases of theft of railway fittings were registered and another 30,000 of theft of booked consignments. As the golden goose that lays the socialistic egg, the Railways are ripped off at thousands of levels. Rail Bhavan at any given moment seems to be acrawl with applicants wishing to bring health to this vast organism by the application of that well-tried medicine—which has the added advantage of falling off when its work has been done—the leech.

Passenger train robbery statistics are rather more difficult to come by and are not considered fit for public consumption, a rather foolish notion since the public, in the absence of trust, is always apt to suppose the worst and must imagine that setting foot on a train in the Cow Belt is to take your life into your own hands. We are given the annual wash of ticketless travel figures that each year sounds suitably severe in its denunciation, but unfortunately the following year announces an increase of ten lakh passengers nabbed. The total is fast approaching a crore of free loaders annually.

Those amused by the righteous postures the government takes up when it hasn't the slightest intention of doing anything serious will enjoy the 'Vigilance' statistics that in recent years have resorted to the rather nasty method of using decoys to trap corrupt railway personnel. Some 299 staff were held responsible in 1987, of whom most were awarded a 'major penalty' (not specified). Of the others, 98 were suspended and 28 were transferred. The total number of those fired was nil, which shows the advantages of a compassionate socialist system over the callous face of capitalism. The revolving if not revolutionary solution to these blots on the integrity of the Railways comes under the heading of 'special steps', namely, the 'rotation of staff in sensitive areas'—so as to avoid more casualties from moral vertigo, perhaps.

Corruption and Connivance

In his history of the Railways in India, G. S. Khosla is forthright in detailing the threat to freight. Under the subheading of 'corruption' he makes no bones about the existence of a secondary business going on behind the Railways' back, with booking clerks falling over one another to please corrupt consignees. The staff being paid to look the other way, with specially lucrative shipments earmarked for a siding where they could be pilfered at leisure. These details emerged from a long report made by the scrupulously honest politician Acharya Kripalani as early as 1953 when the flush of idealism still lay thick on the ground.

One of the abuses reported was the sale of coal by the fireman along the line. As the locomotive steamed by, the client held out the money on a cleft stick and the requisite amount of fuel was shovelled out in this rather efficient example of how subsidiary profits can accrue to those who streamline their distribution network. Colin Garratt describes from the XC locomotive out of Burdwan how the system was flourishing in 1979, nearly four decades after Kripalaniji denounced it. No less an authority than the Guinness Railway Book states that the 'vast pilferage' of coal is a contributory factor to the scrapping of steam from Indian lines. When I was told by a Railways political appointee that this was absurd I concluded that his denial was the best evidence that Guinness, as usual, had got the facts right.

To return to the matter of freight, goods for those interested in records and who find modern container transport too faceless to be worth bothering about (although the first containers date back to 1849) the heaviest single piece of freight ever carried by rail was a hydro-cracker reactor in America (1965) weighing 550 tons. India in 1989 probably won the world record for the transport of non-worldly goods when a 130 tonne granite image of Lord Hanuman, which had taken three years to carve in Mangalore, was hauled to Delhi by broad gauge to be erected in the capital. The 3033 kilometre journey took a month. In another encounter with the monkey god, whose followers have always been a feature of station platforms in north India, one ploy to thin their population was devised by the staff at Saharanpur. A goods train with an empty box wagon had emptied into it several gallons of treacle from the surrounding sugar mills. The bait, with its sweet smell, soon attracted hordes of monkeys. As soon as they were all aboard, the guard flagged off this primate special and the driver steamed flat out non-stop until the train passed through dense jungle on the way to Hardwar. Then it slowed down to enable the monkeys to get off after their sweet traffickings.

Regarding more cumbersome rogue species, the visitor to Delhi Rail Museum who views the bleached skull of the mail-busting tusker might ponder on the ill-advised quartering of the GIPR company crest exhibited alongside. This shows a caparisoned elephant resolutely opposed to the charge of a 'Jenny Lind' lookalike steaming hard and driverless. But it is to the steam archivist Hugh Hughes that the plum of freight statistics falls. He discovered the East Indian Railways erratum slip which hastily reversed the company's remarkable claim to have carried in the first six months of 1897, '26,328 elephants, 1 sheep'.

The Postal Connexion

In the public mind the Railways are intimately tied up with the postal service, yet if you consult Mr Khosla's history you would not know such a service existed. This may be an unconsciously inherited bias against a rival public undertaking. In the early years there was continual bickering between the two speeders of public communications. The Railway Mail Service came into being in 1907 to try and sort out the chaos that surrounded the guard snowed in by unsorted mail bags. Though all big stations have a splash of red to announce the presence of the postal department, it is a subject all IR writers jealously keep off, thus denying the Railways credit for stimulating cheap postage and the democratic urge that follows from the prompt despatch of the morning newspaper. While my bike stood on the platform at Nizamuddin I noticed that its brakevan companions to the south were news magazines for the Bhopal intelligentsia, a bundle of film magazines for the military *jawans* at Kemptee and some Urdu weeklies for the gaze of bureaucratic Hyderabad. We seldom stop to realize the ramifications of freight nor appreciate how much our meaningful moments are made up by the trundling goods train. If we had the eye to sense our continuing welfare at the hands of the Railway we would consider the expression 'goods train' not a boring string of extended commodities but a harbinger of our individual happiness.

≈≈≈ 111 ≈≈≈

CHAPTER TEN

Kafka's Railway Castle

Our search for the Railway miraculous extends from the base of the colossal pyramid where the level crossing keeper braces his muscles to throw open the gates, to the top of the heap where otherwise professional officers prostrate themselves before some political remedy for a transport ill. Between the tiny gangman's hut, bare and isolated on a loop line that comes alive but twice a day to the immaculate polish of Rail Bhavan, the IR headquarters in New Delhi, a million grades of hierarchy seem to intervene. The significant slicing occurs high on the icing of the cake where the officers are differentiated from the staff by the ritual process of 'gazetting'. Under the British the names were actually published in the official list but in keeping with the house philosophy of free India by merely going through the motions it is hoped that the public will summon sufficient apathy to accept that suggestion is a cheaper alternative.

The Unprepossessing Aura of Being a Railwayman

The officers devolve into two main factions, those whose engineering talents led them to a conscious tryst with railed transport (rather than interface brutally with the ten per cent 'cut' inherent in all Public Works Department careers) and those malcontents recruited for administrative chores whose hearts were wedded to a more salubrious central service. A cursory study of the matrimonial columns will prove that in the public mind the Railways lack the vital romantic ingredient that sets aquiver the arrows of cupidity in respectable middle class bosoms. More in demand are the plum home and foreign postings of the Indian Administrative and Foreign Services. Lower in the barrel are the Indian Police, where IQ is suspected to taper off in favour of isometrics. Almost as lightweight in the social pecking list is the Indian Forest Service in which green fingers are assumed to preside over grey matter. In the depths of the barrel remain the unplumbed shades of the economic services, each apple having a worm at its core when it comes to the matching of romantic appetites with the perks of office.

But the lesser calling of these smaller central vehicles are still worthier than the provincial ratings which are allowed no space in the market-place of Sunday morning liaisoning. It is a well known safety device of the Public Service Commission selectors to deliberately abstract a few of the very best groomed genetically to preside at South Block or be monarch of all they convexly survey at Aldwych and deflect their destinies into Railways. Thus no matter how humble the particular service to each is given a leavening of hope in the form of the 'topper'. The fact remains that officers of the upper echelons of Indian Railways fight shy of any 'IRS' letters after their names lest it carry a worse stigma than the American Inland Revenue Service. Though there is little of Mills and Boon in being married to a railwayman at least as the holiday season approaches his professional advantages add to the sum of family happiness.

Just as the socialist ideal of egalitarian utopias is translated into gazetted discrimination and the quarters for the rich and poor railwaymen possess a Dickensian chasm between their facilities, the use of the word *bhavan* connotes the sort of largess that left-leaning governments were elected to redress. On closer acquaintance, however, they obviously find it so fascinating that they feel constrained to allow the lifestyle to continue, at least until their children are old enough to enjoy it. Unlike Baroda House, the HQ of Northern Railways (which is actually a palace taken over by the public sector), Delhi's chief railway nerve centre is housed in a custom-built block, notable for its pleasing architectural simplicity and strength amidst ghastly examples of utilitarian eyesores. Rail Bhavan internally is also unique in Delhi governmental culture—free of *paan* stains in its corridors. One could not be blamed for thinking that this Bhavan is run by the military in view of the conscious shine of its upkeep. Situated well down Rajpath near the roundhouse of Parliament, it is a relief to come across some architecture unaffected by Lutyens's commission to whack out grandiosity from the Saracenic. His uneasy blend of the fawn and fanciful that advertises stodgily the adequately impressive status of an empire over the hump is missing from Rail Bhavan. Nor, mercifully, has it been made to groan under Lutyens's sagging domes— those upturned imperial chamber pots that were carefully graded to indicate descending degrees of importance, ranging from the sola topi lookalike to what appear to be flattened onions.

Flee Hence the Uninitiated

To get into the monastic hygiene of Rail Bhavan requires running through the inevitable rigmarole of governmental confusion. Several queues snake towards the reception counter and as this is a Railway occasion, a resort to elbowing will not be out of place. The receptionist will question you closely on your motives, go through the motions of making secret enquiries (which fools no one since her phone is obviously out of order) and then make out a pass while you sign the visitors book giving a resume of your life's mission within a centimetre-wide column. The pass is in English and Hindi, with the Hindi placed aggressively on top. Some 10,000 books of these passes were printed in January 1986 and mine is numbered 669,265. The receptionist writes in Hindi and copies my name from the registrar which becomes 'Sri Bill Acne'. As well as the bilingual print announcing twice that this is a visitor's pass, a further rubber stamp clarifies that the Government is indeed of India, the Ministry is indubitably of Railways and that the address of the Railway Board is inescapably New Delhi. Exhausted by all these confirmations, clearances and permissions we have now received proper initiation into the rites of Kafkaesque passage.

The Railway security man is more friendly than his airport equivalent and on detecting a can of beer in my day bag suggests it would have been easier for us both if I had drunk it first. Upstairs, at various levels the corridors open out and seem to run broad and unwavering to infinity. It is the same on every floor though each floor grows more carpeted and silent as you gain height. By the third floor it more resembles a five star hotel than the hub of Indian Railways. Working one's way like Kafka's messenger you pass from the cool and authoritative air of professional railway concerns to the more thickly carpeted inner regions where the minister has his throne room. The uncanny silence is now broken by the spill of raucous party workers in their give-away *khadi* uniforms. Milling around in the last limbo before audience with the minister they voice their views on railway employment opportunities bluntly to his assistant—unless the minister fills in their demanded quota of jobs he can expect to do without their votes at the next election.

In the Bowels of the System

On the occasion of attending the release of Khosla's Railway history I was able to see the conference room and get the feel of the spirit that underlies the whole enterprise. In this inner sanctum one could appraise the trophies and guess at the inspiration that kept the system running. The centre-piece seems to be an oil painting of Mahatma Gandhi alighting from a third class carriage, ostensibly announcing the aim of post-Independence rail policy, the closing of tne gap between the way the sahibs travelled and the primitive conditions faced by the ordinary Indian.

On the whole the Railways have come a long way in making travel for the poor man more comfortable. I would go as far as to assert that India's second class sleepers now offer the best travel bargain anywhere in the world. But how many ordinary Indians can afford even that simple luxury! The middle class concerns of Delhi's planning elite have tended to blind the policy makers in Rail Bhavan so that few of the transport improvements have filtered down to the people for whom they were intended. This shortcoming in extending facilities to the underprivileged echoes the situation in other areas of development, and the full enjoyment of freedom and its perks by the articulate section of the nation alone does not answer the real challenge of establishing an economically just society. There is indeed the danger that those at the top are so busy celebrating their new found freedom that they resist the passing on of benefits down the line. One indicator of this vested interest is the excessively grovelling behaviour of senior officers at Rail Bhavan functions. Why should they get involved in these sessions for flattering a minister who is here today and gone tomorrow? At the release of a professional account of railway history how can the mechanically competent chairman of the Railway Board voluntarily reduce his status to that of a *mofussil* cheer leader?

The Dichotomy of Motivation in Rail Deputation

The great divide that Rail Bhavan illustrates to visitors is how the Railway is split between the true sons of rail transport and the illegitimate appointees of the ministerial faction. To enter the office of a genuine Railway officer is to find a true professional concerned for the system and its reputation. He will share information in the hope that all aspects of rail working will receive public exposure and gain from the feedback. By contrast, the office of the fawning favourite brought in on deputation to tell the minister what he wants to hear will only release the statistics that do their mentor proud. They are more concerned to advertise their loyalty to the image of their leader than to the reputation of the Railways—which has to pay for these expensive drags on the system.

The mentality of the sort that gets stuck in these senior postings always assumes that they—the ministerially chosen—are ordained to lecture while you—the public—were created to listen. In a newspaper article I had mentioned how a carriage conductor had illegally charged me five rupees for an overnight berth in south India. I was so grateful to get the berth at 2.00 in the morning that I thought nothing of winking at the demanded bribe and stated that the guilt lay with me for paying, as much as with the conductor. In the same newspaper there was a strongly worded complaint of an air force officer who protested that his confirmed bookings had mysteriously disappeared from the conductor's list to make way for a last minute arrival of a political heavyweight for the overnight train to Delhi. When the grievances officer sent me a routine letter of enquiry for further details of the corrupt conductor—to its credit the Railways investigates every complaint—I decided to meet him with a view to express the public's disgust at something much worse than the defrauding of the railways of five rupees—the demoralization of the nation by queue-jumping VIPs. In the young man's office were the usual background noises of senior governmental perks, the wife on the phone for a staff car, an uncle for a last-minute booking on the VIP quota, and a nephew eager for complimentary tickets for a sporting event. One does not begrudge these perks, and even if one did there's little to be done to prevent them being dispensed since similar conversations occur on the phone of senior officers in every government department I have been to. These are the facts of official life in Delhi—the urge to cream off rather than to labour to grow fodder for the well-being of the livestock. Instead of listening to my strong feelings about the unseated air force officer and learning of the widespread public disgust at the calculated insult to decent values, the young officer predictably retreated into the excuses of his trade and tried the usual bureaucratic prevarications in order to avoid the plain truth that my five rupees bribe was not worth considering in comparison to the damage wreaked by Railway connivance at VIP muscle power.

By refusing to apply his mind this young man extended the suspicion that a policy of cultivated apathy is encouraged at the topmost rungs of the Rail administration. He was paid to explore public grievances, not defend the highhandedness of compliant officials. As with all other vigilance organizations one left his office feeling that the joke was on the public. These spineless milkers of the system lack the will to better the Railway administration, though they do testify to the strength of a system that can absorb their uselessness and neutralize their negativity.

The Saving Grace of Professional Traditions Honoured Down the Line

Needless to say, the ministerial aide who wasted my time was not a railwayman. Backtracking down the spacious corridors to where the pile on the carpets assumes a less lush tread I turned into the office of the Public Relations people. Here one found total helpfulness and the sort of insistence on being kind that led to complete strangers like Colin Garratt turning up in Burdwan and being asked what colour he would like his locomotive painted. Professional officers have fierce pride in their cadre and resent the political interlopers who steal Railway thunder (and possibly much else besides). Most of these genuine railwaymen will laugh at the excessive obsequiousness that socialist ministers have come to demand of them and are always ready to fuel stories of the more outrageous and wasteful idiosyncrasies of their political masters.

The most remarkable thing about Rail Bhavan learnt on our Kafkaesque tour is the subdued atmosphere of the very British corridors. They march before one's gaze in serried immaculacy past the senior brethren of the permanent way who, confined to their gleaming cabins, bask in the glow of panelled opulence. The level of maintenance is acutely at odds with every other public building in the land. Nowhere do you find the *deshi* urge to make a mess. There are no notices urging us to 'Arise and Awake', no wall posters demanding an 'Immediate End to All Social Injustice' and not a single one promising a 'Better Tomorrow'. Austere and emphatically efficient these uncluttered vistas are a healthy symbol of how the railways run so smoothly in spite of the aberrations of a political helmsman. Here one needs no scrawled message telling us 'Discipline is the Need of the Hour', for all around us lay the visible fruits of an iron rule. The virtues of Rail Bhavan are an actual physical tonic, and from this polished evidence of self-respect we can intuitively guess why Indian Railways is one of the nation's few success stories.

The effects of this pervasive political imposition are seen in the most unlikely corners. While waiting for a train at Quilon in Kerala I found posted on the platform wall a lengthy sermon from a new Railway Board chairman who on taking over felt it appropriate to unburden himself. It was a closely reasoned text printed in English and totally predictable in its structure and sentiment. India *par excellence* is the land of exhortation where everybody exhorts everybody else to do the things that no one has the slightest intention of doing themselves. At Quilon the message was that despite aging assets and declining public morality, railwaymen should reflect on the fact that they are better cared for than the average employee. This fact is always hammered home in the official statistics.

The Railway Workforce

The enormous workforce of sixteen lakh employees needed to keep the system running costs the nation around 4000 crore per annum. There are many who feel this is a top heavy organization, especially when with modern transport innovations the need for manpower is growing less. Staff wages amount to 36 per cent of the annual expenditure while passenger earnings only add up to 25 per cent of revenue, representing a difference of 1000 crore of rupees. When wages are forced up by union demands or government commissions, fares are bound to increase to offset them. How can a modern system accommodate such a large work-force when there is a decreasing dependence on their services? Needless to say, in his *Status Paper* for railway reforms, Mr Fernandes shies away from discussing the subject of job saturation. However, he gives us the mind-boggling figure that 100,000 applicants contacted him in a mere two-month period for jobs on the Railways. One of the reasons for the *Status Paper* was to break it gently to the public that the IR cow of plenty was under considerable duress. The railways are in no position to offer more jobs, and were realism ever to penetrate the clouds of socialistic ideology that mantle the Rail Minister's luxurious chair in Rail Bhavan, it would be recognized that a problem already exits in finding the money to pay for the present staff commitments. The hefty wage bill means less for outlay in rescuing an old system from further decay and leaves hardly any investment for the expensive up-to-date technology that could solve some of the problems of waste.

Plastered around the chairman's inspirational poster speech were other railway exhortations painted directly on to the Quilon station wall: 'Keep up the improvement achieved in maintaining discipline and punctuality'. (No one could quarrel with that except possibly a grammarian.) 'Guard national property with a sense of personal indemnification'. (Here one's jaw went slack at the sheer style of the jargon.) 'Develop greater know-how and avoid imports'. (A simple enough third commandment but it did not hold much water in a place like Quilon where, like the rest of India, everyone seemed more crazy for foreign consumer goods than foreign know-how.) The last of the list of slogans was truly imposing since it managed to extract the most meaninglessness from the least number of words—'Make maximum utilization of available capacity'.

Diversions in the South

As one sat waiting for the train it was painful to think that after Kerala's magnificent achievement in making every citizen able to read, these mumbo-jumbo slogans should greet the newly literate. Official jargon seems to be a gas that expands indefinitely until it reaches the limits of bombast, when it turns into a soporific jelly that rains down on the heads of an impervious public. The accumulation of useless information and the amassing of pseudo-scientific formulae for public display is tiresomely unprofitable and induces in the traveller the feeling that if the Railways cannot find better ways to spend its money why should he waste his on a ticket? The public demands useful information not hot air.

On that occasion I had been travelling for three weeks in Kerala and had gone first to Quilon to book a ticket back to the north. I was unable to get a confirmed booking but the young lady who issued the ticket said it was almost certain I would get a berth if I turned up a day before the train left. When I followed her instructions the man on duty regretted he could not finalize the quota list till the next morning when the train left. But he again insisted that my chances were extremely good and that patience was all that was required. Normally these vague assurances would have been taken with a pinch of salt in north India but in Kerala people are much more focused and given to applying their minds. I decided to kill the overnight wait by taking the metre gauge Madras Mail over the mountains to Tenkasi to see the water-falls at Courtallam that evening and come back on the overnight Express from Tiruchi. Next morning, Mr Nair the booking-in-charge, again bade me be patient and said that he would do his best to get me a reserved berth. When the charts were at last pinned up, my name was on them. Here there was no question of a bribe being offered or accepted, just a routine case of the staff doing their best to be helpful and holding out genuine encouragement to a stranger when it would have been just as easy for them to remain non-committal.

It might be noted as a travel tip that, for a surcharge of fifteen rupees, my overnight journey in a second class sleeper saved the expense of a hotel room. Unlike in the north, where the press of population is forever near breaking point, the metre gauge trains in the south run comparatively uncrowded and there is rarely any need to make over-night reservations. Furthermore, there is little of the security fear that lurks around the Gangetic routes.

In contrast, one of the journeys that made me most apprehensive was in travelling by a metre gauge train north of Patna late at night with no other passenger in the carriage except two armed policemen. Every door and window had been locked and none of the lights worked. Next morning the policemen were astonished to discover me on an upper berth. They had got on the allotted coach thinking it was empty and decided the best way to give security to an empty sleeper carriage was to keep out all other passengers along the way and to sleep soundly themselves.

The Breakdown of Railway Jobs

Though it takes all sorts to add up to the sixteen lakhs of Railway employees, this figure does not include the category of casual labour, some of whom contribute critical inputs, as in the permanent way gangs and the knowledgeable red-shirted band of coolies who are of more assistance to a passenger than many uniformed officials. The break up of this vast Railway family includes about 32 per cent work-shop and artisan staff and over 6 per cent running staff. Scheduled castes and tribes occupy about 23 per cent of Railway jobs, of whom some 2000 work at the top levels, which have a total roster of 130,000 officers. *Bahri's Hand Book for Railwaymen* (printed in Delhi) includes a diary whose personal memoranda includes every career statistic—not only one's date of appointment but date of confirmation, of promotion, of increment and retirement. In the columns for 'record of emoluments' are headings that reveal the range of benefits extended by the Railways. One can claim for 'water/lawn charges' and 'geaser/fan hire'. Other exotic allowances are available for 'Bad Climate' and 'Remote Locality'. For the existence of that other lowly category—the Indian woman—no figures are forthcoming, which must suggest naught for the comfort of the feminist lobby. One sees lady booking clerks (indeed one always joins their queue in preference to long-faced male Delhi clerks) and hears of lady ticket collectors and a stray case of a female diesel driver but it looks like a long haul awaits any lady officer who aspires to be a member of the Railway Board.

The most famous Indian railwaywoman, however, is P. T. Usha, the international hurdler who came within a hundredth of a second of winning an Olympic medal. Over the years the Railways have allowed many athletes time off from their duties to train for their events. In return, these high-kicking figures have been used to advertise the drive and goal of the Railways. 'Champions of the track', is one example spotted in a newspaper that shows P. T. Usha hurdling through a hoop depicting the Indian Rail logo (which is, incidentally, an embarrassment now that the decision to scrap steam has rendered it obsolete. Finding a new one is proving to be a problem in spite of a public competition with a juicy reward of 20,000 rupees for the winning design).

'Yes', says an advert, 'Indian Railways have an unbeaten track record as the largest in Asia carrying 11 million passengers and nearly 10 lakh tonnes of freight over a distance of four times to the moon each day.' For once an attempt to make statistics more meaningful has been employed, though very few of us will have any idea of the distance to the moon. Sometimes Railway advertisements can be counter-productive. When the reformed firebrand Mr Fernandes inserted a ministerial appeal to the public not to interfere with the normal running of the lines there was a backlash of cynicism and anger.

'I have been observing with anguish and concern,' wrote the ex-union leader, 'an unprecedented attack on Railway property and passengers ... [which is] particularly distressing because this is being done by educated youth. Railways are the life-line of India and the wheels of our economy.' Against which a most withering cartoon appeared showing a leader in spate: 'You must go back to work. True I used to lead violent agitations before I became a minister. But I never realized then that they disrupted normal life, caused untold suffering and damaged the economy.' Incidentally, the Railway punishment for anyone intent on wrecking a train can be life imprisonment and the minister may have politics to thank for sending him to Parliament instead of jail.

The Need to Project Rail Successes More Professionally

The huge Railway family, with its hundreds of competing craft unions and beset at the very top by political stuntsmanship, nevertheless somehow manages to survive with its morale high. Today, after the defence services, the Railways is the only organization that can hold its head high in getting on with the job of improving the quality of life in the subcontinent. The role of railwaymen is a rallying factor at a time of threatened regional tugs and especially when caste and communal stresses (that have always beggered India's progress as a strong nation) are reappearing. The metals of IR are the best evidence of a welded unity. The Railways weakness is a failure to stress this national role more positively. In our climb down the pyramid from Kafka's castle back to the running staff it ought to be clear that the virtues outshine the weaknesses. The Railway service, which has always seemed unheroic and socially not quite acceptable, needs to view itself more aggressively. A start could be made by officers insisting on the right to use 'IRS' after their names to denote a pride in their calling.

CHAPTER ELEVEN

From Classic to Vintage

To bridge the gap between the almost animal passion of the locomotive-lover and the puzzled indifference to rail transport of the ordinary observer makes any discourse on the subject an exercise of sitting on two stools which are being moved away from each other. Flesh and blood encounters with the subject are more meaningful than paper explanations and for a man to get involved with one woman is usually more productive of the true meaning of love than for him to write an academically correct entry on 'harem' for an encyclopaedia. The great difference between railway love in Britain and in India is on the scale of physical intensity.

Schoolboy Recollections of Train Spotting

By no means an enthusiastic train spotter, as a grammar school boy in Birmingham I did gravitate in my spare time to the end of platform one of New Street station to watch the driving wheels of the departing Jubilees spin frantically or to recognize the arrival of lesser Midland 'Compounds' by their thrashings inside the tunnel. And once or twice I cycled to Tamworth in Staffordshire to spend the day watching the trains go by, a strange luxury to a financially strapped schoolboy. With a sigh of satisfaction my brother and I pedalled back the fifteen miles with some twenty 'namers' underlined in our 'refs'. Funnily enough, I had an aunt in Tamworth whom I visited regularly by bus. On those tame occasions I never bothered to go down to the station, where two lines crossed, but contented myself with putting a penny on the lower line and to wait, with Scots republican truculence, to see His Majesty's profile being polished off by the rush of 6229—the *Duchess of Hamilton*—as she hammered by on her way to Euston. (Happily for my nostalgic instincts this engine continues preserved in steam, though the old penny has been scrapped.)

As holiday commuters from Birmingham to Stirling in our annual clan reunions, my brother and I exulted at Crewe and went ecstatic over Shap. On one occasion between trains an LMS official came up and asked, 'Are you Sandy and Billy?' Our mother's Stirling train had left without us, but by an alchemy I have never been able to work out we were all reunited at Carstairs. The special joys of the North Eastern railway I have already mentioned, where from the top of our local hill Dumyat, some 1300 feet above the Forth, the sight of the 'Wee Puffer' approaching Menstrie meant we would have to descend smartly to catch it on its journey back from Alva.

As a schoolboy too I was exposed to the main Great Western line that passed over my daily Outer Circle bus to Handsworth Grammar. But how many loyalties can a boy have? Crewe was my Mecca and the 'Streaks' of the LMS (which were too bulky for the Birmingham tunnels) were for me the true prophets of steam—even though they retained their wartime khaki livery. The LNER steamliners were runners-up, as they clanked light past the Scott Monument to Waverley. The GWR 'Castles' came a long way behind in my affections though, as with all prejudices, I only know now to my cost what I had missed in not discerning an erotic component in their classical styling.

India boasts few spotters but does have several encylopaedists. The first I met was a young man in Allahabad who lived, moved and had his being in *Bradshaw*. He could tell you the time of any train at any given station, or so it seemed. Since then I have met other similarly enthusiastic collectors of abstract railway lore. It is not that India lacks rail lovers, it is just that they are apt to be more intellectual and metaphysically inclined. You won't find them at the end of grimy platforms wiping off the oil with cotton waste as they seek to read the manufacturer's plate. They will be found in the comfort of their homes with books on the mechanical details, from Satow and Desmond's *Railways of the Raj* to Hugh Hughe's *Steam Locomotives in India* (in three volumes). You only find out the love of these men's lives when you turn up for what was assumed to be an evening's social gathering with small talk of politics where the ladies smile sweetly and pass snacks to conceal their boredom. When the conversation spontaneously turns to the tractive effort of a WAM 4 or a WAP 5 and arguments wage over the diameter of the coupled wheels of a WP and WG, suddenly the evening passes so quickly that even the ladies don't notice their boredom.

A Digression on Scrap via Ranchi

As the steam age leans into the final curve the least we can do is indicate where some of the old favourites can be located—if the auctioneer's scrap hammer does not get to them first. This happened to me at Ranchi, a thoroughly delightful railway town with both broad and narrow gauge activity. I had gone by the Hatia-Tata Express which travelled as dismally as its name suggests until it got off the main line at Mirzapur and entered the fabulous jungled country of the Vindhyas, through which we traversed for a whole day to get to the Jharkhand area. Sitting opposite me was a commercial traveller from Delhi who kept producing quarter bottles of rum, which he held up to the light to make sure were full and then proceeded to empty the contents at one go. Having drained three 'nips' he claimed mournfully that these rituals were justified because he had never wanted to be a commercial traveller in the first place. 'I have the soul of a poet,' he said, looking gloomily at the last half of his fourth nip which he then quaffed to the refrain, 'If music be the food of life—drink on'. Wiping his mouth he would identify his quotations: 'Keats', he would say—or whatever poet he imagined himself to be drawing from. At Daltonganj he made the lucid observation that the train would now enter a long diversionary loop and that it would be quicker to catch a bus. He kindly arranged for me to stay in a hotel run by a friend, but he misspent the evening getting ever more drunk on poetry. His parting mis-attribution— after reciting Hamlet's soliloquy (mixed up with Macbeth's secret black and midnight hags)—was 'If Winter comes can Spring be far

behind'—which he awarded to Browning. Then he keeled over to
announce that the anthologist's barrel had at last run dry.

As I had come to Ranchi to see old steam engines and not com-
miserate with misfit commercial travellers I tip-toed out of the hotel
early next morning and chose another overlooking the station. Ranchi,
along with Puri, has a famous railway hotel. Both have managed to
retain the standards of a more demanding age and when I saw the
Ranchi building's elegant lines spaciously set out in a gracious com-
pound I was tempted to spend a night there. But the cheaper hotel
along the road had the advantage of a flat roof which overlooked narrow-gauge shunting engines as they backed their wagons of ore on
top of a rake of broad gauge hoppers to discharge their load below.

Identifying Your Locomotive

Indian Railways distinguishes its three gauges by the letter— W for
the broad, Y for the metre and Z for the 2 ft 6 in. narrow gauge. Thus
a locomotive with WP painted on it, refers to a broad gauge 'passenger'
engine, just as WG refers to a 'goods' engine. These class descriptions
invented for steam traction have been extended to diesel—WDM 2,
refers to broad gauge diesel 'mixed', i.e. either goods or passenger
engine. (The 2 refers to the developments from prototype.) Electric
traction inserts the letter A to indicate the standard AC system, thus
WAP3 is 'broad gauge electric passenger mark three'.

Throughout India the few remaining classes of steam are to be found
in fairly even numbers, though the availability of coal supplies is an
important factor in determining their distribution. In the 1990s a few
survivors of the heavily manufactured classes are all that one can real-
istically hope to find on broad and metre gauge lines. Incidentally,
never listen to theoretical railway administrators about what you will
find running. Unless you go and check out for yourself they will tell
you, for example, that there is no steam in the south. In fact there is
enough (on the metre gauge) to make a visit memorable.

It is only on the narrow gauge that one can expect to find a variety
of classes and these are of extra interest since the locomotives were

all manufactured abroad for specific duties. Collectors have to be careful of the continual renumbering of these old engines by various hands—at the time of regrouping, nationalization and (today) of redeployment. For example the ZE locos I found at Ranchi were familiar faces to me but were complete strangers to Bihar. They had been sent from the Satpura lines around Nagpur in central India and I had seen some of them in the steam shed at Nainpur just before it was closed down.

Although quick off the mark to become self-sufficient in diesel and to a lesser extent the latest electric traction, it was not considered worthwhile for India to make narrow gauge diesel locos until recently. The decision to phase out steam by the year 1995 made it necessary for Chittaranjan Loco Works to start producing the ZDM (incidentally, now the world's most powerful narrow gauge diesel locomotive). The versatility of Indian Railways emerges from this ability to rise to the occasion without any fuss. Of all the efficient working parts of the IR system, the specialized units for skilled production call for special recognition. We have seen how within the space of a few years a newly founded diesel workshop was into exporting metre gauge diesel units and successfully competing for international tenders against old, tried and reputed combines. The sort of confidence these achievements should generate remains sadly lacking. Anything Indian from colonial habit is still thought to be second best. In their research and constructional competence Indian Railways are amongst the world leaders. Unfortunately, the public is more impressed by speed and slick appearances not realizing that in a non-industrial culture like India's where the public has always regarded the track as a public right of way, it would be suicidal to press for superfast traffic until the people have been educated to the dangers and the track properly secured for sophisticated speeds. Both options are prohibitively expensive, and who can blame the Railways, in the meantime, for using words like 'Superfast' to foster the illusion that we are keeping up with the French and Japanese?

The small line out of Ranchi had been serviced by the 'British Standard' BS class. Originally the line had run east to join up with Purulia in Bengal but some of this has been converted into broad gauge.

Earlier at Nagpur I had been disappointed at the Motibagh shed in not being allowed to photograph a BS and now looked forward in Ranchi to see the last of the species still running. But too late. I was told if I went down the line to Hatia Junction I could see the condemned loco in the siding awaiting the knacker's knock. When I arrived to photograph her, all I got was the echo of her destruction. She had been hammered into pieces a few days before.

The Casual Attitude Towards Rail History

The dog in the manger attitude of IR to its vintage stock is partly the result of working for a public undertaking where there is little call on the pride that stimulated so many private railroad companies to become famous. In the absence of public spirit, petty jealousies and disgruntlement surface to make sure that anyone who appears to be enjoying himself (as amateur loco spotters clearly are) should be pulled down to the level of mass gloom. You can see the apathy of official attitudes in the upkeep of the Delhi Rail Museum, one of the most fascinating collections of steam engines in the world. Instead of being a jealously guarded source of pride, this outdoor display in Chanakyapuri is totally neglected for months at a time until a VIP looms on the horizon. Then staff are rushed in from Amritsar to get steam up on the old numbers to pretend that this is the way things usually are.

The museum collection significantly was the brainchild of Mike Satow, a popular expatriate engineer whose position as head of the Indian ICI enabled most of his suggestions to sound respectable enough for the Railway Board not to veto. But after erecting the show there has been little enthusiasm to expand it or even maintain it as it deserves. Plans were mooted to have other regional museums but nothing has come of them except for a small collection in Mysore. There I was horrified to find no one was on duty to prevent the public from walking away with some of the priceless exhibits on display. Amusingly, I was allowed to walk away with the whole day's takings when I insisted on buying a catalogue and the (sole) gate attendant refused to sell his last copy (with the familiar governmental cry—'Sorry. Out of stock').

When I opened the guide book I found inside several ten rupee notes from the day's gate-money. The attendant received them back with a sheepish shrug. However, Southern Railway is not likely to grind to a halt for a loss of fifty rupees!

Occasionally a journalist visits the Delhi museum and deplores the neglect and after this bad press the very next day extra men are sent in to cut the grass and slap some paint on the locos. The museum staff in turn complain bitterly that most of their clients are parties of school kids out for the day and not the least bit interested in the details of the collection. They clamber all over the exhibits and would damage things if not restrained. One of the biggest problems for visitors is that for most of the year it is too hot to comfortably view metal objects out of doors in Delhi.

The Delhi Rail Museum also has an excellent indoor collection of railway impediments plus a library and sales counter. Monographs by a former curator, R. R. Bhandari, on the history of particular lines ought to be snapped up as priceless oases in the desert of Indian rail information. But what is badly missing is any organized enthusiasm. The sort of people who would love to attend the special occasions when steam is got up (for a visiting VIP) are not likely to be invited by the Railways and even if they were they would find it hard to get past the security that New Delhi amasses on these occasions.

In the layout of Railways priorities the museum comes right at the end of the *Year Book*. Under Mr Scindia's ministership the museum inevitably received even less honour since his interest was electric traction on the fast track and the old steam engines reminded the world that India was still dependent on outmoded coal. In Gwalior, the home town of the minister, I saw lined up for scrapping several unique narrow gauge locomotives dating back to the golden age of the Gwalior Light Railway. When a man of Scindia's background fails to honour his own family stable—there are none of these famous NH class in the Delhi museum—what can one expect from other ministers unacquainted with the public history of Indian Railways? Rather than be sold for scrap these ancient engines would have fetched a good price from overseas collectors, but the Railways are so out of touch with international transport fashions that no one realizes that vintage steam is big business today.

Further Digressions into Bengal, Orissa and Maharashtra

It was with considerable delight, therefore, that I peeped into the Bankura shed (beyond Ranchi) and saw some old Delta and ex-McLeod & Co. Bagnalls, which appeared to have been forgotten by the sentencing judge. On the charming 'ML Railway' of former Mayurbhanj State in Orissa (working my way south from Bankura), I found a line of handsome CC class locos I had come in search of but they were all lined up with 'condum' written on them. At Baripada shed (one of the most pleasantly informal in the whole of India, and accustomed to rail enthusiasts) I met an Anglo-Indian driver posted on an imported ZE who bemoaned the loss of his beloved CC which had been in turn transferred to Bankura. One has to keep up with the transfer intricacies of these light lines and I learnt the local ML class had all been sent 'down country' to the other entrancing little line of Orissa, the Parlakimedi. But when I got there what I saw was the similar PL class (serviced at Naupada) of Kerr Stuart side-tanks dating back to 1928, full of character and proudly sporting a stove-pipe chimney.

Officially steam has been abolished on the Satpura and Barsi lines though I was lucky to see its last gasp on both of these narrow gauges. Both in Kurduvadi (Maharashtra)—the main workshop for NG locomotives—and at Nainpur (M. P.), I was chased away by censorious security men. According to them, no honest citizen should have the voyeuristic need to lust at rusting old birds. Clearly I was up to no good and my permit had no validity until the foreman turned up at nine o'clock. By preventing photography Indian Rail history has suffered more than I. At Nainpur I had the thrill of watching the Satpura Express thrash down the line behind a ZE. This surely was a train the Railways might have thought of preserving as a matter of international prestige. Where else in the world do you find steam expresses on the narrow gauge running to a daily timetable? Unchanged since the Satpura lines were opened in 1905, the 2 Down leaves Howbagh (Jabalpur) at 5.00 in the morning and covers the 224 kilometres to Gondia Junction by 1.00 p.m. At 2.00 she returns as the 1 Up Satpura Express to get back to Jabalpur by 10.00 p.m. This train now hauled by diesel continues to create mild waves on the narrow gauge system, possessing an air-conditioned chair-car coach.

Gujarat's Stable of Steam

The richest haul of narrow-gauge steam is still in the place where it first started, near Baroda (Vadodera in the timetable). Dabhoi in Gujarat is a rail spotter's dream come true with five little lines radiating from it, most served by the handsome and faithful ZB class. Each year the branch lines fall to the problems of drought and flood but the system runs too well to be abandoned for sometime to come. The workshop at Vadodera is said to possess a K class used for internal shunting. Judging by the way Western Railways react to a camera on site you would think the workshop harboured a nuclear bomb not a vintage engine. Typically, my souvenir of that visit is a letter from the Western Railways public relations officer which reads, 'We were ourselves thinking of capturing the narrow gauge steam sections on record . . .' It seems a case of willful negligence that no transport museum in the land has yet bothered to record a single cassette of the sounds of India's steam generation. What sublime apathy is displayed in this official failure to record footplate sounds that in a few years will be heard no more. Video parlours abound in the tiniest village all over the country and yet the nation's largest moving undertaking cannot get round to taping its own history. Of a piece with vested inertia, I suggested to a retired railway manager that his expert opinions be recorded for posterity. He agreed, but when I sent him a list of twenty questions he declined, perhaps deeming the exercise imprudent.

Thanks to the plethora of princely lines in Kathiawad (Gujarat) it is still possible to find some unusual NG locomotives, though after a space of just a few years no doubt most will have given up the fight to survive. At Morvi were shedded two W class locos, one of which had a weather-vane on its dome. Stranded amidst metre gauge replacements, the little line to Ghantila was also out of commission having been washed away by floods. I had a mind to take the metre gauge to Navlakhi for the ferry marked on the old maps and nearly leaped on the YL that pulled up at Morvi. When I checked with the guard about the timings of the ferry he laughed out loud. The ferry had closed twenty years ago. Trying to work out a way round the Rann of Kutch I thought I might go to Dahinsara Junction and change for another short run on the metre gauge to Miyana. This latter junction stood on the new broad gauge line across the Rann, a superb engineering achievement I badly wanted to view. However, to go that way would have taken at least two days by train. Instead, I took a bus from Morvi to Bhuj which got me across on the same afternoon. I had to be content with viewing the rail causeway from a distance.

Thumbing through the timetable in the bus at Gandhidham, I noted that a passenger train was due and that the station was only a stone's throw from the bus stand. Why not end this journey to Bhuj, the westernmost metre gauge station in India (though the Nalia extension was then due to open in a few months time) in style by a steam engine? Sacrificing my bus fare I went across to the booking office, bought a ticket for the end of the line and asked the clerk how many steam engines I would find at Bhuj. 'Here we believe in progress', he said—'No steam'. This was a blow, especially as Bhuj turned out to be quite one of the nicest Indian towns I have been in. The budget hotel was beautifully clean and the food they served elegantly Gujarati with the most tempting vegetarian delicacies. All it needed to make this the perfect small town was the flourish of steam.

Touching Upon the Deccan

The remainder of the metre gauge steam fleet are almost entirely YPs, or its goods version, the YG. With their blinkers these engines, no matter how dirty, make for handsome profiles and are always summoned up to show off India's famous domes, the Taj Mahal and the Gol Gumbaz, to good effect. The latter happens to be amongst the biggest in the world incidentally, second only to St Peter's in Rome and bigger than St Paul's in London. It also enjoys some heraldic rail glory in being depicted on the official shield of the old Southern Mahratta Railway Company. There is a Gol Gumbaj Express, involving an epic trundle across the Deccan to Bijapur from Bangalore, and since it also stops at Badami, the visitor can view India's most scintillating temples too. (Taken together the Deccan architecture of Bijapur and Badami knocks Agra and Delhi resoundingly into the shade.)

It should be noted by aesthetic followers of steam that the metre gauge engines of the South Central zone are the most beautifully maintained of subcontinental locomotives. From Khandwa in Madhya Pradesh to Guntakal in Andhra Pradesh it is a joy to see the love lavished on these YPs. One of the loveliest rail scenes I have seen was to pass the tiny rural loco shed at Akola (midway in Maharashtra) and mark the gleaming livestock aglow with the outward signs of mechanical affection in the afternoon sun. Purna, further down the line, took the prize for maintaining the most sparkling locomotives in India, while Guntakal easily won the competition for artistic decoration of loco bodies. For example, the Tirupati Passenger had a beautifully painted board set on her front buffers showing the famous temple of Balaji and the joys of a pilgrimage to probably the richest shrine in the world. All the engines around Guntakal have artwork on their cab sides and tenders, and the blinkers invariably carry some dynamic motif like a springing tiger or an unleashed arrow. One dilapidated number surely in line for the scrap-yard hammer had optimistically painted across her bows 'God saves'.

Rajasthan Recalled

The smartest run loco shed I have visited was at Bikaner where Sardar J. S. Murari ran the operations with military precision and an abiding enthusiasm for steam. There is a fine little museum of mechanical parts for trainees at Bikaner and I was shown an ancient G class loco tucked away at the back of the yard. Apart from YPs and YGs the only other metre gauge engines around in any number are the MAWDs (noticed, for example, in Guwahati), and a few of the YL class for lighter lines and more modest duties (e.g. in Gujarat). If you are puzzled by what looks like a YG without blinkers hauling passenger stock—that's exactly what it is. Nowadays these goods engines (with or without blinkers) work passenger trains and (if you do not count the cost of the coal) make excellent travelling companions when the driver gives them their head.

The last steam engine built in India was YG 3573 which steamed away to her home shed at Banaras on 5 February 1972, sadly without any ceremony for what had been a thoroughbred performance from a class totalling 1074 locomotives.

The broad gauge *Antim Sitara* (whose name had been borrowed from British Rail's *Evening Star*) at least had a name-plate attached when unveiled in June 1970 though she was a mere goods engine (WG 10560). Perhaps this handsome class of loco - still the most visible on Indian Railways and full of steam magic with its rugged Yankee looks—deserved the honour since it is believed the total number manufactured—2450 engines—is the largest single class of steam locos ever built for any Commonwealth railway. Bhusawal shed may possess another Commonwealth record in once holding almost 100 engines of this class.

Broad Gauge Survivors in Steam

The ubiquity of the WG and the thrilling bullet nose of her companion passenger model, the WP, guarantee that a lot of character will attend the very last pantings of steam in India. The most famous broad gauge class HPS with its pre-war preference for British looks has long been withdrawn and the oldest BG steam class is the very American war-time WDs. Those from the USA are known AWD, while their sisters manufactured in Canada are labelled CWD. (The metre gauge WDs, to distinguish them, are referred to as MAWD class.)

Occasionally on the lighter lines one may bump into a WL. Recently, on detraining from the Punjab Mail at Kotkapura Junction to catch the metre gauge branch line to Fazilka, my ears tingled to the sweet prairie music of an approaching WL Pacific from Ferozepur bound for Bhatinda. Most were allotted to sheds in the Northern region for branch line duties.

In general, as with the cultural pattern, the better looked after engines will be found in central and southern India. The north is too beset with problems of population and politics to be able to bother with the self-respect that comes from polishing official artifacts that may at the drop of a hat become the objects of public ire. Nevertheless, where you have a northern engine crew attached to their locomotive and a depot foreman with a keen sense of competition you will find particular locos from his round-house fitted out with distinctive grills and markings. It is common for an imaginative crew even in the inartistic Cow Belt to bedeck their WG chimney with a fluted coronet and to paint a silver star up front. Colin Garratt has captured the mood in a WP laced with a crown and bearing a board in Hindi that reads *Sanjay*. The significance of this is lost on the outsider which refers again to the chronic infusion of politics into anything that runs in India. The picture can be dated from this reference to Sanjay Gandhi, the Emergency strong-man, whom his mother Mrs Gandhi allowed to rampage—not unlike a runaway locomotive—on the rights of decent citizens. The significance of the board may mean either that a driver wanted promotion by way of this crude expression of flattery or that his running superintendent had an eye to similar prospects. The politics being north Indian, the board would no doubt have been repainted *Rajiv* as soon as his younger brother's political fortunes had expired.

The east coast is a good place to see WPs running at speed and often in colourful livery. As one works one's way south from Orissa the cultural upswing is evident in the turn out of all categories of transport. Trucks and buses in the south are painted with finesse, in matching colours, while the rest of Aryan India tends to slap on the paint garishly and loudly, the pinker the better. If the important areas of industrial Bengal and steel-citied Bihar have been given the go-by this is not from any lack of railway interest but simply from the writer's conscious avoidance of hassle-prone destinations. Jamalpur in Bengal is the Crewe, Swindon, and Doncaster of India rolled into one but it would be a brave man who travelled in such wild and woolly areas without a railway chaperon. This is a pity in view of the tremendous historical importance of West Bengal to the growth of the Indian steam fleet.

The Oldest Working Loco in the World

The sugarcane tracts west of Bihar and north of the Ganga still yield the odd industrial locomotive. Over the border in Nepal at the Kosi Barrage I nearly fell off my motorbike to come face to face with a 1908 BC class. It seems this old Bengal Nagpur Railway engine had been sold to Nepal in 1958. At Janakpur, a pleasant surprise awaits the brave steam enthusiast who will find two rusting NG Beyer-Garratts. An even more exciting find lies near Gorakhpur (back in India) at Sardarnagar. Here, at the Saraiya Sugar Mills, is a fleet of ancient and adapted steamers that will gladden the heart of any rail enthusiast. Privately owned, the industrial estate also happens to be the ancestral property of Amrita Sher Gill, one of the first great modern Indian artists in oils. Sorting out the provenance of these vintage models, which get up steam in the cane season (November to March), will keep the most agile of Masterminds busy. It appears that *Tweed* can claim to be the oldest steam locomotive at work anywhere in the world and that she arrived in the *Purbia* outback (to the very civilized attentions of Dr Victor Egon, the Hungarian-born husband of the artist) via the predecessor of the 'Old and Tired' railway (Oudh and Tirhut)—Tirhoot State Railway. The 0–4–0 'D' class no. 8 was sold to the Sikh industrialist family at Sardarnagar in 1926. The romantic confusion surrounding her parentage has not been helped by the theft of the manufacturer's plate by an enthusiast who betrayed Dr Egon's trust. Apparently *Tweed* (and her sister *Mersey*—said to be working on a neighbouring sugar mill) were built by Sharp Stewart in 1873. When I saw her in 1986 the distinguished nameplate continued to ride high on the boiler while her tender had painted on the side a supplementary Indian name—the Hindi rendering of 'Emperor Ashoka'.

CHAPTER TWELVE

Broadly Speaking

Having outlined the sort of pleasure that awaits the desperate seeker of steam, we can now enjoy ourselves and travel behind these aging loco-motives to compare the ride they give with the new breed of traction.

The broad gauge is an echo of the political lines along which India is laid. The teeming (and some would say civically tottering) Gangetic culture depends heavily on the snarl of track that knots the railway map. Though not entirely synonymous with the Cow Belt and its heavy-weight political presence, the role of the broad gauge is very much akin to the stridency of the Hindi fanatics who claim to speak for the whole country. The brute statistics of the 5 feet 6 inches gauge certainly sug-gests a major slice of the cake of rail traffic—82 per cent of the passenger flow and a whopping 90 per cent near monopoly of freight movement.

The Clash Between Emotions and Reality on the Ground

The (1988) track length of the BG is 54 per cent compared to the 38 per cent of the metre system. Two crucial facts of life militate against the exaggerated belief that the broad gauge is the only one that counts. It still does not link up the entire Indian land mass, as does the metre gauge, though Minister Jaffer Sharief has recently taken the drastic decision to phase out the metric in favour of 'uniguage'. What we are left with is similar to the place of Hindi in national calculations. Both the language and broad gauge of the Gangetic Valley *ought* to be the ideal standards but are not—for obvious political and physical reasons which narcissistic north Indians find hard to face. Since Independence, a lot of India's problems have marked time stymied by notions of idealistic nationalism that refuses to face religious and ethnic complexities. At least when the Railways took a decision in 1988 to make the metre gauge more productive they acknowledged the inescapable logic of financial contingencies. Unfortunately, to those concerned with the realm of political and religious ideology such clear thinking as to 'Who will pay?' escapes their schemes.

Too often prescriptions to improve the condition of India are based on empty assumptions, the most common being that the remedy agreeable to most must be the best. The secret of India's enduring unity, however, has been based on the ability to assimilate and reconcile disparate points of view. Only in the splendour of the many can the fullness of the one be enjoyed. Traditionally, India has held herself together by an elastic cultural ease of intercourse that was strong enough to overcome the stretch of widely varied regions and the stumbling block of many tongues. The British administration used the Railways to strengthen the underpinning of culture with administrative steel, but since Independence the drift towards regional and communal divisiveness has been set in motion at the urge of power-seeking leaders who whip up an unlettered constituency by feeding them assumptions about India that are not borne out by travelling reality.

It is a sad comment on the priorities of the government that it is only during events like the Nehru Centenary that 'All-India Rail Integration' tours are tub-thumped to political advantage. Though there are concessionary tickets for circular tours of the country, the public at large feel, perhaps rightly, that they are intended more for the commercial traveller than the student of Indian culture. Certainly there has been no enthusiasm to launch *Bharat darshan* ('See India') schemes and the concessions that exist involve enough paper work to make candidates think twice before applying. For a teacher, the 25 per cent saved on the discount will be lost in his efforts to elicit a certificate from the issuing authority. I remember when I taught in Bengal (some thirty years ago), how I waited for hours outside an education office in Calcutta for the inspector to sign my application. Nobody had told an innocent from abroad that the actual authority was the peon at the door who existed to trim all 25 per cent concessions back to the 15 per cent mark.

For all its potential, therefore, the broad gauge takes the easy way out and hugs the coast, leaving the smaller lines to come to grips with the real gradients. However, the new ore lines are impressive evidence that the broad gauge when called upon can meet the challenges of troublesome terrain. And the 5 ft 6 ins. slot is undoubtedly a good working compromise between Brunel's extravagant, fast but safe 7 ft. and the cautious British standard track of 4 ft. $8\frac{1}{2}$ ins. (incidentally lowered by 3 mm in 1966). The journey by broad gauge for long distances is much more relaxing than by the smaller lines and the exercise is over quicker, thanks to the greater speed the engines can risk. But speed is a very subjective sensation and to most people the painting of Turner's *Rain, Steam and Speed* of a primitive tall-stacked engine of the 1840s looks more flat out than the blurred shots of today's high-speed French and Japanese units. It is of interest to note that in the painting Turner's engine is running on the Great Western broad gauge of Brunel which bore speeds of 90 m.p.h. in the early days of steam. India inherited the virtues of this safer gauge when Dalhousie compromised between the needs of a subcontinent and its ability to foot the bill. The 'something intermediate' was to be a long term boon to the people of India for had the British standard been applied, it would have meant a system that would today be overwhelmed by human demand.

The Dismal Side of Fast Travel

It was to escape the press of bodies that my metre gauge journeys were made. If I had to travel along the broad gauge trunk routes from Calcutta or Bombay to Delhi it was never a flavoursome journey to be remembered. In a three-tier sleeper there would be so much activity and interference that it was easier to opt out and cling to the uppermost berth all the way. The chair-car is an even bleaker alternative where, set at prescribed angles like patients in a dentist's chair, the passengers try and convince themselves that this, because of the coolness of the compartment, is the most desirable way to reach the capital. In fact you freeze at night and cannot see out of the window by day thanks to the double glazing that air-conditioning demands. The experience is more like emulating a trussed chicken in cold storage than of tasting India's rich rail heritage. On one occasion at Bharatpur, where the train pulled in early in the morning, I leapt off on an impulse, unable to stand the confinement any longer. Because of the early hour I sleepily surrendered my ticket which was booked through to Delhi. After a visit to the bird sanctuary and being marvellously perked up from seeing birds in the untrussed state, I went back to the station to see if I could retrieve my ticket. It turned up eventually but bore the fatal clip of the ticket collector's punch. The M-shaped tooth mark indicated it had been 'mutilated'. According to the station master I should apply for a refund to the headquarters of the Central Railway in Bombay which would take about three months. Instead, I caught a bus to Agra and bought a seat from there. As I had been a ticketless traveller on my very first foray in the subcontinent, it was only right that atonement should be paid for by adjusting under-journeying against former excesses.

When the Rajdhani Express was introduced I tried that and while not as clinically austere as the 'de luxe' chair-car it had the whole feel of a government exercise in civic fatuousness. We were bombarded with visual and audio warnings against the evils of alcohol as though it was a temperance outing. Considering that several passengers were contentedly swigging their gin and vodka from the innocent clarity of a water bottle it might have been more sensible to change the warnings to 'Consumption of *Ganga jal* neat is injurious to health'. On another occasion the diesel broke down outside Baroda and I walked forward to find out the cause. The smartly uniformed train supervisor was standing there with the fixed smile that accompanies all official stonewalling of public enquiries. 'What went wrong?', I asked. 'The train has broken down', he said.

The Smart Turnout of the Western Zone

As the most modern of the zonal Railways, the Western is apt to be the least interesting to the traveller not looking for bland passage and uneventful discharge, though neither of these possibilities can be held against the Western Railways in respect of their toe-clinging suburban traffic. To show how far I am from the normal concerns of railway users I once deliberately entered Churchgate as the morning rush hour disgorged. Battling my way to a fully empty EMU rake I concluded that for the greatest human tidal wave in the book of transport the Bombay commuters were either too individualistic or too kind-hearted to deserve the title of mass movers. I had expected to be mown down but everyone gave way.

Rail addicts tend to give Bombay a wide berth (despite its historical pull of being a railway cathedral city) because the traffic is entirely diesel and electric and even the tickets have dispensed with the thunder box of the past. Superbly organized, by these very virtues Bombay railwaymen hardly qualify as typically Indian. Your WR man is altogether too smart, too brainy and too personable to give what the statistics might call an 'average customer-kilometre yield' of satisfaction. As an example of the intelligent interest the WR staff takes in the world around us, one of them came and sat in my compartment after his ticket examining duties were over and gave a running commentary on the metre gauge line climbing up from Nathdwara in Rajasthan to the crest of the Aravallis where it reaches the highest point on the Western Railways. Later we passed a small impregnable looking fort-town and the TTE identified it as a 'national stronghold'. Apparently a former prime minister's mother-in-law hailed from there.

Before leaving the WR for more exotic zones, mention must be made of the double-decker carriages that seem like a desperate modern solution to stem the flow of passengers. In point of fact these double-storey coaches had been introduced by the BB & CI Railway as early as 1862. I travelled on one from Valsad to Bombay Central in the 'Flying Ranee' against a theoretically reserved seat, the promise turning out to be something of a joke as I could hardly enter the compartment let alone find my seat. The double-storey sensation was a bit like being part of a tank crew as you prepared for battle stations. Everything was cramped and painted khaki and any vendor who wanted to pass (and they all do) insisted on climbing up and over you. The number of vendors was in proportion to the seething passenger presence and one admired the Houdini contortions they perform to steeplechase over the crowd. My lasting impression of this cheek-by-jowl mode of travel was of a man complaining bitterly to a neighbour on another level: 'Do you mind? You are standing on my head'.

In the old days, one of the choicest ways to inter-city was to slip into a first class coupe, usually sited at either end of the carriage and immune from spiritual exhortations to lay off the bottle. Pet owners found this an ideal way to transport their dogs without banishment to the quarantine of the brake van where all the tortoises were desperately striving to stick their necks out while the sub-metric calves kept theirs in so as not to exceed the limit. To prove that the old joke about the guard booking dogs according to their literal circumstances is still applicable, I have a receipt—'Way-bill for booking of animals and birds at other than parcel rates'—from New Delhi to Patna Junction. It reads 'Dog and pup with owner in Cups Ist class'. The original story ran that a station master had entered against a similar travelling duo: 'One bitch and one son-of-a-bitch'.

A Ride on the Puri-Tirupati Pilgrim Express

Compared to the turn-out of the western zone, the railwaymen of the northern and eastern regions rate only fair. To approach similar WR standards you must go central or south. The broad gauge leading south is always a pleasant experience from whichever metropolitan city you depart. From Calcutta I would (after learning to tip the peon for my teacher's concession) take the overnight train to Puri and then continue to occupy a weekend berth in a camping coach parked in the siding. From there I have caught the Tirupati Express which caters for those interested in the Hindu goal of *moksha* (salvation) but who are not in a desperate hurry to achieve it. For a railway lover this is a journey to relish, for the ample train ambles along with none of the usual furious overly businesslike concern of the broad gauge. Pulled by a smartly painted WP you soon get cinders in your hair as you exult in what turns out to be a 'Stopping Express', a bolder variant of the

'Fast Passenger', for here the driver has a willing racehorse to flog between stations. Note that the new numbering of named trains has a useful logic behind it. The first digit refers to the zone from which the train originates, the second the division responsible for servicing the rake and the last two numbers codify the name of the train.

Our Pilgrim Express 8079 halted for twenty minutes at Kharagpur which enabled us to get a sampling of this remarkable railway settlement. First I crossed the overbridge to buy a platform ticket to remind me of what pleasures lay in store when later I needed to recall the actual day of my visit. Then to the station's most famous feature—its long platform. I asked several of the station staff the actual length which once made this (but not any more) the longest platform in the world. Like me, everyone was confused at having to translate feet into metres and estimates veered so wildly that I decided to pace it out for myself. This went well for the first half but ended abruptly when the sprawl of luggage and passengers prevented further advance. At least I learned the logic of its great length. In catering for the merging traffic from Bombay and Madras, the station often needed to park two long trains alongside the same platform. Half way down, the line wriggles free to bypass the train parked in front.

On the overbridge I was stopped by a boy selling official railway literature that included plastic-sheathed identity card forms. He insisted I buy something from him and as a souvenir of this bustling rail centre I chose 'Form no. 558 E/119 (Act.App.Rectt.)/87 KPA (Notice)'. This was an application to become a railway apprentice on the Eastern Railway—'last date 31.12.87 within 14.30 hours. Sealed drums to be placed at the Loco and Carriage & Wagon shops'. The caste and sub-caste of certain candidates was demanded, while the sons of serving Railway employees enjoyed a privileged status. Amongst the questions put to the would-be 'Winder, Cable Jointer, Welder or Moulder' was one that was surprising when addressed to an innocent apprentice: 'State number of wives living'.

The driver of the WP was a bearded man with the traditional knotted handkerchief tied round his head. I said casually that his old Telco bird probably could not run faster than 30 m.p.h. and that she must find it difficult to keep up with the trucks on the highway that ran alongside between the Eastern Ghats and the tossing ocean. The driver took the bait and glanced meaningfully at his two firemen to check that they had heard my impudence. The first fireman retorted by spitting into his hands and clanging open the grate to enable his understudy to slug in some coal for a session of proving this critic wrong. The fourth member of the crew raked the coal forward and broke the bigger lumps. The train thereafter seemed to fly down the coast in exultant abandon. The best evidence that the crew was angry was the smattering of unburnt cinder that blew in our wake. It was a passage of joy with the demented pistons flashing in broad gauge bliss. The rods belted out their own music of heavy metal hysteria and to make the symphony complete another WP approached us at high speed on the Up line. These two bullets on trajectories of physical predetermination met for a moment of psychic fusion, then hurled themselves apart. Their mechanical potential had reached the perfection of its design and only transcendental images remained of this magical conjunction. When the divisional end of the line appeared the crew changed. The driver stroked his beard thoughtfully as he looked first at his lovely old engine then askance at me. Behind him the fireman grinned broadly while his assistant showed the thumbs-up. Nothing more needed to be said. I showed the other thumb and the crew ambled away with the honour of their stable intact. The WP had done what diesel and electric can only hint at. She had provided the raw sense of speed that the broad gauge can best give. Never during that insensate beat down the edge of the ocean did the old lady lose her composure. One felt more relaxed the faster she got, though it has to be admitted that with an old locomotive there is the real danger that things may start dropping off!

That happened once on a broad gauge passenger pulling out of Saharanpur bound for Delhi. For a start the WG engine had been married to a WP tender, and did not like the forced union one bit. The track took a terrible pounding as the tender thumped up and down in protest—and the driver kept looking back to see what the problem was. *Ka-boom!* A brake housing sheered off from a tender wheel and exploded onto the track. The bucking continued and at the next station the driver felt the wheel, pronounced it unheated and continued the thumping. To protest against this cruelty to the track I got off at Muzaffarnagar and caught a bus to Delhi.

The Social Fallout Between Broad Gauge Tracks

One aesthetic criticism of the broad gauge track-bed must be that when it is not in use its scale tends to deaden any human feeling. All along the 2 ft. Darjeeling line you find the hill people interacting with the track, children trolleying down it and housewives drying their winter vegetables along its length. Somehow the main line is too big to relate to and remains not quite friendly to our step. I have noticed in Tamil cinema that when the heroine wants to commit suicide she will always choose a broad gauge crossing before which she parks her Daddy's open white convertible. This is chased by Daddy in a Buick or Chevrolet, who always manages to rush up and put his arms round her as the WP engine crew slam on the brakes. One wonders what film makers in the south will do when the superfast electric WAP 3 enters service since it has a braking distance of over a kilometre when it tops 100 km.p.h. In north India the fashion in suicides is for the heroine to jump off Lakshman Jhula bridge into the Ganga at Rishikesh. This is safely a few miles upstream of the rail-head which, incidentally, is served by the occasional WL—not quite the locomotive for heroic gestures of the last-stand variety. And thanks to the gradient, the would-be victim would have plenty of time to think about changing her mind.

Hindi films also favour the broad gauge for their flash-back scenes, the hypnotic clack of a Pacific wheel-layout invariably used to conjure up memories of how the rags-to-riches story of a stowaway boy began. It would be difficult to think of a best-selling formula that entirely left out the railways from a script. From the classic *Pakeeza* to *Sholay* some action by train is *de rigueur*. The smaller lines are reserved for romantic interludes and I was told that an old armoured ZF class engine was kept in Kalka sidings solely for those film-makers who wished to inject the passion that only steam can give rise to, in a repeat of *Love in Simla*.

Owing to their width, the lines of the broad gauge require higher platforms, and that favourite rural habit of taking a short cut across the track is fraught with immediate danger when a steep wall looms before one which one has to scramble up. A year or two ago, at my local Delhi station, Okhla, gruesome carnage resulted from a party of villagers detraining from the wrong side and being cut down in the path of an approaching diesel. This was exactly how the very first train accident happened in 1830 at the opening of the Liverpool and Manchester Railway. The local MP alighted away from the platform and caused an enlarged version of the *Rocket* to engineer a re-election.

The Exhilarating Eastern Ore Lines

For the impressive beauty of the broad gauge one has to see it against the odds on the ore lines of the Eastern Ghats. The KK Line of the South Eastern 'Blue Chip Railway' is the most enthralling broad gauge section in India, and important for our theme of Indian virtue since the three sections were entirely constructed by Indian labour and designed by Indian engineers. The carrying capacity of these profitable rakes that rumble down to the port of Visakhapatnam with several heavy electric locomotives in tow (braking round the screaming curves as the flanges wear out from the excessive weight of high-grade iron ore), is better seen than described. The tiny tribal township of Koraput is a good place to view the line from. Here, in the most backward belt of India, is manufactured the latest jet fighter and amidst anthropologically undeveloped tribes runs a top-rate railway system incorporating the latest technological advances.

This, the highest broad gauge line in the world, crests the Ghats at 997 metres (3272 feet) while the highest broad gauge station in India is at Shimliguda, 120 kilometres above Vizag on the way to Kirandul (via Koraput). Only one train a day runs for passengers and that too is 'mixed' (which means half of it is made up of goods stock). From 7.00 in the morning to 10.00 at night this trundling line soars through dramatic ghat scenery. But be warned, when you reach the end of the line at Kirandul (late at night) there is nothing to see apart from iron ore (according to one disheartened enthusiast I met who travelled the whole stretch). It might be advisable to get off at Jagdalpur, the fascinating capital of the old tribal state of Bastar, and spend the night there. This is still 150 kilometres short of Kirandul, but after 5.00 p.m. (when the train arrives at Jagdalpur) what are you going to do for the next five hours?

Unacquainted with the workings of the government when I arrived at Bastar I went straight into the palace grounds and began to take photographs. The building has now been taken over as a government office and bears all the signs of municipal culture—that which is not falling down has been painted bright blue. I noted that my activity brought forth a lot of stares and elbow-diggings from the staff, but true to their apathetic traditions none of the clerks on duty did anything to prevent me. It was only later back in Delhi I learned that in Bastar it is forbidden to use a camera without special permission, in view of the extremely sensitive situation regarding tribal exposure. These rules have been in force from British times and were introduced to protect the unclad people of the jungle from any salacious outsider who might take prurient delight in viewing savage breasts. Today, Jagdalpur seemed just like any other rural town in Madhya Pradesh except that there are no cars in evidence on the roads. The hotel where I stayed boasted of an owner who wore a white khadi cap. To prove his ideological credentials, above the bed was painted the first sign in Hindi I had seen all day: *sharab pina munna hai*—'Liquor is forbidden'.

The broad gauge strives to live up to its billing as the mainstream line and continues to inch its way north beyond Jammu in another of those heroic engineering onslaughts Indian railwaymen do not fight shy of. Already the broad gauge has penetrated fully to Kanyakumari and if one is obliged to use the metre gauge to get to India's eastern and western extremities at least the broad gauge can give us the regal north-south sweep. Actually, progress by the Himsagar Express which covers the 3730 kilometres from Jammu Tawi to the Cape (on specified days) is more symbolic than businesslike, unless you prefer the term 'molecular' for its bouncing between the coasts of Coromandel and Malabar—definitely a train for the retired couple who wish to avail of their senior citizen concession. The leisure this train gives will

enable them to wear down the arguments of the TTE—'No certificate required at the time of booking for citizens of the age of 65 years
and above. The persons falling in borderline cases are advised to carry
some documentary proof of age while travelling'.

The Southernmost Rail Fantasy

The Kanyakumari railway station that marks the ultimate southern
buffers of the broad gauge system is a giveaway of the sort of the false
self-importance the main line—like the 'mainstream' citizen—is
prone to adopt. Proud of its distinction as 'the best kept station' on
Southern Railway (all of whose stations are extremely well-cared
for), obviously the awarding committee did not trouble to step beyond
the lavish pillared portico, a far too pompously endowed structure for
this modest but refined terminal town. Above the soaring columns of
broad gauge fantasy can be seen a whole line of leaking latrines, the
damp and disfigured wall indicating VIP bathrooms and abysmal
plumbing standards about to greet any visitor to *Bharat* who sets foot
on its southernmost point.

As if to rub in the lesson, the island across the choppy waters where
the oceans meet and where the Vivekananda Memorial has been built,
is so astoundingly hygienic that a Dutch or German houseproud *frau*
would approve. Unfortunately, the price of this non-mainland experience is the feel of heavy fascist propaganda and one was chilled at
the level of Hindu chauvinism almost as much as amused at its muddle-
headed understanding of actual Indian culture. For example, none of
these enthusiasts who wished to convert the local Christian fisherfolk
back to Hinduism (as defined by Shankaracharya) seemed to be aware
that Christianity (and Judaism for that matter) had taken root in south
India several centuries before Shankaracharya had been born.

Such brash assumptions are the bane of modern India and it is only
organizations like the Army and the Railways that can rise above the
self-serving perspectives of the politicians who wax powerful on a diet
of deceit. The reality, as any traveller can find out, is totally different.
For example, in Kanyakumari I bought a cassette of hymns to Lord

Ayappa who sits in the popular Kerala shrine of Sabarimala high in the South Sahyadris. This tough pilgrimage is preceded by stiff discipline and all over south India in the appropriate season can be seen the bare-bodied devotees from several religions clad only in a black *lungi* as they prepare for the climax after forty-one days of penance. The cassette mentioned had been recorded by the popular singer Jesudasan who, as his name suggests, is a Christian devotee of the Hindu Ayappa. Muslims likewise join in this energetic pilgrimage. However, the traditional religious harmony of the south is under assault by fascist forces who seem to argue that the broad gauge religion of India—their version of Hinduism—is the only line that counts in the land. What they overlook is that the real glory of Hinduism has been to host several gauges or ways to the goal. The broad gauge should not be viewed as the Big Brother of Indian Railways bossing the lesser lines and arrogating all the funds to itself, as it has been prone to do. It should be seen rather as the background *atman* giving life to the entire system and uniting on one string all the conflicting cultural facets that lie along that great arc of the subcontinent between Kashmir and Kanyakumari.

CHAPTER THIRTEEN

Elate Metre

The gauge is the width between two lines measured from their inside edges. Any break in the gauge and the system will come to a standstill. In Britain the chaos of competing gauges led to a war between the companies and the bigger (but not better) gauge won because of its economic clout. What most transport historians have conceded is that the best railway ever to run was probably the Great Western on Brunel's extra broad gauge of 7 ft. It made for speed and safety but in a land as insularly attached to its estates as Britain there was never any real chance that muddle as a policy would be superseded by foresight. The spectacular clash of gauges at Gloucester where milling passengers from the standard fought their way past crowds equally intent on putting the broad gauge behind them, led to high level commissions and a slugging-out match between rival claims. In 1845 locomotive trials were held and while Gooch's 'Firefly' class (captured in Turner's famous painting) outshone the narrower competition, the latter had by no means disgraced itself. Fighting a losing battle despite better performance, the Great Western was forced to allow the standard gauge to invade its territory. In 1892 it threw in the towel and almost overnight the broad system gave way to the lesser. The last broad gauge train to leave Paddington was that most classic of locomotives, a Gooch 'single'. It was the end of an era of what might have been for Britain. The UK would have been a richer and happier nation had Brunel's vision been allowed to mature.

The Reconciliation of Dual Gauges in India

If happiness is a uniform gauge, then the Delhi Rail Museum must qualify as the outermost circle of transport misery. It has six. As well as the broad, metre and two narrow gauges it has a toy train line for children and a monorail with the startling gauge of 0 ft 0 ins. India gave the world the zero—and also the lesson that dual gauging was not the end of all hope. While Britain was striving to minimize the damage, the metre gauge inaugurated twenty years later was soon chasing the mileage of the Indian broad gauge track. The fact was, that though British power in the subcontinent was paramount, it was not as legally pervasive as it pretended to be. The rulers of Indian states were quick to react to the benefits of railed transport and the Gaekwad's narrow gauge lines predate the decision to go metric for the feeder traffic in upland terrain.

To show the possibilities under a vertical sun the Maharaja of Jodhpur proposed a line in his state in late 1879 and by early 1881 it was operational. The Government of India learnt of its existence only in August 1881 and hoped the Viceroy would put the Maharaja in his place. Lord Ripon took an enlightened view of the initiative and over-ruled the negative reactions of his advisors. The Jodhpur State Railway (later allied with neighbouring Bikaner) turned out to be the chief early pride of Indian Railways. It ran so well and made such profits that for the first time in imperial transport history the British entrusted the company with a section of their own railway to run.

If politics is the art of the possible, railway economics is the craft of bowing to the inevitable and no matter how much the introduction of a conflicting system put a spanner in Dalhousie's works, the demand for secondary lines of lighter loading was a reality that could not be wished away. It remains to be seen whether the recent uniguage initiative will prove more cost-effective than the earlier plan to up-grade metre guage running. It never gets stressed in the wrangle over what constitutes an ideal railway system for India that an emphatic plus point for Indian railwaymen was to conquer the fatalism engendered by duality. By their works they have overcome the disastrous potential of a twin system. (For all practical purposes the 4000 kilometres of the narrow gauge hardly affects the issue.)

The Yogic Aspect of Rail Integration

Making a going concern of mutually hostile gauges has been to snatch away an excuse for inefficiency. The poison of an antagonistic and incompatible pair of tracks has been swallowed whole and if you did not know where to look in the annual statistics for the breakdown into broad gauge and metre gauge no one would ever think of advertising the difference. The basic reality is that for the whole of the Indian public the Railways are one. As such, they are a mighty symbol of yoga, the art of the individual integrating himself by devotion and *sadhana* (discipline) to become part of a more meaningful whole. What better parable of national life could there be than the life of the average railway worker contributing his share to the wealth of the nation?

Yoga, we are told, is skill in action and surely he who travels over India's network, not fast but friendly, has an inkling of what is meant by the 'Knower of the Field'. The rail experience exemplifies the yoking of disparate elements into useful harmony at many levels. Fire and water are yoked in the engine and tender just as the loco is linked to the rake and sections along the line are made susceptible to the flashed signal and Neale's tokens. Like a well-ordered organism, the railway animal flexes its muscles each time a train sets off. From section to division and from zone to region the body performs the required *asanas* (postures) and the goal is brought nearer. The passenger is winged on his way and the nation made stronger by such efficient despatch. Behind all, the Rail *atman* watches as the spirit of integration fulfils itself, every part functioning according to its needs and each enabled by the network to receive what is its due. Only when travelling by train does one gain the distinct impression that it is in these civil works that the average Indian can witness the unified nation of his dreams.

For the railway aesthete the addition of another gauge is a source of pleasure. The metre gauge is very easy to relate to, its confines more designed for the wiry frame of rural India. Beware, however, of using the expression '*chotey* line' in the presence of undergraduates—it is their idiom for deviant sex. In one sense the conservatives were right about the dirt and grime of railways and their propensity to defile. Fire and passion publicly proclaimed and the promiscuous angle of the fireman's shovel could do no good for a submissive society, and the Duke of Wellington's fear that the railways would encourage the lower members of society to erect their desires seemed a sober assessment of their threat. Note too the young lady's enthusiasm turned on by the heat and drum of Stephenson's *Rocket*, whose cylinders were also angled most suggestively. A current best-selling British lady author who leans heavily on the hormone count has described the stimulus of a visit to a rail museum. She talks about the incredible sexual energy of throbbing pumping pistons and hot fluids oozing down pipes. To get to that fever pitch she must have possessed a galloping imagination or been too close a friend of the curator of working models.

The Subtle Credentials of the Metre Gauge

To see only the animality of the steam chest is to miss its other subtle dimensions. It is my contention that the metre gauge is the ideal medium to express the poetry of rail travel just as the broad track speaks of the businesslike end of the undertaking. For a start, the metre line (except for 166 kilometres in the south) is so far uncontaminated by the anonymous sterility of electric traction. It has fire and it has range. Penetrating beyond the stretch of the broad gauge it resembles a good beer—it gets to the parts the other brands do not reach. The far south, the far east and the furthest west, the metre gauge links up India's cultural extremities which, it must be said, are far in colourful advance of the dreary norm set by Delhi and Uttar Pradesh. Rajasthan, Gujarat, Assam and Tamilnadu, all regions of individual character, are largely serviced by the smaller line. What emerges from this common bond is that the metric system owns its own identity and is in no way an imitation of the broad gauge. Its character and flavour are distinct and easily recognizable. Suffice it to say that these lines seem more Indian in their relaxed and modest strivings. The smaller lines have evolved their own atmosphere—not so much that of a poor relation eager to please but more of an easy-going country cousin, less rushed and more reflective in character.

To travel long distance on the metre (with the exception of the lone superfast Ashram Express) is to experience something of the classic age of steam, a lifestyle now departed from the faster lines where slick imitation of foreign travel habits has sanitized and cajoled the *deshi* mood into one of surrender. As a friendlier system, the feelings of the metre gauge always seem preferable to me. Intimacy is a fact of size. Man relates to wasted space with a swagger. Confine him to proper conventions and he turns more homely. It is this human property that I always feel to be the tangible difference between gauges. The metre lines have a benign quality reminiscent of the welcoming villager, in contrast to the self-absorbed standoffish feel of the broad gauge, with its touch of urban aloofness.

These subjective soundings are never to be taken as unshakeable. You can have bad trips on the metre gauge with surly companions on a rattletrap conveyance just as you can recall pleasurable trunk memories of the Karnataka Express with the 'Thomases' and 'Josephs' forever dashing back and forth with *vadas* and vegetable '*cutlates*'. It is the sum of one's pleasures that accrue to the smaller line by virtue of its snug measurements—the perfect *via media* between broad and narrow.

The metre lacks the vulgar gape of hoardings since its clients are not deemed big spenders. (Most fast travellers to Gujarat prefer the broad gauge as do the passengers bound for Guwahati.) Those matrimonial hoardings that greet the eye for broad gauge arrivals from Calcutta, Bombay and Madras are missing on the metre gauge spin past Delhi Cantt. *Riste-hi-riste* ('Relationships forever') announces Prof. Arora in two-foot capitals from Faridabad (or Chipiyana Buzurg West) onwards, and gives his address in Karolbagh to prove that he is not just willing but raring to go.

The starting station is the best introduction to the flavour of the lesser vehicle. At Old Delhi you pass from the large, modern but not very soulful broad gauge waiting hall to the scaled-down platforms of the metre. The architecture is ancient and true; pointed Gothic stone arches and wrought iron trellis work for struts that hold up a pre-Raphaelite world of steam. Unlike the main platforms, where baggage heaves and forms are draped in wraith-like attitudes, here every load and gesture has a human wrapping. There is less of everything destructive in the search for yoga. The competition is less fierce, the brushing aside by coolies less brutal. Though smaller, there is room for all and a sense of generous sharing pervades the scene. Both time and space have slowed and spread themselves, but little panic attends the thought of being left behind. The absence of the main-line tension and the casual flow of country air allow *pranayama* (the art of breathing) to find its level.

A Languorous Diagonal Across the Deccan

This sense of getting the best out of India's rural virtues can be easily verified by a ride in the curiously named Meenakshi Express which covers the longest diagonal on the metre gauge system—1462 kilometres from Jaipur to Kacheguda (Secunderabad). Against the broad gauge 'total track kilometres' of 70,000 plus, the metre gauge barely scores some 33,000 kilometres. In route kilometres, however, a more balanced picture emerges. The broad gauge in 1988 (and increasing nominally by the year) ran to 33,831 kilometres while the metre gauge shadowed it at an ancient and respectable 23,839 kilometres. The difference between the track and route distances being the fact that the metre lines tend to run singly in less populated areas while broad gauge tracks in industrial situations lie thick and fast on the ground. We have already noted the puny contribution the small lines make to the national exchequer—and as expected the input of the metre gauge's 38 per cent of Indian rails is a measly 17 per cent of passenger traffic and a dismal 10 per cent of goods freighted.

Some Statistics of the Metre Gauge

As it happens, the metre gauge in international reckoning is by no means a despised solution. Its total comes second to the British standard gauge, which happens to be used in countries as far apart as France and Germany, the USA, China and North Africa. The first metre gauge line was laid by the junior Stephenson to a Derbyshire limestone quarry in 1841 and was worked for over 100 years. The first passenger metre gauge line in the world was the Delhi-Rewari section, over whose lines we have already travelled in the Farukh Nagar Passenger. The line was opened in 1873. Apparently Lord Mayo hit upon this compromise because the topic of going metric was fashionable in his day. The rest of Indian life went metric only ninety years later.

Though the image of the slow track now clings to the metre gauge, this gauge once monopolized the scenic beauty of India. Now it has been upstaged by the coming of the broad gauge in its tracks to Dwarka and Trivandrum but prior to the age of conversion the metre gauge outshone the broad in giving you India as it really was.

The long slash through the hinterland from Rajasthan to Hyderabad remains my idea of the perfect journey by any means of transport. The journey started off badly under a booking office notice that screamed 'Punctuality' in Hindi but where the clerk arrived fifteen minutes late and spent the next fifteen closing the previous night's accounts, interrupting his duties to answer two ringing phones, neither of which ever merited more than a series of 'Allo-allos'. If India had done to the railways what it has done to that other western invention—the telephone—the population problem would be well under control because of all the resultant crashes. The fatuousness of the phone makes it akin to a South Sea animist icon; respected, feared and abused but never used for what it was intended—the conveying of simple communication. In the best homes in Delhi, the most powerful people in the land still do not know how to use a telephone. Most of them pick up the receiver well aware that 90 per cent of numbers dialled are apt to be wrong yet continue to practice the superstition that by demanding stentoriously '*kaun hai*'? ('who is it?')—somehow the right number will be arrived at. It is assumed that the feudal urge to bellow must triumph over a patently passive instrument.

To add to my problem I wanted a confirmed berth the same day. This is unthinkable on the broad gauge but on most metre gauge trains it is a working possibility—another big advantage to the traveller who plays his itinerary by ear. However, I could only get 'waiting list' but would be accommodated on tomorrow's train. Rather than hang around Jaipur with its overblown princely style and sickly pink architecture I thought I would move along the line to Ajmer to see the famous metre gauge workshop and board the Meenakshi Express next day from there. But I had to pay again for the section between Jaipur and Ajmer. Railway rules were so inflexible that I would have had to go all the way up to the Supreme Court before anyone would admit that injustice had been done. The same day I read in the newspaper of a citizen who had done just this and fought his case successfully against the Railways who had caused him to miss his connection and then penalized him for travelling in a faster train to try and make up for lost ground.

The difference between the timeless fatalism of the administrative side and prompt delivery of the loco running staff was brought home to me at Bikaner. I thought to save money on a long route (broken into short stretches) by availing of the convenience of a commercial circular ticket. After finding the authorized babu 'on his seat', another five minutes elapsed while he looked for the key to the drawer that contained the key to the cupboard. He then had to grope for yet another key to another drawer to enable him to locate the key of the first drawer. Realizing that what I saved in rupees would be lost in heart-burn I backtracked to the platform and announced to a parked steam locomotive crew my desire to see their engine shed, which lay some miles away. Immediately they made room for me on the footplate of a beautifully maintained YP with a 'splasher' nameplate, and when the signal dropped, off we went whistling our way light. The contrast between the work-shy attitudes of the clerical staff and the get-stuck-in philosophy of the boiler-suited was further evidence that Indian Railways' success rode on the backs of its *mistris* and artisans; the upper echelons in many cases just going along for the ride.

An Interlude in the Ajmer Workshop

This was again hammered home in my visit to the Ajmer workshop where too I managed to hitch a ride, not on the footplate but on the rear coach of a backing rake. The security was both severe and somewhat racist. At the sight of the unfamiliarly pigmented the office staff went rigid with fear. When I asked to see the man in charge, his peon looked me up and down deliberately, then dismissed me to have an interview with the junior-most accounts officer. At least that enabled me to see why babus are such an unpleasant and unfulfilled breed. When up to one's necks in ledgers in gloomy Victorian warehouse surroundings, whose milk of humanity would not curdle and eventually dry up? Everyone I saw reminded me of badly packed tortoises peering from their self-induced brake-vans. Eventually I was shunted back to the door of the man from whose step I had originally been shooed. The sour-looking peon reluctantly took in my letter of authority (without which I would never have got past the guards on the gate) and within a minute he was back beckoning me in with a newly-discovered rubbery smile.

The bright young officer inside was amused at the fawning charades of official hierarchy but could do little about the extraordinary elasticity of his peon's face. Having been in government service for twenty-five years, this man was a hopeless case. The officer told me about the halcyon days of the RMR (Rajputana Malwa Railway) and its dependence on imported rolling stock until the Ajmer Workshop began to turn out some beautifully classic numbers of its own. The very last of these was spotted rusting in a siding and rescued by Mike Satow for the Delhi museum. It is now no. 162 of the elegant 4-4-0 M class, which is unusual in having their cylinders inside the frame. (Other Ajmer engines on show in Delhi are an F class Pacific of 1922 BESA design and the very first metre gauge loco manufactured in India, F 734 built at the workshop in 1895. India had been assembling locomotives from imported parts since 1868 and the broad gauge workshop at Jamalpur was renowned for 'producing' engines from an assortment of spares.)

Today the Ajmer shop floor is much reduced but maintains the old level of efficiency despite its lesser role as the doctor of sick carriages. Targets are displayed around the room as in all other government offices. The difference with Indian Railways (Ajmer is now under

Western Railways) is that most of the targets are met and a few ar
exceeded. This pride extended to the rake attendant who gave me th
lift. No repair is allowed to take more than a week he told me. Th
flavour of past performance follows this line down to Khandw
where the BB&CI lines (which took over the RMR) met those of th
GIP. On most of the stations along the way you can spot old metr
gauge rails used for supports to the platform awning, bent int
elegant shapes with the name of the manufacturing foundry and dat
clearly preserved. Those at Khandwa of the Great Indian Peninsula
date back to 1887.

One of the nice effects of a single-track journey that takes tw
nights to cover the Deccan is that under a good crew (steam took ove
from diesel at Khandwa) you arrive well ahead of time at most station
This enables you to wander around and acquaint yourself with pa
glories and derelict memories. I made a special note of those particula
railway pleasures that are in danger of being sacrificed to progres
At Neemar Khera I tasted superb railway tea served in the earthen cu
and laced with cardamom. At Tukalthad the driver waited patientl
till we had finished our *thali* lunches, a memorable meal with tw
vegetables and curried eggs for the non-vegetarian. The up-to-dat
serving of 'casseroles' suffers from the absence of a tray. Man
passengers end up with the urge not to compliment Mr Madhav Ra
Scindia (the innovator) but to send him their laundry bill for dal spi
from inadequate containers.

A Digression to Dhanushkodi

To disprove the notion that the metre lines only cater to rural char
and appeal to those of rustic intent one should travel on one of th
most dramatic stretches in the south, which crosses over the chopp
seas of the Bay of Bengal as they force their way inland to form th
Palk Strait that severs Rameshwaram from the mainland. Only i
recent years has a road link been built to this famous temple town an
for most pilgrims the metre gauge was the easiest way to the feet
the gods. The train steams gingerly over the sunken piers in the lee

he exalted new road bridge, as fine an engineering fling as any in the
world. After all the ugly PWD bridges India has put up in more public
places it seems a pity that this truly wonderful example of *deshi* skill
and daring should be tucked away and forgotten in the furthest corner
of the land.

You get some idea of the power of the meeting oceans as the waves
surge against the piers of the rail bridge, delivering an awesome
pounding. Safely across, the train picks its way over drifting sand and
badly corroded lines where the salt in the air greedily eats into any
metal surface. Beyond the temple town, a spit of sand nearly twenty
kilometres long and wildly beautiful in the tropical intensity of the
encroaching seas, once hosted a metre gauge track. Today you can
catch a bus outside the Rameshwaram temple and drive for sixteen
kilometres till the sand closes in over the road. Most pilgrims bathe in
the sea here but the more diligent will trek the four remaining kilometres to the shattered settlement of Dhanushkodi. This hot and
laborious trudge through the loose sand turns into an end-of-the-
rainbow venture when you learn to skirt the dunes and pace out along
the ocean edge a path instantly reclaimed by eternity. Perhaps a railway line amidst this blindingly blue beauty was too rash an assault
on the territory of the gods. Never have I been more uplifted by the
grandeur of the sea nor has my soul drunk in such a surfeit of strong
colour. What had started as a dismal slog to check out a typhoon-flat-
tened terminal ended as a choral sea symphony: the simple joy of being
electrifyingly alive with the wind in one's hair and the sand between
one's toes being a transcendant act of communion.

The grim poverty of the few fisherfolk who now manned the ruined
terminal could not dilute these exalted feelings. What little fresh water
they could scoop from the sand they offered gladly to a stranger. I
climbed over the drifts of sand into the ruined walls of the station
building and saw the pillars that once supported the water tanks for
this doomed railway colony. Halfway along the spit where the Gulf
of Mannar in its metallic blue almost touched the green hiss of the
Palk Strait a gaunt and tilting obelisk marked what may have once
been the site of a train swept away. The plaque has been washed off
and the days of the monument are numbered as the twin seas combine

to erode its base. An exquisite shell of a tiny chapel stands in majestic silhouette on the coastline overlooking the tragic events, its empty bell tower seemingly pointing a finger against any who dared to repeat the Dhanushkodi experiment.

Metric Matters in the Sub-Himalayan Tract

Railwaymen do not consider it auspicious to talk about the dead and some may recall the early British engineering argument that recommended the broad gauge on the strength of its greater stability in high winds. One of the world's worst accidents, with the most casualties in any rail disaster, is attributed to the metre gauge line in Bihar that runs over the normally mild river deriving from Kathmandu, the Bagmati. Some 800 passengers were feared drowned in a freak accident which occurred in June 1981, a season that might well have produced the sort of unpredictable wind that buffeted the entire rake into the river which, unluckily, is surprisingly deep at this crossing. When I saw it in December 1988 it looked deceptively benign, a river incapable of turning against man. A vendor whose father had survived the wreckage—the locomotive and the leading coach managed to pull clear— said there had been a cow on the line and the sudden braking may have added to the side-swipe of the storm. The rest of the compartment made ghoulish jokes about a marriage party that went down with the train, suggesting that the groom had been saved from a fate worse than death.

In the vicinity of these weaving old lines north of the Ganga that reach to the border of Nepal some mountaineering history was made to add to the epic content of the metre gauge. In his account of the thrilling and desperate climb to the summit of the first 8000 metre peak, Maurice Hertzog in his *Annapurna* excels in describing his team's heroic retreat, Hertzog himself on the back of a tough porter. He describes the terrible price that had to be paid for their exertions in the small train that took them to Gorakhpur and international acclaim. On a metre gauge passenger, in a temperature of 113 degrees F, the expedition doctor amputated several toes of Lachenal, a summiteer.

As the big toe was about to be amputated, the train jerked to a halt, causing the doctor to curse when the surgical knife flew out of his hand and disappear down the back of a seat. Amidst the dust and flies of the Terai, the doctor can hardly be blamed for echoing Edward Lear's *Merde* which he enunciated while waiting for a train near Madras: 'O beastly row. O hateful Indian travel!' But since Lear spoke these words only six months after the opening of the metre gauge line from Delhi we can blame his affliction on the broad. As it happened, Queen Victoria was more optimistic about Indian Railways. On taking up his governor-generalship (after Dalhousie but before the Mutiny), Lord Canning had visited some railway works in Madras. When his wife, Lady Canning, informed Windsor Castle of the many great works in hand the Queen (by now a confirmed believer in the Great Western) wrote back, 'How like a dream it must all appear to European eyes. If it was not for the heat and insects how much I should like to see India.'

Lear had already discovered the Englishman's way round the heat and bugs and resorted religiously to a Railway repellent found at every junction worthy of the name: 'Good evans. If any of my old friends could know how much beer, brandy and sherry this child consumes, would they recognize me?'

CHAPTER FOURTEEN

Steam Kindly Light

The diminution of railway stature is marked by an increase in affection. Parked side by side at the Delhi Rail Museum is a 234 ton Beyer Garratt and a 14 ton Darjeeling saddle tank. Somewhat protectively, visitors will always yield more to the economically less visible. Small is not only beautiful but it seems acutely vulnerable and provokes a surge of human feeling. The sight of the Ooty tankers wheezing up behind the four coaches of the Nilgiri Passenger calls forth admiration and blinds most watchers to the fact that this is not (like the Darjeeling and Matheran trains) a toy. The Ooty rack is part of a metre gauge line. The change of engine at Coonoor is not so much to give the locomotive a rest as to utilize those engines whose rack mechanism is out of order but which are otherwise serviceable.

The affection light railways stimulate is due in part to their willingness to work. It is hard to appreciate that in its time the Darjeeling Himalayan Railway gave handsome dividends, because it is difficult to believe that this unlikely challenger to the world's highest range arrived well before the advent of the motor car. Fussy, ridiculous and, as uneconomical as India's small lines appear, they continue to run on the strength of genuine public sympathy. The narrow gauge, as far as most railwaymen are concerned, is an expensive joke. The Z lines of 2 ft. 6 ins. gauge (the bulk of the narrow gauge system) are bad enough, but the Q designation for the 2 ft. gauge (a classification rarely used) makes them positively quaint. Unremunerative branch lines cost the Railways 78 crores annually.

My first contact with the little lines was to look at them longingly

Once the pride of India's steam fleet, this WP-class locomotive,
seen at Kazipet, looks distinguished even in its cannibalized state.

Tweed is believed to be the oldest locomotive in the world still at
work. It performs seasonal duties at a sugar factory near Gorakhpur
in Uttar Pradesh.

CC 682, a North British narrow gauge locomotive,
having served faithfully for eighty years, lined up
for scrap at Baripada in Orissa.

ZE 95 from the Nainpur shed in Madhya Pradesh collects
a pointsman at Mandla Fort before reversing.

Sporting the Bengal Nagpur jubilee crest on its boiler front, this narrow gauge Bagnall tank engine (manufactured *c.* 1920) awaits repairs at Bankura shed. BDR refers to the former Bankura–Damodar River Railway run by McLeod.

The metre gauge YG-class locomotive used for working the Khamblighat gradient edges onto the turntable at Phulad, Rajasthan.

Grandiose but deserted—the southernmost station in India,
Kanyakumari in Tamil Nadu.

Cast iron manufacturers' plate acquired from the Delhi Rail
Museum by the author.

Two views of the princely family in the Maharaja of Jind's saloon,
constructed *c.* 1932.

Bearers wearing traditional Rajasthani turbans standing outside the
'Palace on Wheels' luxury tourist train.

A fireman stoking his metre gauge YG-class locomotive on the western zone.

Northern Railway fitters from Amritsar work on the boiler of Delhi Rail Museum's most remarkable exhibit, the German locomotive of the former Patiala State's monorail system.

ZB 58, a British built locomotive of 1983 vintage rumbles over
Karzan bridge into Rajpipla, a former princely state now part
of Gujarat.

Thanks partly to a diet of shale, white smoke belches from the
chimney of a YG-class locomotive as it eases its rake of seven
coaches down the side of the Aravalli Hills in Rajasthan.

Two locally built (and badly
sprung) diesel railcars cross at
Chintamani on the former Kolar
Gold Fields line.

A kilometre post on the narrow gauge
Satpura line indicating the distance
from the former headquarters of the
Bengal Nagpur Railway company
in Calcutta.

A selection of tickets from Indian Railways narrow gauge and
metre gauge lines.

as the main line train flashed through Dhaulpur and Gwalior on its way south past Agra. Just before I came to Delhi a narrow gauge line ran along the east bank of the Yamuna from Saharanpur to Shahdara but this was so comprehensively converted to broad in 1968 that few traces remain. On the way to Bombay via Baroda you pass a whole necklace of these little feeder lines branching off, often with a ZB standing across the platform as, for example, at Ankleshwar where half the station suddenly does an Alice in Wonderland shrink to meet the reduction in gauges. It seems another world where the wooden carriages and even the passengers appear to belong to a different age. They appear unhurried and look out of the carriage windows at our surging speed without a flicker of interest. There was a quality of re-pose around those old coaches that I was determined to savour. One day, I vowed, I would get off and take a ride in them.

Acquaintance with the Satpura Lines

The chance came on a return journey to Delhi from Bangalore. I decided to get off at Balharshah which was the nearest halt the KK Express (as it was then called) made to the southernmost station of the narrow gauge Satpura lines. All the passengers looked at me in astonishment as I humped my rucksack out on to the empty platform. Nobody ever got off or on at Balharshah. It was simply a convenient refuelling station for passengers' stomachs. Here all the tin food trays were piled on and clashed down at the end of the sleeper coach (before the era of the silent, sploshing casseroles). A few miles up the line at Chandrapur in Maharashtra the narrow gauge from Chanda Fort sets out bravely on a scenic interior route across the Satpura Range to Jabalpur in Madhya Pradesh. A few steam engines were then left in action and I badly wanted to test the motion of their narrow gait and compare it to the high stepping clack of the broad to see if both could keep time with the hypnotically relaxing beat of the metre. It turned out to be a day of railway marathons. The KK had wafted me 360 kilometres in five hours, now the narrow line would take twenty hours to transport me another 470 kilometres to Jabalpur. As only one train

a day set out from Chanda Fort to Gondia I had to wait till next morning
and chose to spend the night in the interesting walled market town of
Chandrapur. This seat of the tribal Gond dynasty still retains a measure
of its royal layout. Literary students of the railway will recall that
E. M. Forster's *Passage to India* was set in a 'Chandrapore' full of rail
references. It's engine went 'Pomper, pomper, pomper' which sounds
a lot like the cautious tread of the narrow unremunerative lines. Also,
Forster mentions that his engines stop to take water in their tender
which certainly suggests the Satpura fleet. All three of the steeper
hill lines went in for tank engines. On the other hand, Forster says
you can hear the wail of the passing Punjab Mail, whereas real-life
Chandrapur resounds to the rush of the Grand Trunk Express. Again,
he talks about the flowers in the station master's garden; the heat of
south-east Maharashtra would have soon made these wilt.

Next morning, an undistinguished ZDM diesel arrived to pull a rake
of fascinating vintage. The oldest coach bore a plate stating that the
underframe had been originally manufactured in 1909. When I bent
down to snap this delightful detail I heard a disdainful sigh and looked
up to find an elegant arm languidly draped out of a ladies compartment, hinting that there were more photogenic subjects at hand. The
train jarred off into the bamboo thicknesses leaving behind the dumps
of lime and pulp refuse of the paper factories. These lines were built
to farm the bamboo and after their opening in 1904 the system spread
around Nagpur to become the longest narrow gauge network in the
world. Most of their 1005 kilometres passed through Kipling country
and rode south of the Narmada amidst the broad-leaved species that
surround the jungle of Seonie.

On the train I met an Anglo-Indian schoolteacher with his sons
born of a tribal mother. Travellers all over the world have to learn to
distinguish fact from fancy and in no field is this easier than in cutting
down to size the boasts of one's fellow men in their claims to sexual
prowess. Middle-class Hindi film makers often cash in on the theme
of savagely fulfilling encounters with sultry tribal beauties and my
raconteur was evidently out to stretch out the same fantasy. Anyone
who has entered the tribal tracts knows that while their instincts may
be unimpaired by the inhibitions of urban convention, their urge to

find food and dignity is any day more pressing than any hankerings after romance. Funnily enough, only the day before in Bangalore a young man—Anglo-Burmese this time—had come up to me and broken out with such an accomplished spiel that one was immediately on guard against his motives. He told a story of having had to leave Rangoon overnight on government orders and was now starving and down to the clothes he stood up in. But neither did he appear to be starving nor did his clothes give that slept-in rumpled look that every rough traveller is familiar with. One learns to let con men trap themselves. Soon the story began to contradict itself and the facts he had stated earlier now stood plainly implausible. No doubt he had once been a victim of eviction, but by inventing an update of an old family tragedy he spoiled what sympathy he deserved. He said he had flown in a few days earlier by Indian Airlines so I asked casually what type of plane now flew the Rangoon route. 'Caravelle' he said glibly then laughed when he realized he had been found out. The plane had been withdrawn from service several years earlier and he had forgotten to update the aircraft. (A similar character continues to work this hard-luck line in Delhi's Connaught Place.)

With the Anglo-Indian teacher—who claimed he had been to kindergarten with Indira Gandhi in Allahabad—the facts seemed to hold together. During the war he had been part of a bomber crew with the RAF and a member of the dam-buster squadron. It just so happened that as an air cadet at school I had occasion to hear a lecture from a leading pilot on these sorties and every detail my informant recounted rang true, including his rank of 'Flying Flight Sergeant' which is exactly as high as a bright Eurasian could hope to fly in the delicately racist ordering of the British wartime services.

Comparisons with the Ride to Shimla

The diesel grind through the overlapping jungle was too slow to admit of any music and it is sad to think that future travellers will forever miss out on the sibilant beat of a flashing piston, expressing harmony with the motion and ricocheting exultantly off the passing scene in a song of praise for energy made visible. Anyone who has tried to type in the dull monotony of the Shimla railcar will know the unpleasant friction of diesel grindings.

This experience, by the way, echoed for me an abbreviated Palace on Wheels in the extent to which the paying public is taken for a ride. To get on to the railcar at any station beyond Kalka is a problem because the driver, a morose operator conscious of his status, locks his passengers in. Even with a ticket against an empty seat the Solan station master had to cajole the sour-faced tram operator to accept a passenger on board. (Perhaps the vibrations had given him ulcers?)

The diesel-hauled Kalka-Shimla Express gives a much smoother run. Similarly, the ride through the Kangra Valley (also in Himachal Pradesh) on a sister line is a pleasant undertaking made easier by the absence of continuous climbing curves. This little referred to line must count among the loveliest railways of any system in view of the sylvan mix of mountain and stream against a backdrop of resplendent snow peaks. For some years the line was out of operation owing to a bad alignment which allowed road transport to bypass its advantages. Now with a re-laid section to Jogindernagar it makes for a soothing run for the most demanding of tourist tastes and provides a thrilling occasion for students of engineering, possessing some exalted bridges. It possesses the steepest gradient in India outside the Ooty rack. Here, adhesion is taken to the limit.

Perhaps the rail-car suffers from the pall of its VIP clientele. The timetable bristles with extra definitions to cater to their needs and cleverly conceals the surcharge they are to pay by stating 'Chargeable distance to First Class passengers'. The actual distance by rail to Shimla is 96 kilometres but the ordinary passenger pays for twice that distance and the exclusive rail-car user much more. I found the sun in winter trying and the conversation of my fellow passengers even more wilting. The wives of a politician and business man sat in captive glumness the whole way as their husbands sounded off on how the world could easily be put to rights if they were consulted. The train driver, meanwhile, smirked as if to imply that he would not be found wanting when Utopia issued its summons. The politician intoned how happy he was that the government had decided to flush out black money. The businessman agreed but spoilt the effect by giving a nervous guilty laugh as he added unconvincingly, 'We all hope the Prime Minister will be successful'.

The Branch Line to Tribal Mandla

The diesel to Gondia in Madhya Pradesh arrived at the ancient junction at 9.00 p.m. The contrast between the face-lifted broad gauge station and the sooty backwardness of the narrow was palpable even at that late hour. Just before midnight I caught a passenger to Jabalpur and had the satisfaction of seeing a steam locomotive back up to take us to Nainpur which in 1985 boasted of a loco shed that still homed ten ZEs. Like all narrow gauge carriages the fittings were old but full of character. The wooden seats of the lower classes gave a pleasant enough ride for me to have no regrets on that overnight journey which ended at 4.00 a.m. when the train, which was running to time, halted for water and a change of engine at Nainpur Junction.

Rather than catch the first train to Mandla (on a branch line to the back of beyond) and miss seeing the loco shed and Nainpur's attractive little railway colony of narrow gauge interest, I decided to go later by bus and catch the train back. At Mandla I made friends with the station master who ran the one tiny platform and who was aided by a pointsman who helped the engines reverse on a triangle. Being part of the old Bengal Nagpur system (now the South Eastern zone) the station master was a Bengali with a love of statistical stockpiling. His office was full of charts and diagrams and outside, locked on to the wall, was a 'Scotch Block' which is a device to restrain over-enthusiastic drivers from setting out when the weather is unfavourable. Inside his office he could swivel from the compilation of his statistics to service the ticket hatch. I bought a platform ticket and sent his sales for the month soaring by 100 per cent. Last month he hadn't sold any.

He agreed to let me stay the night in the first class waiting-room cum temporary parcels office. The interior was being painted a bilious apple green, and while the paint dried (evidently old stock) I would have to share space with the parcel 'smalls'. Imagining the high security that went with this trust, it came as a surprise to note that instead of unlocking a series of padlocks he simply put his hand through a broken upper pane and opened the waiting-room door from inside. An inner door opened to reveal the bathroom, a most impressively endowed area with plumbing pipes that could have graced a Gooch single. These wreathed their way up and over three steps to the WC which had embossed on its china a florid coat of arms that might have been by appointment to the Queen Empress. Further formidable reminders of the colonial imperative to do things in style and to impress the natives with the naked splendour of civilization included a large zinc bath-tub hooked firmly to the wall, bearing its railway serial number stamped on the side.

Next morning I understood the significance of the broken windowpane when the resident railway person, dressed only in a towel, admitted himself, said 'Good morning' and passed inside to make the plumbing vibrate to his Sanskrit recitations. He was followed by several other members of his family, all of whom carefully locked and unlocked the waiting room door through the broken window. At last, with everyone finished, I was permitted to perform my ablutions. We all gathered on the platform suitably spruced up to await the arrival of 1 NM mixed. She was pulled by the very handsome German built ZE 95 but there seemed to be some confusion over the reality of this beautiful Marlene Dietrich number. According to the official list no. 95 had already been scrapped. I could only hope that railway justice would borrow from civil law that you cannot condemn a person twice for the same offence. That way ZE 95 might survive the breaker's hammer.

The tremendous character of these small lines stays alive in the memory, while all the fast track we cover passes into speedy oblivion, each journey more bland than the one before. The steaming properties of the ZE back to Nainpur were totally different from those of other engines on the same gauge. Built for rugged country, the 2-8-2 wheel arrangement indicated the beef of a goods engine. Compared to the lighter 2-6-2 configuration of the ZBs on the Gaekwad's lines, the extra tractive power of the Satpura engines clearly showed but unfortunately their muscle outweighs their music. If that sounds unfair to my German Fräulein ZE 95 for whom I worked up quite a passion (and I continue to keep her photo on my desk), let us say it was the difference between Beethoven and Mozart.

The Aural Satisfaction of the Gaekwad's ZBs

My dream engine, judged entirely on the criterion of *sounding* poetic, was ZB 58 by which I travelled from Rajpipla to Ankleshwar in Gujarat. On the score of visual ravishment, I earlier had the luck to find shunting at Khurduvadi one of the last of the Nasmyth Wilson F class, which combined the ruggedness of the Satpura engines with the music of the Gaekwad's. Also, inside the Barsi Light Railway carriages I found (at Pandharpur) the most charming fittings and seating arrangements that proved Engineer Calthrop's genius extended to passenger comforts—using the tried seating formula '16 to the bum, 16 to the ton'.

I had hoped to get to Dabhoi, the nerve centre of the Gaekwad's narrow gauge system (the oldest in the world and still running) by the line that ran in from Chota Udaipur, a former princely state of largely tribal subjects. However, transport does not run at night as some of the Bhils use passing buses for target practice in order to hone their hunting skills.

Narrow Gauge Lines to the Narmada

The Rajpipla-Ankleshwar line runs parallel to and south of the River Narmada. Most conveniently there is a line out of Dabhoi that takes you to Chandod, a pilgrim town on the north bank from where, for ten paise, you can be ferried across the serene river to catch connecting transport to Rajpipla. The afternoon Chandod 'mixed' was an attractive experience after a fascinating morning spent poking around the rich narrow gauge loco shed of Dabhoi. The ZB ran beautifully and with symphonic grace to the very river bank. A short walk through the old religious bazaar brought one to the ferry ghats. But first I bought a platform ticket which had printed on its back *shubh yatra* —'Have a nice pilgrimage'. Thanks to the friendly melody of the well-maintained loco it was an afternoon of transport magic capped by the unfurled sails of the ferry that tacked across the river's placid evening face.

The architecture of princely Rajpipla struck me as being amongst the easiest on the eye I have seen anywhere in India. The station was a little way out of town but done solidly as befitted its royal stature. The station master, when I turned up next morning, was the epitome of efficiency, reeling off facts, most of which held gloomy portents for the future of the railway. He was embarrassed to admit he was out of platform tickets but to save face—since I only wanted one as a souvenir—he issued a ticket for the first station along the line— for the same price. The narrow gauge line came to a dead end at Raj-pipla and when I asked how the loco reversed he told me how in his grandfather's day (being the Rajpipla station master was a family monopoly) the line had earlier only come up to the river bank. In-itially the Indian princes assumed the distaste shown by British noble-men towards the defiling influence of railways and kept their works at a proper distance from their palaces. Later, when the lines proved profitable, the station was moved to a more central site or, as in Gwalior where His Highness Scindia extended the state railway, to the palace door itself.

The bridge over the Karjan river built by Baillie of London exhibited in its stout black metal piers the confidence of an age willing to invest in railways. Room had been left for an optimistic second track. I as-sumed that Karjan was a local variant of 'Curzon' but for once coin-cidence took precedence over corrupted diction. The stout structure made for a superb shot of the approaching morning passenger train. Unfortunately, the track ran down quite sharply to the bridge and the driver had to cut off steam and let ZB 58 coast into the station. That meant instead of a following plume of smoke all we got was a smudge of exhaust. Because of its thinness on the ground and the primitive state of interior facilities, narrow gauge steam on the run has hardly ever been captured in its rarer moments of abandon. Foreign spotters are always delighted when their official rail chaperons arrange for a 'run-past' of their host train. Often, to their chagrin (and disbelief) the scene is ruined by all the local passengers getting down and running alongside the train as well—not wanting to miss out on the chance of a family photograph.

The British-built ZB trod softly with scarcely a clank. At each station she ghosted in to halt with the sigh of valves snugly housed and glands smoothly content. Nowhere did the steam mechanism falter or offend. It worked utterly benign and its expansiveness had infected the attitudes of the driver and guard, both of whom had put in more than twenty-five years on this line and were now ready to retire gracefully rather than be retrained for diesel. The train rocked its way smoothly with a complement of tribal passengers who stacked their luggage in the WC. Quaint no doubt this line was, but for more than a century it had proved its worth and added to the sum of human happiness.

Arguments For and Against the Narrow Lines

It is usually overlooked that the 2 ft. 6 ins. gauge running in the plains performs sterling service for the rural poor. If these services continue against the Beeching instinct (to axe the weaker transport brethren at the root) it is because there is a real demand for them. The speed of the bus has now rendered the train fit only for those who have too much luggage to put on the bus roof. Each year these feeder lines pant along less convincingly and some are put out of their ailing cost-effective misery by the excuse of drought or flood conditions. No one can prevent their going and India so far lacks the class of romantically inclined preservationists who could pump in some capital and turn short sections into tourist lines. This way IR could continue to run them at no loss to its balance sheet.

The hill lines should survive as long as tourist imperatives demand it. Shimla's switch to diesel may mean this narrow gauge will outlast all others, though diesel also plies the 2 ft. line to Matheran. Darjeeling simply wouldn't be the same without its heroic saddle tanks, but possibly the attractive diesel rail-cars of the Gwalior line could break public habit into the cause for a diesel takeover. Ooty presents insuperable problems of conversion but it is quite possible the tourist bait is big enough for the genius of the Coonoor shed mechanics to keep their Swiss tankers in steam for another few years so as to see the twenty-first century in.

The light railway was devised to be a cheap form of transport for a poor area and the use of narrow gauge enabled a small engine to progress powerfully into places where a cart driver would think twice of going with a load. Later, the benefits seemed more from the internal combustion engine but it is not impossible that things may veer back to steam. The harsh sentence served on British branch lines by the Beeching Report apparently solved little. By shutting down all the country stations he only increased the misery of the vulnerable sections of society, the young and the elderly (and for those visitors from India and elsewhere who do not possess a car). The short-sightedness of these easy surgical exercises that remove an organ—and leave the patient even weaker—was revealed by the oil crunch that floored all optimistic projections of universal road travel.

As a boy in Scotland, I had the choice of both train and bus to go to Alloa or Stirling, the county towns, for shopping. In those days the travelling baker, butcher and vegetable seller daily brought his van around. Now one has neither train nor convenient bus. If you are no longer young, able-bodied and successful the real stigma haunts the traveller that society has little time for you. Lord Beeching's decree was the thin end of the wedge for the most brutal capitalist viewpoint. The current social tensions in Britain, the poor reputation of British . Railways in the eyes of those of the public who can afford to use it, and the extraordinary resurgence of enthusiasm for steam-age values all make Beeching's place in the history of human welfare far below that of his vaunted status as a transport trouble-shooter.

Whatever its socialist credo and its inbuilt capacity for wasteful management attitudes, Indian Railways at least retains a balanced concern for the human fall-out of far-reaching cut-backs. The much maligned object of professional railway scorn—the minister—is a valuable check against a purely mechanical view of railway running. The loud and uncouth who foregather outside his office in Rail Bhavan are not entirely a blot on the railway landscape. Their presence is a guarantee that democracy works and evidence that the common man (who 'owns' the railway—as he is always told) can get past the outer workings to place his point of view before the inner mysteries.

Sentiment for Small Lines: A Losing Cause

The aggrieved note in the Railway *Year Book* about the money wasted on the narrow gauge lines is toned down in the Fernandes *Status Paper*. He talks about these uneconomic lines as having become part of the 'socio-economic environment' and wonders if they do not justify being operated despite losses. The people for whom these lines are intended do not possess the voice to give their affirmative. The poor on the Ankleshwar train have already had their land taken away from them for the Narmada project and their tribal culture wiped out by the stroke of an urban pen. Sacrifices have to be made by the nation, and those with the least voice can trust to have such sacrifices imposed upon them. The politicians may not like the swarming poor any more than the middle-class planners do, but at least they are forced by their lip service to Gandhian ideology to go slow on sacrificing unpaying lines. It is because of Indian Railways' size and mixed tradition that the narrow gauge continues to get an extra lease of life.

For the railway student the narrow gauge is fascinating since it resembles a Rip Van Winkle experience that stopped developing at the beginning of this century. In its day to day working, more than any other gauge, it has seen the fruit of improvisation where Indian mechanics have kept its wholly imported fleet running in defiance of all known mechanical laws. From these engineering miracles lessons should be drawn. In the quaintness of the toy trains setting out to climb mountains can be detected great maintenance skills and some brilliant pragmatic answers to daily snags.

The mood of the narrow gauge is of defiant cheerfulness. Wherever you go on the Z and Q gauges the staff own a quiet pride in keeping an impossible system running. It must grate on the ears of the yuppie statistician in Rail Bhavan that most foreign visitors equate India's railroad talents not with the Shatabdi superfast to Bhopal nor the Iron Ore specials to Vishakapatnam but with the little lines to Shimla and Darjeeling. In continuing these affectionate tokens of regard lies a lesson of Indian striving that could teach Lord Beeching transport wisdom. Transport systems exist to make profits but they also serve to stimulate the priceless gift of civilized intercourse. In any narrow gauge economic survey we risk underestimating the feelings of the ordinary citizen to his steam heritage. It is a fact that nowhere is railway culture so essentially Indian as in the informal traverse of the Darjeeling train, with the carriages rattling by inches away from the potted geraniums on the window sills of the houses in Kurseong's main street. Here truly is a people's railway.

CHAPTER FIFTEEN

Down By the Station

The centrality of the railways to Indian life is brought home to any-one crawling along in the jam of Delhi's rush-hour traffic. On the backs of buses are advertisements ranging from 24-carat gold jewellery to Hakim Kishan Lal's *shafakhana* where your virility will be toned up to match the starched cockade on the Hakim's turban and your restored confidence will be slung like the bandolier of LG cartridges draped symbolically under two fountain pens in his breast pocket (the pen mightier than the double-barrelled shotgun?) For most of these buses their ultimate destination is *Relway Isstation.*

The railway station is indeed the place most citizens fix their bearings by and comparisons with cathedrals begin to make sense when we realize that these nineteenth century public buildings had effectively usurped the place of the medieval parish church as the central focus of a community. Life had speeded up and religion had become more adventurous with steam now paddling missionaries to the prospect of untold harvests. (Some of the routes of the metre gauge line in Rajasthan were altered to suit missionary tastes, though this did not mean any spiritual arm-twisting. It was the result of the secular apathy shown by other invited lobbies.)

The Social Significance of the Railway Station

Just as the Roman church had gone out and flourished along the Roman roads, the Victorian belief in its mission to civilize the savage by the imposition of British law followed the iron way. Unconsciously perhaps, the London terminals were designed to inspire confidence in the Empire administrators departing from them, since the chances of Zulu warriors or Afridi frontiersmen being impressed was remote indeed and confined to jubilee occasions. That conspicuous critic of the railway's overadventurous policies, Dr Lardner, had been disarmed by the size of the stations and doffed his hat as though in a church or a bank: 'It is impossible to regard the vast building and their dependencies which constitute a chief terminal station of a great line of railway without feelings of inexpressible astonishment at the magnitude of the capital and the boldness of the enterprise. Nothing in the history of the past affords any parallel to such a spectacle.'

For once Lardner is right. These 'great theatres' as he called them sprang in their girdered arrogance to announce the spanning of both time and space by mechanical ingenuity. The church buildings had spoken of a power on high, distant and beyond easy communication. The station pile with its imperious command over a city's skyline announced that the railways were prophetical of the age of the ordinary mortal and that religion with its once-weekly institutional formalities was being challenged by a searching mobile creed unashamed to recognize the hand of God in the crude endlessness of a metal track. The railways jolted the human soul as much as they jarred its body. The virtue of punctuality was only possible where communications were reliable—and the roads of Britain had been appalling. The demands of precision could only come with finely machined tolerances and such manual compulsions drove mental discipline towards ever greater transport refinements.

The Religious Symbolism of Stations

The medieval age and its faithfulness was also the era of drudgery with the human mind set in tiresome grooves unaware of the exciting world out there and unable, except for the very adventurous (or criminal) to break through the bonds of its stationariness. By demonstrating the possibility that a man could go out of his valley and come back again the same day, the railways had effected a mental and religious revolution. The imagery of salvation now lay in the lines at one's feet and the way forward opened up the prospect of liberating destinies. By their sheer permanence the railways had become a potential deliverer of mankind. From the bombastic talk of their civilizing mission to the hill boy who runs away to Bombay hoping to become a filmstar, the effect of the railways, if not exactly a new religion that enabled the individual to see things for himself, was of a heavy dose of laxative on the old. In India, it both stimulated pilgrimage to traditional Hindu *tirthas* (holy places) and silently struck at the debilitating influence of caste. The irresistible appeal of journeying immediately overwhelmed the conservative instinct to stagnate and the railway station was in business.

If the subject of railways can become an object of love the place of stations easily occupy a special romantic niche in our longings. 'One of the most beautiful subjects in the world' and 'the last refuge of happiness' are some of the more exaggerated bouquets thrown at these prime erections of the railway urge. These and a lot of psychological insights emerge from an exhibition staged by the Georges Pompidou Centre of Paris in 1978. According to the Gallic view (which, if one has seen the *Monsieur Hulot* films puts French railway platforms on a par with the Indian ones for the spontaneity of their passengers' reactions) the station expresses both the wonder and tragedy of life. The modern French sponsors of the exhibition, with its marvellously colourful collection of paintings of every conceivable school, seem to have thought more in terms of the sad modern drift from a vibrant industrial past to the contemporary hopelessness of the 'inner city'— where coloured immigrants and architecturally sterile acres of redevelopment are in turn surrounded by the special soulless horror of suburbia where the smug and salaried bury themselves away from the urban crisis behind a TV screen (fitted to a burglar alarm).

The Flavour of Indian Stations

India has different pressing problems but the same socialist irony hits the eye in the grading of facilities on platforms to make sure that the lucrative Victorian ideal—the first class passenger—is properly tucked in for all his needs. Prior to Independence Indian stations had the complication of religious segregation extending to such basics as drinking water. A lingering touch of such spiritual oneupmanship is still to be found in the 'non-veg' restaurant with its western style menu. Some years back I shared a taxi with what seemed the very last of the *burra sahibs*, whom I had been detailed to put on a train in Bareilly. Finicky and upset by the long winding road down from the hills he arrived at the platform restaurant with his opinions against any oily article of diet firmly established. Addressing the beturbanned bearer (who looked far too dramatic in his turn-out to be authentic), the Englishman minced out his instructions in Hindustani with the painful air of the perpetually aggrieved colonial. 'Toast and marmalade', was his order. The bearer, turned on his heel beaming, without repeating the order (disastrously, I thought, as experience has taught me that the over-eager salute in Avadh often means that the injured tone of a foreigner's delivery has not been identified and the true cause of his complaint only guessed at). Within seconds (it seemed) the gauze-grilled doors leading to the kitchen burst open and the bearer plopped down in front of our horrified sahib a cold, greasy omelette reposing on a slice of stale bread. 'Toast and *armlate*', announced the waiter proudly.

Arrival and departure rites were formerly in the care of the priest and pundit, but in modern travel we are faced with the coolie and ticket collector. Stations for the most part are a mix of the military and the respectable and to dream of a station master is akin to the awesome confrontation with a guru. In psychic terms the station is the way in to the unknown; those tunnels awaiting us at the end of the platform symbolizing the world of the unconscious with its tortuous overhang on our destiny—the real journey through this waking world. The station master is a warm guarantee that one will re-emerge from the plunge and for those who need the extra touch of respectability to their assurances he used to be marked by the wearing of a top hat.

In 1989 one of the railway wonders of the world celebrated its centenary and Indian Railways lost a chance to advertise its cultural treasure in the honouring of a 100 years of service by Bombay's Victoria Terminus. The Rail Minister no doubt did attend and make the proper noises and the Post Office did release a special stamp to mark the occasion but it was left to the *Times of India*, also celebrating a milestone of public service in Bombay, to bring out the full significance of one of modern transport's finest structures. It is a measure of the philistinism of Railway officers that few seemed aware of their splendid architectural inheritance. This indifference to railway history by its custodians ought to be cause for public concern.

The Virtues of Victoria Terminus

'What is timeless art doing at Victoria Terminal?', asks the *The Times of India* and proceeds to do the Railways' job for it by advertising succinctly and creatively, resisting the urge to batter in the heads of the public with freight statistics. '100 years of the *Times of India* coincides with 100 years of the Victoria Terminus. Both institutions located in the same neighbourhood, both hub centres of communications and connections, in a city that's a confluence of the nation and active witness to history from horse carriage to railway coaches. Some 25 lakh passengers flit back and forth each day in the VT making it an unprecedented gallery of life where amidst magnificent stone facades you can see friezes of faces from all parts of the country.' Though this only gives a fraction of the overall impressiveness of this marvellous station building and the minutest indication of its splendidly worked detail, it is enough to set on fire the public imagination that here is an extraordinary structure, the like of which is unique and confined exclusively to the Railways.

The VT is a masterpiece. You may not appreciate its lengthy amalgamation of the Indo-Italianate-Gothic and may well find its ornate knobbliness too cloying and exotic to be taken seriously as a transport model, but its impressiveness close-to silences most critics who, once more familiarly introduced, keep discovering minor delights in every embellished nook and round every lovingly wrought corner. It is the sort of building that deserves to be laughed at on paper yet cannot be, on confrontation. Described, it sounds splendidly ridiculous but in the flesh this emporium is ridiculously splendid, a one-off stroke of genius that destiny has donated to Central Railways.

One could expand on the quality of Indian workmanship revealed in this minor art gallery but in view of there being 7000 other stations in India we must content ourselves with a parting compliment to the architect, F. W. Stevens, whose genius was sniffed at by Lady Dufferin, rather in the manner of those born aristocrats who chide the Almighty for granting the lower orders the pleasures of sex.

In Kathiawad, with its legion of princely lines, the stations reflect many Indian virtues not appreciated by the more staid British. Junagarh manages to combine proportion and style into its elegant platforms after an almost zany brush with megalomania at the gate. On the whole working clock towers are an unfamiliar part of the subcontinental station scene, reflecting the timeless reality of rural concerns. At Jamnagar the deserted metre gauge station still boasts some fine workmanship now falling to bits. Sadly, the shoebox style of modern railway architecture indicates the brash progress of the unpedigreed broad gauge which offends with its 'take it or leave it' finality.

The Decline of Indian Rail Architecture

But it would be wrong to confine to the broad gauge what is actually a defect to be witnessed all over India. No doubt the broad gauge station at Quilon thoughtlessly tacked on the metre gauge platforms is a faceless barn favoured by a railway budget that thinks solely in terms of economy, but no architecture need be quite so tasteless as modern India is resorting to, slapping up concrete imitations of regional styles and, where these do not exist, building cheap and loveless cement boxes. In Assam, along the little used metre gauge section to Murkong Selek I shuddered to see the unimaginative aspect of the wayside stations almost thrown at the heads of the local people—oblongs of plastered brick given a coat of paint and as lifeless as the minds who thought them up. Do these dismal central images help cause insurrection in the North East, one wonders. Shortly after I witnessed these horrifically banal buildings the Bodo agitation started and some of them became targets of its terrorist wrath.

The metre gauge has the same modern ersatz tastes spread all along its lines. Whether it is Ajmer and Jaipur getting an imitation Rajasthani roof of a royal pavilion done in drooping cement, or Madurai and Tirupati lazily and badly copying the *gopuram* architecture of Tamil-nadu, the effect is of barren design habits and builders devoid of ideas. The disease that threatens the whole spine of IR from the Railway Board down to the painter of the notice board is of passive attitudes to the creative challenge in any given piece of work. Everything they put their hands to architecturally seems too late or too little, their public reactions either too palsied or too carelessly bland. Until it becomes more professional in advertising itself as an aware organization the Railways can only invite cynical comment on their declared concern to get the wheels of their empire turning more smoothly.

Station architecture is the instant way to diagnose the health of the system and anyone concerned to analyse the quality of stations fleeting by these days would find it hard not to conclude that the main inspiration for any rail building—probably the only one—is cheapness. It is because it is such a socialist creature with so many udders (most booked in advance), that the Railways never get round to contracting out its station designs to young, innovative and exciting talent. That is not to say that all modern facades are unpleasing but as with the new frontage at Banaras which is neat and inspiring enough, there is no excitement, no sense of being attuned to a changing society where the young generation may not necessarily relate to the motifs of their seniors. The point being that it is to the interests of the next generation of railusers that today's designs should be aimed, to win them over to an understanding of what the system is capable of.

Unwise Impositions

If the modern run of terminals bore us with their lack of inspiration, it is still possible to collect examples of the fine quality of those days when private railway companies were concerned to be advertised by the quality of their stations. Saharanpur, surprisingly, still has the elegance of early interiors with barrel vaults and some fine metal

work. Princely Patiala, not so surprisingly, has some truly royal platform furniture and a fetching overhead bridge that perfectly sets off
the wrought iron trellis work under a delicate continental canopy.
When I complimented a Patiala railway officer on the easy style of his
raised waiting hall he thought my judgement cock-eyed. For a real
station one should go to Lucknow and see imitation Islamic he argued.
It is a terrifying thought that such officers who are blind to their heritage could issue an order to remove the Patiala canopy and replace it
with asbestos sheets, unaware that art had been destroyed and railway history vandalized. The sort of thing that seems to make these
officers happy is the cement pillared monstrosity bullying the landscape at Kanyakumari, a lack-lustre building pretending to be something it is not. Clearly its design could only have been passed by
someone close to the minister who wanted the Railways to seem
important at the Cape. The tragedy of this vulgar climax to IR architecture is that visitors do not notice its vaunted echoing halls—for
the simple reason that there are few visitors. It handles three passenger
trains and one express train a day, an example if one needed it, of the
splendidly ridiculous.

Plenty of stations along the lines far from the baleful trowels of
Delhi patronage continue to delight in their modest integrity. Built to
last, these halts need the luck of having no political leader on their
doorstep to survive the paintbrush of progress. The old friendly wayside station, unhurried and neatly kept, is a characteristic of the south,
where the pressure on the land has not caused the locals to walk off with
all the moveable railway property which is remotely useful. By contrast, the new stations on Delhi's ring railway tend to be as bland as
the commuters they serve, but the other metropolitan platforms are
always worth having a peer at as one passes through. (Note the name
boards borrowed from the London Underground.) Generally the furniture on the smaller gauges is more intact, since these lines do not
attract the enthusiasm of ministers and their whims to create 'model'
stations with a slick appearance and no real soul. In Quilon the old
metre gauge station has now been turned into a parcels office, its tiny
porch sealed off from public access. Yet this is a gem of railway architecture, done royally in the style of Kerala, a good model for the new

stations coming up as the meagre tracks of the state expand. In contrast, it is a shock to find the old station at Trivandrum looking like something seconded from the Stockton and Darlington Railway, an extraordinarily ugly building to be found in what is aesthetically one of India's most sensitive cities.

Style Not Yet a Thing of the Past

Other big cities have appropriate and well-known show-piece terminals which are suitably impressive in their dimensions and which are not so far swamped by the modern swell of travellers. An early version of Sealdah was designed by Brunel and he made several engineering notings for the Eastern Bengal line that operated from there.

However, none of these appraisals of the buildings' outer impressiveness really catches the palpable flavour of an Indian station nor gives any clue to how different it is from its European original. For that we can dip into the first impressions of *Kim's* lama. 'This is the work of devils', he declared, as he beheld third class passengers laid out sheeted as though dead. Kipling, however, is using the old man to put across the western view wherein draped bodies littering the platform always seem the best evidence of oriental cussedness, when in fact their dispersal on the stone floor is the simplest and most sensible way to keep cool. Western photographers continue to click these cliches of the East. However, Englishmen on such exclusive flag-waving missions as climbing Everest, are considered heroic when they resort to sleeping on the ground and bivouacing before the elements.

I have slept on several station platforms—preferably on a bench, which over the years has become kinder to the flesh. Earlier cement, then wood and now moulded plastic forms are to be found on the better equipped junctions. At Guwahati I had a ticket for a train that left next morning but was down to my last few rupees after a sudden urge to visit Shillong, where I gambled on staying with a friend—who was out of station—and hence my cut-price bench. But there was a platform television to watch as I lay back to let clanking 'MacArthur' locomotives lull me to sleep. As the station grew quieter the only sound was that of security men doing their rounds and clacking their sticks on the platform. What I have found to be a curious common denominator of railway stations all over India (especially in the early hours of the morning) is the appearance of a young madwoman with bobbed hair. Quite why you are awakened by the harmless giggle of this particular apparition in places as far apart as Guwahati in Assam and Palani in Kerala may be a question for the social psychologist to answer. Anything at that hour is apt to appear uncanny and one takes comfort in the patrolling footsteps of the Railway police. Calcutta in recent times has had the sensational 'Stoneman' series of murders. Many of the victims found with their brains bashed out were sleeping on station platforms. Though the rail authorities are fairly strict (by Indian standards) in not allowing vagrants to sleep on stations, the latter are so persistent and numerous that some are bound to permeate past security. Stations are also the gathering place for runaway children who find odd jobs in the bazaar outside when the pickings of petty crime do not seem more remunerative. Delhi has even staged a play produced for these children revealing their actual lifestyle, and the Bombay station children have featured in the film *Salaam Bombay*. If Delhi streets are callously indifferent to the plight of the young and unemployed, at least the lighted railway station seems friendly and offers some warmth in the shadowy company of other feckless travellers.

Memorable Station Facilities

The waft of platform food is too well known to Indian travellers for comment, though it is often considered to be too hot and unhygienic for foreign tastes. Letters of complaint forever blame the travelling meal service for poor quality food but I have never seen a platform stall ridiculed for its lack of savour. Almost invariably one notices the passenger unsuccessfully fighting the urge to enjoy a second helping. Of all virtues that distinguish the Indian platform from the austere fare of British Rail, the stall-holder with his hot fresh food rates highest. His attitude is entirely professional and his cooking as reliable as his knowledge of railway timings. For a fraction of the cost of a full meal one can feast on a selection of snacks and retire content having sampled some of the tastiest food prepared anywhere under the sun. The secret of this is the affection that holds between the stall-holder and his public. The passenger wants his food hot and tasty and immediately accessible. This minor miracle is accomplished a thousand times a day on railway platforms, yet the fashion of fast food is deemed to have arisen in the West. And how ghastly junk food tastes in comparison to the delicious Indian fare sold at a tenth of the price.

Stations, according to the book, are listed with a letter after them to indicate their possibilities. The *S* denotes, at the very least, a teastall. *B* announces bigger things with a bookstall, while *W* is the sign of a station that has really arrived and boasts of a waiting-room. For those who take their stations seriously an asterisk before the *S* and *N* (a non-vegetarian refreshment room) indicates that the facilities are departmentally run by the Railways themselves. The absence of an asterisk means one is at the mercy of a private contractor unprotected by the canopy of socialist catering ethics. Other hieroglyphics, according to region, refer to the presence of water coolers and that ultimate platform treat, the retiring room. Stations are also graded according to the sophistication of their signalling equipment. The subject of signalling, so crucial to railway operations, is a specialized passion and the professionalism of its initiates guarantees that its study among the laity will be restricted to the lovers of chess. The lore of 'Lower Quadrant', and mysteries of 'Multiple Aspect Upper Quadrant' sadly escape the gape of agitated commuters.

For those addicted to the poetry of lists and who go through the index of stations with the joy of a parent hoping to alight on the most appropriate name for a genius soon to be announced, sound advice is to tune in to the musical vowels of the Telugu language of Andhra Pradesh. For anyone with the Miltonic urge to declaim from the moving window, a run-down of the line between Secunderabad and Tirupati will provide the twin thrill of assonance and alliteration: Gollapalli, Poodoor, Linganenidoddi, Tuggali, Zangalappale, Mudigubba, Tummanagutta, Damalcheruvu, greet the ears. What must count amongst the longest station names in the world is another halt some

fifty kilometres south of Tirupati on the broad gauge to Madras—
Venkatanarasingharajuvariapeta (or VKZ to railwaymen).

Platform Profiles

As already mentioned, regarding the longest platform India has several
contenders, though the winner at present is in Chicago where it runs
well beyond a kilometre. Kharagpur is second at 833 metres and
Sonepur fourth at 736, Lucknow is sixth, Bezwada seventh and Jhansi
eighth in the world. India probably also holds the record for the most
stations without any platform at all, and this by no means applies only
to the smaller gauges. One of the most delightful wayside halts that
always reminds me (in the rainy season) of Wimbledon is between
Muzaffarnagar and Saharanpur, called Bahman Heri. It boasts neither
a *B, W* or *S*—hardly surprising in the absence of a platform.

Those inseparable understudies of station masters and whose information on railway matters is unbeatable—the porters—are by an
irony of circumstance not officially railway employees. In their red
shirts, flashing a brass token on their arm, they are fringe beneficiaries
of the Railways but lack anything but a casual relationship with the
official system. This anomaly arises from the assumption that a socialist undertaking would automatically absorb those whose labours
the private companies availed of but would not codify. IR has the
problem of where to cut off from what constitutes actual railway involvement. Had employment status been granted to the Garibaldi
brigade, the rickshawpullers might also demand that their custom
was an integral part of the arrival and departure pattern. Tongawallahs
(the horse-drawn taxi) could similarly lay claim to indispensability
and possibly the shoe-shine boy, followed by the travelling busker
who has been described by one unpoetic ear as producing 'coarse
music' to allay the 'heavy sound' of the running train.

The station as a magic arena always offers a poetic helping of railway delight. No less important is its admirable physical translation of
passenger and parcel chaos into orderly channels. Its sounds, smells
and the intervals of silence between the tumult of the passing train,

enable the station to claim a life of its own providing friendly memories in a life that too often get boarded up from indifference or contempt. And encouragingly, it seems the lesson has at last been learned that an aesthetic concern and the desire to build with pride wins instant public admiration. All the earlier disgust at the teething problems of the Calcutta Metro have been swept away by the winning elegance of its outward manifestation.

CHAPTER SIXTEEN

Paperwork

Was Kipling making it up when he suggested 'the sheeted dead' had bought their tickets the night before? Most of us second class passengers are kept waiting by the ticket babu up till an hour before the departure of the train, and then are forced to join a scrum which is vigorous enough to have made Gandhiji willingly suspend his disbelief in violence. The babus locked inside their booking office may take three hours to make out a circular ticket and at the end of it decide you should go to the Chief Commercial Superintendent's office two miles away (since they lack the 'jurisdiction' to issue a letter of authority for a 'non-standard journey'). You can at present travel from Shimla to Kanyakumari via Dwarka, Goa, Bangalore, Trivandrum, Madurai and Madras—a journey exceeding 9000 kilometres—for 550 rupees on a ticket valid for two months (so it is hardly right to complain of the two mile initial walk). These extraordinary travel bargains spill out of the back of any regional timetable, but because of the smallness of the print the public is deterred from following them up. Indian Railways happens to be the best value for money transport system on the face of the earth. But owing to the ingrained habit of whining about the dal slopping out of a casserole travelling at 100 km.p.h., the bargain gets overlooked. (What you save on long distance tickets you can easily afford to re-invest in laundry bills.)

A Salute to George Bradshaw

Part of the problem is the public fear of *Bradshaw*. To his followers this Manchester printer, circa 1840, is one of the great intellectual joys of railway travel. Like so many other pioneers of the Industrial Revolution, George Bradshaw was a Quaker forced by the narrowness of established church attitudes to follow his inner voice and do his own thing. His Railway Companion included 'the times of departure, fares etc. of the railways in England and also hackney coach fares from the principle railway stations illustrated with maps of the country through which the railways pass and plans of London, Birmingham, Leeds, Liverpool and Manchester'. For a shilling the traveller certainly got his money's worth. Bradshaw was also a meticulous mapmaker and a first-rate printer. It was from his creed as a Quaker that this timetable was produced to help passengers and for years his 'correct account of arrival and departure of the trains' continued to use antiquated Society of Friends conventions, such as 'First Mo.' for the month of January.

A somewhat similar example of religious inspiration is that of Thomas Cook who, at the same time Bradshaw was getting into print, organized the first excursions for the masses, also for a shilling (which may sound excessive for the ten mile trip from Leicester to Loughborough). Yet 500 passengers crowded on to his special train and the junket included a visit to a stately home and a chance to take on the lordly hosts at cricket. Cook's brainwave derived from his fanatical belief in temperance. It is possible that the phrase 'on the wagon' derived from his urgent concern to divert the hand that raised the bottle to the seat that bypassed the local. On the strength of his original motivation Thomas Cook (who now appears on his own travellers' cheques) could well claim to be the patron saint of those compartments on Indian Railways where prohibition notices (in a flagrant denial of natural justice) seem to threaten more those of modest means.

One can sympathize with the average passenger on being presented with a railway timetable, for its consultation involves an acquired skill. You can find your way through only after you have learned how to get in. But most of those who need to use it lose their way from the remorseless details that distract from their desired cut-and-dried itinerary. For a public educated on newspapers where the lead story is abruptly 'continued on page 7' the timetable ought not to be such an insuperable challenge, but the layout of a newspaper has the advantage of allowing the reader's attention to wander on the traverse of tangential interest. For a *Bradshaw* addict such diversion may be a heady tonic but the ordinary user, beset by columns that resemble Wisden batting averages, tends to curse the directory and phone the enquiries counter at the station instead.

Like all good things in life, the soul of a timetable does not unfold until the love of its mysteries has overcome all resistance to the oft-turned page. My current *Bradshaw* runs to more than 300 pages and also gives information to 'Airway travellers'. Its proper title is *Newman's Indian Bradshaw* published monthly and a necessity for the compulsive journeyer since the Railways have stopped the sale of a bound edition of their combined regional timetable which was eminently consultable by virtue of its contrasting zonal colours. Now we are palmed off with *Trains at a Glance* which claims to be an 'abstract of Mail and Express timings' but could more accurately be called a 'Bourgeois Rail Companion'. Concerned only for upmarket tastes it caters to those most likely to complain of casserole fatigue. In bold type its limitations are announced—'For branch line services, stoppage at smaller stations and slip coach services, consult zonal timetables'. In other words, the producers of humble railway revenue can get stuffed.

The Deplorable Decline in Indian Mapping

Something else that would make Bradshaw blanch are the shoddy maps that come with current railway publications, though recently the railway map of India inserted with the *Trains at a Glance* has improved, it still appears on an excruciatingly fine scale (thanks for the breakthrough must go to the The Art Shoppe, Aziz Mulk IIIrd Street, Thousand Lights, Madras and not to the Railways). Some of the zonal maps are disgracefully unprofessional. The sheet supposed to show the layout of the Northern Railways divisional structure, for example, serves only to suggest the imminent breakdown of the system. It is next to impossible to convey the Indian network on a reduced map, but instead of dividing the subcontinent into manageable proportions the Railway *Year Book* prints a colourfully meaningless sheet that obscures more than it reveals. Only the person who has travelled the lines (and hence is in no need of a map) will be able to understand it. What purpose is served by printing 'Bodinayakkanur' across the width of the peninsula?—and that too illegibly. Such things lends a shoddy air to our concerns, as does the absurd 'Kanniyakumari-Cape Comorin (Kanniyakumari)' triad, with the stress on getting the Sanskrit diacriticals right. Station collectors may perk up on finding an unlisted entry between Salem Market and Villipuram, but it seems more likely the halt called 'Magnesite' is a stray fallen from a passing map of mineral deposits!

Not all zonal maps are equally abysmally drawn though most are rendered indecipherable by the amateurish insertion of 'corresponding timetable number'. Even if the NE Frontier Railway map is as crudely jostling in its layout as that of the Western zone, things show a definite improvement with the South Central. Its timetable is characterized by a more intelligent approach all round and, significantly, it opens with the list of the 'Railway Users Consultative Committee' (Northern Railway manages to stifle the existence of its advisory public up to page 158 where they find a place after 'Vigilance', 'Complaints' and 'Tourist Spots'). The South Central Railway possessed of a mind of its own applies it and gives us at the outset a map showing the table numbers of sections over the SCR. That simple solution results in the end map being free from clutter. But to indicate that the South Central is not exactly a typical ride, the same timetable exhorts passengers 'to desist from exhibiting gold ornaments which are likely to attract unsocial elements'.

For the best zonal map we have to go further south (back to the 'Art Shoppe of a Thousand Lights', in fact) where the cartography is superbly clear, and the legend free of the customary gibberish. To show that the Railways can print well when the need arises the zonal timetables are usually put out by the regional railway presses. And to show that the Railways are serious about 'Any suggestion for making an improvement in this book or in the timings will be welcomed', I find that after earlier complaints of the poor quality of NR timetable maps their offerings have been made their more legible, thanks to the appointment of an assistant.

The Cartographic Genius of J. H. Trott

In the good old days map making was as thrilling and romantic a subject as steam. From a second hand bookshop in Bangalore I acquired a sumptuous railway map for 1920 'corrected annually and issued with Administration Report by the Railway Board'. On a scale of 1 inch to 64 miles it was difficult enough for J.H. Trott (the map's 'proprietor' from Aligarh) to get in all the detail. Yet what glorious detail this four-foot square sheet, mounted on cloth, goes into. Titled 'Railway systems in India, Burma and Ceylon' its scope extends through Siam and Malaysia to Singapore. The first thing I looked for was the extreme westerly station of Zahidan where I had joined the system but the line into Persia from Baluchistan was yet to be constructed in 1920. The wealth of information is fit more for an encyclopaedia than a map. Insets abound—Calcutta, Agra, Lucknow, Delhi, Bombay, Simla and Madras. A special enlarged map of Bengal showing its coalfield lines is included, as also a long list of the names of private railway companies, most of whose narrow gauge works have been swallowed up by time.

To catch the imaginative outlook of a railway public conditioned to see the train as the most meaningful mode of travel, Trott has drawn up cleverly (in the open space of the Bay of Bengal) a world map showing routes by rail road and water, giving all the distances between points along them. The information is supplemented by tables of travel totals which tell you that by road from London to Delhi is 300 kilometres longer (500 if you divert to Mecca) than if you travelled by boat (6095 miles). Unless, of course, you chose to wear woollens and travel via Vladikaskov, Krasnavodsk, Kushk and Kandahar. That way you could slice another 500 miles off the road to Delhi.

The dedicated rail traveller who liked to reach Singapore by the roundabout route would take the Trans-Siberian to Harbin (some 500 miles short of Vladivostock), then wriggle his way down via Peking, Yunnan, Hanoi and Bangkok to notch up 12,202 miles out of Piccadilly. Not content with traipsing the length of Asia, Mr Trott somehow also manages to fit in a separate map of the world that discloses the most magical route by which to circumscribe it—'From

India to India 22,222 miles in 80 days'. If you are short of time he provides the alternative 'Round the world via Siberia in 37 days'. The catch here is that all the 'world' amounts to is a three week traverse of the Steppes followed by a fortnight's grind through the prairies (which might almost add up to a Cook's theme tour—'40 days in the wilderness').

What the mass of exciting content cannot convey is the spectacular artistry of Trott's map. The various railways are shown in contrasting bright colours. Not without cause does the proprietor advertise under his name 'Exhibited by Government at the Franco-British Exposition London 1908'. And to complete its superb railway credentials the sheet has been 'Helio-zincographed at Thomason College, Roorkie'. (*Thomason*, it will be recalled, gave his name to the first working locomotive in India).

From the art of J. H. Trott to the squigglings of the zonal 'Sharmajis', the railway map has declined miserably and reflects seriously on what Nehru called the lack of a scientific temper. (Certainly Trott's map would be proscribed in an age more preoccupied with prestige for he shows the Chinese border running within fifty miles of Tezpur!) Slovenly publication schedules have ruined the reputation of India's cartographers who once were hailed amongst the world's best. Railway maps like road maps see the light of day ten years after their survey and with obsolete information and sluggish sales have become just another expensive joke at public expense. Because of its international repercussions, shoddy mapping attitudes reflect badly on India's image. Apathy on sovereign matters is one commodity no nation need export.

Mention may be made of the latest official Railway map of India on a scale similar to Trott's. The depiction of the states of the Union in dully contrasting colours, with the lines of the Railway's different zones imposed over them in various other shades, leads to a very unsatisfactory visual experience. Why should a railway layout anyway be superimposed on a political map? The professional way to depict Indian Railways would be to shade the zones in strong colours that emphasize the divisional break up. The public never has a clear idea of the basic structure of the system because of the lack of such information and can hardly be blamed for showing a lack of interest in railway organization.

A Ticket Collector Extraordinary

Having explored the delights of *Bradshaw* and experienced the despondency of current rail maps we can turn next to the rites of ticketing. Anyone who stands in a short line at the air-conditioned reservation counters (that now open at hours convenient to the public) will bless the Railways for overcoming the primitive and endlessly fatiguing queue system that obtained in the scruffy booking halls of yesteryear. In the middle of one's agony the babu would invariably close down for lunch, each customer seemingly demanding at least ten minutes of his time. Great thumpings of muscular folios would announce that the appropriate reservation had been located and several more minutes would elapse before it could be got open at the right page. Getting a ticket was rather like having a baby. Small wonder that the *deshi* solution to one's affliction—the 'ticket tout'—put in his appearance and was viewed by those to whom time was precious as more of a saviour than a parasite.

In the early days of ticketing, the paper coupons of the stagecoach companies were imitated just as surely as the horse drawn carriage was the model for the railway coach. (On the early lines you parked your carriage on a float, container style, and drove it off at your destination.) The time-consuming system of filling out a ticket form led to the invention of the Edmundson dispensing machine which simplified the issuing, kept a check on the numbers, and stamped the date with a definitive clap of thunder. Edmundson was a station master in the north of England and came up with his idea in 1837. However, entry to Indian platforms only began after public resentment was voiced in the 1880s. The wheel has come full circle and a little over a hundred years later the travelling public have begun to demand the exclusion of the traditional clan seeing-off rites. Just one station in Madras issues 11,000 platform tickets daily!

One had always valued the humble platform ticket as the best

reminder of a journey but it was not until I met a serious collector of
these railway items that I realized what a fascinating world they open
up. While resting after a round of the stupa at Sanchi I met John King
from Hove in England. He comes to India most years primarily to
boost his collection of platform tickets. By urging me to study my
own tickets a bit closer (his collection extended to all categories of
tickets sold by the railways) I was able to make out the tremendous
scope for individuality that is a feature of Indian Railways. We assume
every ticket is the same when a closer look will reveal that even a small
collection yields the astonishing fact that tickets are more like finger-
prints. Obviously the colours differ for first and second class travel
tickets but also in the realm of platform specimens you can find a bewildering array of shades. Some are white, some are green, some are
grey, and one is yellow (Ledo in Assam). The overprinting can be in
black, or various shades of red or orange (a colour that distinguishes
the cleanly printed Central Railways tickets). The disgracefully printed
examples predictably all issue from the north, and New Delhi was
amongst the worst for shoddy illegibility. Southern and Western
tickets are acceptable, though the South Central specimens rival the
Northern Railway's for smudginess. The narrow gauge stations around
Dabhoi go in for very cleanly printed tickets in wholly orange type.
The broad gauge NR stations of Dehra Dun, Kotkapura and Varanasi
betray a watered down brown ink which might suggest the mixing of
dwindling stocks of scarlet and black.

No two tickets are alike. All have the regional language in addition
to the Hindi and English name. Only one ticket in my collection is
entirely in English—Chandod on the Narmada in Gujarat. The overprinting of several languages hardly helps rail efficiency and the need
to repeat all forms in a bilingual format is a demonstration of Hindi's
imperial pretensions. Every ticket tells its own story of professional
attitudes, political interference and the levels of local culture. Those
marked 20 paise and cancelled to read one and a half rupees testify to
rising prices. Ten years ago the *Indian Bradshaw* cost ten rupees. In
1992 it had gone up to 35.

Curiously, the most modern ticket in my assortment is a throwback almost to the Stockton-Darlington coupon type with the date

and month filled in by hand. The only thing missing is the old fashioned instruction 'Please to hold this Ticket till called for'. The place of issue of this latest thing in IR ticketing (that takes us back to the 1830s) is Gwalior, home of the latest 'model' station.

At least the new computerized journey ticket is a less flimsy fare. Some Railway Notes from the *Statesman* of September 1890 ('By a Railway Man Dating Tickets') infer dubious motives to the smudger of tickets: 'I suppose station masters and booking clerks are to blame for illegible dating but in most cases the economy of the head office is responsible. As imperfect dating puts a good chance for cheating in the hands of dishonest persons, greater attention should be paid to the dating arrangements'. A glance at a wide variety of travel tickets in my care reveals that the complaint of a hundred years ago about the need to ink one's ribbon or type remains valid for modern booking offices. Not a single ticket bears an inked date and many have been stamped dry, in a kind of railway braille. Most have been overwritten by hand. Now with the computerized ticket-form, less is open to guesswork but the ephemeral feel of a print-out lacks the special touch of the Edmundson 'two by one' card.

Personal Encounters in Being Punched

Many tickets come in voucher form and it is common in a reserved compartment for the TTE to sit down beside the passenger and up-grade his cardboard ticket with a surcharged flimsy. My excess fare ticket issued by P. Madhavan Nair (TTE/TVC, badge no. 2119) for a second class sleeper berth on the Kerala Mangala Express to Delhi was called forth by my RAC booking that entitled me to board the train and occupy a reserved seat while the TTE discovered if there were any berths available against cancellation (if there weren't I would have had to sit up for two nights).

Journey tickets form a vast lore and John King introduced me into some of the preliminary mysteries. The first recorded fare-paying passenger was Jonah in the Old Testament who 'went down to Joppa and found a ship going to Tarshish; so he paid the fare thereof' (Jonah 1:3).

Red wavy lines on most long distance tickets are a throwback to the age of private companies when this was the device used to indicate that the journey passed from the home lines of your local railway to enter the tracks of the 'foreign' competition. Indian zonal timetables continue to refer to other zones as 'foreign' lines. Whether Jonah's ticket was valid for the onward journey by whale is not clear, but the likelihood of wavy lines cannot be ruled out.

In Lumding on the NEF Railway I witnessed an unusual act of enterprise by a booking clerk. When I asked for a platform ticket, instead of falling back on the listless 'out of stock' refrain of the habitual defeatist, the young babu proceeded to make a platform ticket on his own initiative. Taking a slip designed for booking luggage he crossed out the word 'luggage' and wrote, 'In lieu of a platform ticket Lumding'. Perhaps he was new to the assignment and had not yet contracted the creeping palsy that overcomes so many in his job.

Soon the only memory of the Edmundson card may be the platform weighing machine. These have been made more lively by the addition of disco lights and it is always a joy to watch village children on their first visit to a station step on these machines and wait with marvel and anticipation for the magic act of telling their weight. The last time I weighed myself was in Behrampur in Orissa, and the ticket contained a photograph of the Hindi film actress Poonam on one side and a long screed in Oriya on the other. Did this mean I was fated to meet a beautiful woman as I stepped out of the station? Apparently not. The traffic policeman posted there offered to translate. He indicated a more pragmatic destiny: 'You are prolific in original ideas and impatient of old methods'. But that still left a bold bottom line untranslated and when I insisted, the policeman read out some excellent advice to the romantically inclined railway user—'Keep off the track'.

One railway ticket that did do me service when in a tight corner was the Ministry of Railways photography pass which I flourished when an officious person in Jaipur questioned my *locus standi* to snap ancient steam locomotives. The glimpse of *Rel Mantralaya* in Hindi was sufficient to turn his opposition into fawning co-operation. What he did not notice was that the pass was only for the Delhi Rail Museum and not transferable. Often on one's travels when brandishing the proper permission from Delhi the sight of this letter-head from Rail Bhavan is enough for simpler members of the railway staff to follow you around in the hope that you can take up their case and have them transferred far enough down the line to be out of earshot of their mothers-in-law.

CHAPTER SEVENTEEN

Wheeler and Dealers

To illustrate the hold the railway has on our literate faculty we can take recourse to any level of literature and constantly find a wide range of references to 'ferriferous equinity'. The examples quoted are all from the shelf of my own rail user's library. Railway literary alignment got off to a good start in England when Charles Dickens' *Dombey and Son* (1848) gave a vivid and sometimes painful account of how brash rail technology would carve out for itself a whole new lifestyle. 'The railroad trailed smoothly away upon its mighty course of civilization and improvement', he wrote as the new line was dug out of Euston. After initial hesitation at the mess and inconvenience caused by the digging, Dickens leapt aboard to record its music: 'Burrowing among the dwellings of men, breasting the wind and light, shower and sunshine, it rolls and roars, working on in a storm of energy and perseverance with a shrill yell of exultation, tearing on through the purple distance, resistless to the goal.' The symbol of the Euston Arch (properly *proplyaeum*) spoke not just of the pre-eminence of the railway but of British industrial enterprise. When it was dismantled in 1961 few then were aware that this symbolized the official announcement of the liquidation of British economic superiority.

Dickens had the misfortune to be involved in a violent derailment near Staplehurst in 1865. He was writing his last novel *The Mystery of Edwin Drood* when the carriage left the line and it seems in spite of the cool he displayed, the shock hastened his end. Indeed, the novelist had a bad run of luck with his rail journeys. On his way to Ireland the train was snowed in for four hours. In America floods put back his time of arrival by seven hours. We owe his railway ghost story—*The*

Signalman—to a further calamity that detained him at Rugby when his carriage caught fire.

Another novelist who got in details of the railway's early impact was Disraeli (in *Sybil*). Robert Louis Stevenson's famous lines *From a Railway Carriage*—'Faster than fairies, faster than witches/Bridges and houses, hedges and ditches' (set to music nearly a century after they were written) has overshadowed his blow by blow account of a journey by train—*Across the Plains*.

Early Poetry of the Railroad

The early poetry of the railways seems a bit puffed up in its heavy philosophizing (wherein 'annihilation' was a favourite image). Bertram Dobell's 'Devouring distance defeating time A common sight but how sublime', sums up the message—and its shaky quality. Charles Mackay was the first to declare the poetic associations of the steam locomotive: 'Behold smoke panoplied the wondrous car'—which flowered into the mellifluous metaphors and 'elate metre' of Spender ('the black statement of pistons') and Auden (whose *'Night Mail'* 'shovelled steam' over her shoulder). 'Tis freedom's song the train is singing', exulted George Bungay and to the Beatnik guru Jack Keouac, the thought of steam conjures up 'India in a dream'.

The railway companies themselves could wax literary in their brochures. If the far-out proposition—'Railways are supplying you in the mere facility of locomotion with a new motive for classical study' sounds like a script for 'Monty Python', the reference was in fact unearthed by that avid spotter Michael Palin whose creed, 'The Importance of Getting Excited About Railways' we share.

Someone who would not have been amused at such light hearted voyagings was the original bookstall proprietor W. H. Smith the Second. At the time he was contracted to open a bookstall at Euston he was known as the 'North-Western Missionary'; his motive was to provide serious reading at a time when the traveller could only expect to find pornographic offerings to while away his time and warm his freezing extremities. Some companies actually had Bibles chained to lecterns on the platform (this had the approval of W. H. Smith who aspired to be a clergyman). The family line on what constitutes literature continues and the flourishingly respectable bookseller runs no risk of becoming part of the contemporary history of what was once called 'swinging Britain'.

In India, the Allahabad concern of A. H. Wheeler & Co. (Pvt.) Ltd. has for more than a century been 'bringing knowledge and clean entertainment' to some 264 stations in the northern half of India. In the South the name of Higginbothams is to be seen on the railway bookstalls, recalling the rivalry of John Menzies to W. H. Smith in the North British scheme of things. Wheeler provides a livelihood to 5000 people and brings good reading matter to an audience that runs into many millions. Also seen on selected platforms are booksellers of a missionary persuasion who stock literature of a morally uplifting nonsectarian kind. One notes for example Sarvodaya bookstalls that sell Gandhian books and the Gita Press, Gorakhpur, that promotes the Puranic wisdom of popular Hinduism. (To judge from the widespread immorality of ticketless travel the circulation of these tracts is limited, however.)

Normally it pays to have a good look at the station selection for here you may find a forgotten title that has long been sold out in the town bookshop. No matter what station one is in, the same international best-seller authors will be on display—Jackie Collins, Jeffrey Archer, Harold Robbins, Sidney Sheldon, Robert Ludlum, Frederick Forsyth, Alastair Maclean, etc. As a tribute to the genius of Indian writing skills, names like Forsyth and Maclean have inspired Delhi's pirate printers to commission fictitious titles written under their names. For the ladies, Mills and Boon paperbacks abound but the bulk of passengers prefer the single most popular read—the legion of film magazines—*Stardust, Cineblitz, Filmfare*, etc. They fill the ordinary traveller's heart with all the wonder real life denies it—wealth, fame, romance, a glittering wardrobe, a marble-clad flat overlooking the sea, liveried bearers, faithful slim and doting wives, chubby spoilt children, and elongated limousines with a press-button fold-down hood (to enable the neighbourhood to share your latest blaring film music). It is a harmless and desperately needed placebo that caters to the fantasies of rich and poor alike. Film stars become larger than life, their every step watched in a compulsive love-hate relationship. Their fans weep when they fall ill and gloat when they face tax problems. Their public image turns them from ordinary human beings into terrifying slavish archetypes forced to behave according to the idolatry of their masterful audiences.

To attract this vast passive gallery waiting to be stimulated, an 'in-flight' railway magazine was started but it never found a slot in passenger affections. Most travellers indeed were unaware of its existence. On the Shatabdi to Gwalior when I asked for the magazine the conductor said it was 'Just coming' but after a reminder he admitted there had been a snag. Either the platform staff hadn't bothered to load it on to the train so early in the morning or the train staff hadn't bothered to distribute it. The fact that the magazine, called *Rail Yatri* was free, doomed it from the start. Its glossy pages would make strong paper bags for the fruit sold outside the station. Why lug piles of literature on to a train—where the public will only throw it on the floor—when you can get a better price from the waste-paper merchant for clean copy? I saw the blurb for this project—which was most professionally researched—to 'unleash the power of India's largest captive audience, a bored audience that is literally behind bars'. What might have been a brilliantly useful source of information to give travellers a pride in their rail system turned out to be a non-starter.

The Regional Character of Railway Bookstalls

Bookstalls cater to many regional languages and in Assam, for example, you have the NE Frontier timetable available in four different tongues. The only station I have come across that vetoes entirely an English stock was Marwar in Rajasthan, though many small stations contain publications only in their regional tongue. Bookstalls easily identify the region you are in, and the sale of Marxist textbooks announces Calcutta just as surely as the wall slogans and 'Proutist' pamphlets declare the station to be in the West Bengal hinterland where the Ananda Marg socio-religious movement is deployed. The higgledy-piggledy layout of the unkempt Dehra Dun platform bookstall could only reflect the cultural chaos of Uttar Pradesh and where else but in Kerala would one pick up a *History of Railway Trade Union Movement?* (And where but at the other end of the country would you hear the Bengali aristocratic refrain: 'One would rather borrow money than travel second class'.) Bengalis can claim to be the expert travellers of Indian Railways. They have usually travelled the furthest, know much about its workings, complain more vigorously than most, and rise to literary heights in their letters to the editor. Travel pieces written on the train by a Bengali are as succulent as their sweet-meats, with rich descriptions of the rhythms of life; the mood of the observed given along with the emotions of the observer. They are always witty and full of lust for the immediate and contrast with the usual western traveller's uninvolved commentary where all the juice has been strained out. Indian railwaymen have begun to record their own history and R. R. Bhandari's monographs on the more exotic lines gives an excellent resume of archival material out of reach of the layman. S. N. Sharma has compiled a fascinating survey of the Great Indian Peninsular records and by his emphasis on British attitudes reveals the level of resentment felt by many Indians at the indignity inherent in a colonial relationship. Francis da Costa's *Introduction to Railway Operation* is a standard reference work first published in 1963 and now in its sixth edition. On lighter lines, K. R. Vaidyanathan has released a book on railway jokes.

To show that expatriate opinion is by no means obsolete, the best general work, *Railways of the Raj* is by Michael Satow and Ray Desmond while the specialized mechanical lore of steam locomotives largely derives from the pen of Hugh Hughes.

Railways became such an instantaneously accepted part of the Indian landscape that already by the 1860s primers for regional languages were showing 'singles' and giving the equivalent of Elsa Stamp's 1929 geography lectures on how quickly the white man could travel without having to change his bullocks. A *Cannerese First Book* gave a spirited woodcut of a 'Copper-knob' named *Rapid* and scored further points against the bullock lobby by emphasizing the former's lack of sway.

The development of the railways and the speeding of the morning news gave a boost to literacy and the serious paperback filled in that vital gap between the chained Bible and the furtively pocketed pornography which remains, in its yellow cellophane wrapping, a characteristic feature of bus stations. Fifty years before the paperback imprint of Penguins, Wheeler & Co. had started at a rupee a time the *Indian Railway Library*. Popular titles included the works of Kipling and the logo of the series was an elephant smashing its head through a hoop to dispel the darkness. (The waving trunk no doubt beckoned long distance passengers.) Visitors to the Delhi Rail Museum are shown another elephant that sought to make an impact on the railways. It derailed an Up mail and its skull testifies to the danger of not heeding those warnings in Oriya on the back of weighing machine tickets.

Reading Matter for the Ladies Compartment

Children's reading matter can vary from the sensitive stories of Ruskin Bond, often centred round the strange magic of a railway station where romantic moments not acted on flee our life for ever, to the crude comics echoing American tastes in heroic violence and sex fantasy. Oddly enough, the Rail authorities commissioned a series of comic books, one of which called *Rel Pari ki Kahani* (Rail Fairy's Story) is a garish fancy dress account of railway history. The aim is to capture the child's attention by introducing *Rail Fairy* as a guide, but perhaps with a view to stimulating wider audience support the artist has depicted the fairy as a nubile blonde with enough oomph to compel octogenarian interest. (If *Rail Fairy* entered the 'Miss Universe' competition she would get a bye to the final. Fleshed out like a bathing beauty in an outsize red bra and diaphanous nether attire, W.H. Smith II might have had trouble focusing on the medallion at the end of her bouncing garland.) It is the logo of Indian Railways, probably the only accurate rendering in the whole strip. To indicate the origin of gauge we are shown Roman chariots taken straight out of the Hindu epics. The coal miners of the north of England are confused with cowboys of the Wild West and James Watt is made to dress like a medieval squire. Instead of using the chance to correct the early artist's mistake in depicting the first locomotive's contours on the run from Bombay to Thane, the present illustrator proves to be afflicted by the same unscientific outlook. The lines are drawn without sleepers and the indifference to detail and accuracy are precisely the sort of dangers such primers should guard against.

By way of contrast we might refer to an example of getting too near the truth for children. In *The story of our Railways* published by the National Book Trust (1971) the author notes that in more advanced countries people have been trained to obey rules instinctively, whereas in India a lot of time is wasted by the need for a second man to check on the work of the first. In this book, supposed to create affection for Indian Railways, the author cheerfully suggests that the reader's contact with the system should be 'intermittent, short and (hopefully) sweet'.

Lady writers prefer the passenger content to the mechanical in their description of rail journeys and at least one English woman has published a book (*Third Class Journey*) to offset the predictable cleverness of those travelling the easy way—from Mark Twain to Paul Theroux. Mollie Panter-Downes who with a name like that could hardly go wrong in writing a well-received book *Ooty Preserved*, cannot fight free of the 'toy train' illusion. Her choice of book jacket is to view the lake at Ooty from the railway line itself thus obviating any need to record its charm. Accidentally, a title in the same Century series of travel books brings to the fore the fatal feminine unconcern to get hard facts right. Maharani Gayatri Devi of Jaipur in her assisted autobiography *A Princess Remembers* does not remember too well the railway detail of the princely state she married into. She refers to the metre gauge in Jaipur as 'narrow'—a usage that went out in the 1880s. It must seem astounding (at least to those unacquainted with the unrealistic lifestyle of the former princes) that you can live for the best part of a lifetime in a city and still not register the transport facts of life under your nose.

For the most genuine railway flavour of India's steam age, John Master's novel of Anglo-Indian life *Bhowani Junction* is unlikely to be bettered. He gives you the authentic clangour of the bucking footplate as the crew, amidst prodigious sweat, rhythmically perform their parts. His characters are as recognizable as Forster's.

As with the former princes, the Anglo-Indian presence has now been wiped clean from its once privileged status in Indian society. Both groups were (to adapt a phrase from the Maharani's autobiography) 'trained parrots' of the British. But no one can dishonour the memory of those whose honest endeavour went in to all their works. The Anglo-Indians provided the foundation for today's running virtues of Indian Railways.

Jim Corbett's Railway Background

Jim Corbett, better known as a big game hunter was by calling a railwayman though perhaps because he hob-nobbed with the great from Lucknow his 'country-born' profession was never bandied about with quite the same enthusiasm as his *shikar bandobast* (wildlife excursions). In *My India*, one of the best books ever written about India by an Anglo-Indian, Jim Corbett includes a lot of railway detail. He describes the less dramatic encounters of his days in the plains working for the Bengal and North Western Railway. In the exciting account of the snaring of the bandit Sultana who operated in the jungles around Najibabad (U.P.) he describes the usefulness of the Railways in helping to track down crime. One ruse used to surround the local Robin Hood was to march the policemen fully armed each evening through the Hardwar bazaar and then unexpectedly divert them on to a waiting train to be offloaded in the jungle. The last scene in this thriller was enacted at Moradabad station. The remainder of the gang could not be identified and the English police officer playing for time invited them to his bungalow to share his supper. When they reached the spot, where the police officer had kept the pet of the captured Sultana, the gang's identity was betrayed by the affection of the dog for these who claimed to be complete strangers.

When the film of this story came to be made with Yul Brynner playing the role of Sultana there were several railway scenes, but none that would fool anyone who knows the line from Najibabad to Kotdwara. The Indian Government, not wishing to advertise notorious bandits, refused to give permission for the movie to be filmed and so the location chosen was Spain because of its romantic steam engines.

This was a pity, because the Kotdwara branch line is very photogenic, running over several girdered culverts as you approach the foothills of Garhwal. The road runs alongside the line and on one occasion I chased a shuttle on my motorbike, sprinting ahead to get a photograph of the WG and then again overtaking the wheezing engine for the next shot. Each time I took a photo the driver, enraged at such liberties, shook his fist at me. Eventually we met up on the platform at Kotdwara where the line ends and his aggression was mitigated when he read my camera permission from the Railway authorities. I was curious to know why he had got so worked up about an old imported engine being snapped. Was it security, xenophobia or just officiousness? 'Duty' he said. 'It is against the rules to photograph railway assets without permission.' It was only then I realized how close Indian Railways comes to military discipline. Their devotion and loyalty make railwaymen part of a fighting brotherhood and they do not like outsiders entering their mysteries. The disadvantage of this feeling of solidarity is that the individual too often does not feel that he is paid to think.

Corbett's account of his life trans-shipping goods across the Ganga for twenty-one years (starting when he was twenty-one) is full of these qualities of loyalty and devotion, albeit arising from the labours of the casual railway staff. It is quite startling to be reminded that the greatest empire the world has seen ran smoothly not because of the efficiency of the foreign managerial whip but from the inherent virtue of the Indian peasant. Against the 'evils of trans-shipment' Corbett's men displayed a courage that transfigured the subject. His first duties as Fuel Inspector supervising the felling of timber for sleepers allowed his love of the jungle to be fulfilled, but it must have soon dawned on Corbett that the Railways would be the ruin of India if alternative technology were not devised to safeguard the crucial asset of forest wealth. Now cement sleepers are consciously part of Indian Railways track culture and in an added awareness of how close the early policy of timber extraction had brought the environment to the verge of collapse, tree planting on railway properties is vigorously encouraged. Some 200 lakh trees were planted in 1988 to help make green the permanent way.

Corbett's work allowed him to sample a range of railway duties from driving the engine to guarding a goods train. When he was posted to Mokameh Ghat to try and clear the backlog of freight piling up from the gauge break he did not flinch from the challenge and nor did his excellent assistant Ram Saran, the station master. Corbett allows himself to digress on the immoral habits of one railway doctor and relates how that person had been lured to a pointsman's hut in the hope of carnal gratification—only to find himself locked in with his equally randy wife. Some would argue that Corbett's satisfaction at the couple's discomfiture tells us as much about his own sex life as it does of the doctor's!

Psychic Phenomena on Rails

In an intriguing example of extra-sensory perception Corbett relates the story of the Nepal Prime Minister's entourage (who adopted the style of royalty at that time) whom he had seen off on their return from Calcutta after a shopping spree. Soon afterwards the official in charge of the Nepal party's luggage returned to Mokameh in extreme distress to share his problem with Corbett. A suitcase of jewellery was reported missing and the desperate official had taken recourse in his misery to consulting a yogi who had the gift of clairvoyance. The old hermit had a vision during the night of the suitcase with its seals intact hidden under other luggage in a room near a great river with a door that faced east. Mokameh Ghat had no such room but Corbett recalled that the parcel office at nearby Mokameh Junction did. The suitcase was located exactly as predicted under other luggage and had found its way there when the carriage sweeper cleaning out the Royal Train from Nepal had discovered it under a seat. He had taken the suitcase to the parcel office and not finding anyone on duty had left it there. After all the stories of corruption and dishonesty on the Railways this simple example of a sweeper's devotion to duty warms the heart.

Running past the junction where the missing jewellery was found is the main line to Delhi from the east. On an overnight train, the author Somerset Maugham tells us of how he had met an Indian scientist with his American wife, both of whom practised yoga and in a convincing demonstration of its advantages on a crowded train had slept peacefully sitting up while the author went through the discomfort of waiting for the morning to come. It was on the strength of this conversation on the train, plus a visit to the saint Ramana Maharishi in South India, that Maugham's novel *The Razor's Edge* took shape with its theme of Larry the *karma yogi*. The scientist was Dr Boshi Sen, a disciple of the first follower of Vivekananda, Swami Sadananda. Some say he was a station master who, like the great fisherman before him, dropped everything to follow his master. Boshida was a widely travelled student of life and his marriage to Gertrude Emerson (another philosophically inclined wanderer) made a remarkable modern couple who combined the best of East and West, science and devotion for half a century in their idyllic bungalow in Almora. The Kumaon Hills also host other religious railway stories. South of Almora near Bhowali the ashram of Kanchi came up in the sixties following similar temples at Bhumiyadhar and Hanumangarhi near Naini Tal. It was said if you looked down from the U. P. Governor's House (a building incidentally built by F. W. Stevens whom we had last met finishing off his masterpiece at Bombay's Victoria Terminus), you could see straight into the heart of Hanuman at Bhumiadhar below and behold Lord Ram. This was quite literally true for the builder of all these modern temples around Naini Tal was a holy man called Neem Karoli Maharaj who had a pair of cupboard doors fitted into the chest of the monkey-god to facilitate the U. P. governor's devotions. Known as the 'government guru' Neem Karoli was an unsophisticated mendicant who assessed what his devotees (mainly government servants) wanted and then proceeded to give it to them. The thing a government officer wants more than anything else is promotion and this hierarchical perk once achieved guaranteed that the higher a man climbed the more grateful he would be to Neem Karoli who had acquired the *siddhi* (skill) of commanding favours of the official kind. It is not known if the mirrors installed at Bhumiadhar to reflect the presence of Lord Ram were due to the grace of the governor or the favours of the guru but Neem Karoli's influence was so pervasive that it would have been surprising if aspiring gubernatorial material had not gone to him for furthering their careers.

An Enquiry into the Spiritual Folklore of Railways

Like so many 'Godmen' risen from the ranks, the miraculous powers attributed to the baba stemmed from his supposed ability to control that most visible symbol of government—the railway. His career began (and this was related to me by local Kumaonis long before revised American versions were put about) near a U.P. village called Neem Karoli when the baba had prevented a train from starting. Apparently he had been turfed out of the compartment for travelling without a ticket and to remedy this insult to the sacred cloth he had cursed the train crew and threatened that unless he and other ticketless holy men were allowed to travel, the engine would be held back by his yogic power. And lo! this is exactly what happened. The engine driver (an Anglo-Indian) had given the holy man a mouthful of his ire and opened the regulator. But the engine instead of moving ahead spun on its driving wheels vigorously as if to indicate some greater power was restraining its motion. The Railways had to admit defeat against the traditional power of the yogi and from that day onwards the nondescript baba (indistinguishable from millions of others until this incident changed his luck) became a feared and respected figure, known to possess powers that could influence, if not the destiny of the nation, at least the turning of government wheels in Lucknow.

More sophisticated *sadhus* I have spoken to who have lived in the Kumaon area much longer than the later crop (who appeared conveniently with their transcendental gobbledegook at a time when the American market opened up for spiritual merchandise) told me that the holding back of the steam engine was a common archetype you can meet with all over India and represents the fringe of Luddite orthodoxy. Near V. T. Bombay a fakir, Hazrat Bismillah Baba resisted railed progress, his miracle at a hundred years of age, extended to pushing an engine off the track with one hand.

The villagers want to believe these miracles since the physical explanation sounds so much flatter. The psychology of an Anglo-Indian driver (based on a split within himself of having to reconcile a superstitious eastern mother with a western father of equally humble caste) might be agitated enough to open the regulator more than necessary and if the lines were wet or greasy the driving wheels would spin from bad handling not from yogic forces. (Significantly, with the introduction of heavier diesel and electric locomotives the incidence of 'miracles' has fallen.) No one likes to have his family cursed by a holy man and while an educated railway officer might disregard the threats of a saffron-clad beggar, most of the lower staff would be in mortal terror lest some black magic might not be unleashed against their children. I was told that other stories of trains not being able to start were not the result of spiritual powers but of anti-social elements disconnecting the vacuum. The derailment by the fakir was presumably assisted by a wily pointsman-devotee.

On the whole Indian Railways displays a sensible regard for the numerous holy men who take rides in the belief that the system will earn merit by their conveyance. The foot soldiers of other religions, however, are less likely to get away with the doctrine of sheer numbers. While travelling to Bhagalpur in Bihar the train was so crowded I decided to buy a first class ticket. However, this happened to be the day that Pundit Pant, the Home Minister, had died and all government servants in a remarkable demonstration of official solicitude had promptly downed tools and steamed off home in high spirits. The train was jammed full and passengers were seated on the locomotive frame. I found conditions in the first class compartment equally squeezed and the ticketless intruders suggested I bear with the exceptional circumstances of this sad celebration as they were soon getting off. At last as some seats presented themselves I indicated to the only other legal tenant, a white lady missionary (all her mien advertised that calling) that the compartment would soon be empty. 'I hope so,' she said with the withering confirmation of her spiritual memsahib credentials. 'This is a Ladies compartment.'

On none of my travels have I encountered the theft of luggage by those specialists who stand by the window of a departing train ready to slip their hand in through the bars, nor have I been offered drugged morsels to announce a more professional tribe of relievers. Almost invariably, travelling by second class protects one from the profile of appearing a soft touch. Only once did I lose a small steel water bottle which I had placed on the floor of an empty compartment near Tenkasi on the metre gauge prior to crossing the South Sahyadris. Somewhat surprisingly, the thief was probably a well-dressed young man who had been the sole passenger when I had got down on to the platform. Within minutes I returned and found him missing along with the bottle.

To end on a more Corbett-like note, I was told by the yogi who analysed the railway claims of would-be Godmen that while it was extremely rare to find a swan amidst the crows he had once stumbled onto a great soul on the platform at Lucknow. He had struck up conversation with the venerable Sufi imagining his remarks would be of the conventional sort, repeating how impossibly difficult it was to search for reality. But instead, the old man had surprised him by saying there was no difficulty in finding Truth. How could this be, asked the questing yogi? 'It's simple,' said the old man. 'When two become one—that's Truth.'

CHAPTER EIGHTEEN

Prosaic Mosaic

On long distance trains I have always deplored the absence of a railway guide for travellers which would identify the places along the way and indicate the significance of the scene that coasts past your window. One of the advantages of India's stolid interpretation of what constitutes an express is that one can drink in the scene and not feel as one does, for example, on a British Inter-City, slightly queasy at the flick of undigested countryside. From the day I made my first long distance journey I have felt cheated that we steam by unlabelled sites of historical importance, geographical significance, architectural uniqueness, geological profundity, and religious beauty, deprived by the apathy of habit from expanding our vision and gainfully doubling the value of the ticket. The *Indian Bradshaw* does give a formal salaam in the direction of tourist sites but tends to raise more queries than it dispels—'Delhi is a fusion of India's yesterday and tomorrow', 'Mussoorie is a gay hill resort on the southern slopes of the Himalayas', 'Ajmer is a historical city in Rajasthan', etc.

Shortcomings in Meaningful Interaction Between the Railways and Their Public

At no level is there any real interaction between the public and the Railways concerning useful information. The Railway Board does produce a general monthly magazine for the lay reader called *Indian Railways* which at three rupees is excellent value but like all largess from official sources it runs late and no one is much concerned to push sales. Railway advertisements, as frequently noted, tend to bemuse rather than inspire for they come with the insipidity of dutiful insertion, driven by events rather than guiding them. Sloganeering, conflicting sentiments, yo-yoing between threats and boasts and the pointless-ness of addressing lessons to an educated audience already alive to the problem gives an air of unreality to government publicity. With all the funds at its command, why cannot the Railways hire a top ad-vertising consultant to get its message across professionally? The answer might be that IR is not serious about its destiny. Occasionally films by well known personalities are funded and these, at least help stir the popular imagination. It is just as well the public does not see the lengths to which the Railways go in their hospitality expenses. One friend who made a film at the Railways' invitation confessed that he had run up a bill of 8000 rupees on cognac for just one night on the Palace on Wheels. As a cow of plenty the system is too big to check abuses and it would be unrealistic to expect that those who are paid to trumpet the achievements of IR do so primarily from a love of railed transport. One of the basic problems is how to stimulate more affection for the railway system. A start could be made by encouraging a fan club to put some life into the Delhi Rail Museum. Members at least would not have to pay five rupees every time they enter with a camera. Talks could be arranged to hear professional railwaymen.

But there is a doomed air about New Delhi that kills all enterprise. The stale breath of government is a kind of blight that enters a man's soul the day he applies for a job and there is little hope that public en-thusiasm will ever get off the ground burdened by so much official un-concern. A real need is to encourage a well-informed public to monitor positive railway happenings and get them reported in the press. Gov-ernment officers are acutely allergic to the fireworks of newspaper ex-posure and have developed instantaneous reflexes to avoid any public searchlight falling on their—more vacant than pensive—chairs.

Miscellaneous Suggestions to Reduce Public Indifference

We have already stressed the point that no statistics can be made too simple for public consumption. To win the common man's sympathy the Railways must relate their achievements on a scale anyone can comprehend. Most of India still thinks in terms of rupees and miles and to talk in terms of grams and kilometres (while necessary for the growing generation) is to alienate an influential section of your audience. Other lessons include the obvious need to keep the system geared to its primary job and cut down on the parasitical effect of socialist side transfusions to boost language or family planning or similar bright but wasteful ideas.

Above all, a confident pride is needed that the system, in spite of its defects, does a commendable job. With positive attitudes things can only get better and the urgent challenge is for passengers to make constructive criticism to strengthen the vehicle. In a collection of *Ideas to Take the Country Forward* published by Lt.-Col. Kul Bhushan (Retd.) of New Delhi, members of the public sent in their suggestions for improving the national scene. On the subject of the Railways several correspondents reacted to the scourge of ticketless travel and thought the best way to tackle it would be to 'auction traffic segments to private parties'. The fare would be handed over to the local station master while the fine would be used to pay the private contractor. The theory is sound but since the problem is not the dishonesty of railwaymen in particular but of society in general why should it be supposed that the private contractors would be any more public spirited than the TTEs? Other ideas included advertising inside carriages, attaching passenger coaches to goods trains, the provision of passenger trolleys on platforms, surprise checks by members of the Railway Board on ticketless travellers, recovery of unused railway material dumped along the lines, and 'a closet-type hole in the ceiling of three-tier carriages to provide ventilation'. This latter suggestion recalls the report that emanated from an official of the Oudh and Rohilkund Railway after they had introduced lavatories in the third class in 1891: 'The hole in the floor was only 5 inches—apparently the designer had taken a first class closet as his standard and had made the diameter of the orifice in proportion to the fare'.

The Diversity of India Witnessed from a Train

Just as the air of my Scottish childhood had been exhilarated by the ardent evaporation of whisky fumes, the railway track in India is made fecund by the processing of alimentary transformations. Surely here is a cycle waiting to be completed, and those rotting timbers of a sleeping past are today planted with new growth in green progression. The countryside forever speaks of the sparse yield of India outside the delta alluvium but the national flag is discernible from a train window. It is echoed in the strident redness of the southern gravel after the green cover of the north and east; while the sands of Rajasthan supply the neutral tone that divides the contrasting soils of Aryavarta and Karnataka. It also separates the Persian type (and a few Abyssianian strays) in the west from the Mongol touches that lend fascination to the north-eastern frontiers. Look out of the train window and you do not see India as much as a microcosm of the human race. From Ledo to Bhuj and to the Cape from Jammu Tawi the impression is much more of a voluntary conglomeration of sub-nations than any localized entity that can claim to be more Indian than the rest or more typical. For their comfort, politicians at the centre will always stress the primacy of what is actually a shadowy ideal, a 'mainstream'. To the traveller there is no meaningful India apart from the contrasting regional flavours. These are all essentially Indian in their variety and their vigorous identification with a regional tongue. Many people are beginning to recognize that the parrot call from Delhi about the need for national unity is only part of the solution. The Indian comity of cultures also needs its diversity honoured and it is fears of losing regional identities that lead to ethnic agitations and minority mistrust. Too often the face of what is called the mainstream conceals an urge for high-caste aggrandizement.

To make out that mainstream modes must monopolize any viable India is to ignore the syncretistic nature of Hinduism. From but one direction Persians, Greeks, Parthians, Huns, Turks, Afghans have influenced Indian life, while racial inputs on the eastern flank have come from Indo-China, Tibet and the Pacific. (Indeed the continent itself originated from across *kala pani.*) The European flags that followed trade and religion obscure the fact that small centres of both Judaism and Christianity had flourished in south India several centuries before the classic age of Hinduism. India's strength today, as always, has been in the self-expression of her myriad cultures which strike the traveller by their spontaneous folk inspiration, as opposed to the heavy application of a supposed national culture—which pretends all good Indians aspire to wear a white homespun cap which in reality has turned into a symbol of hypocritical power abuse. Travel the whole length of the subcontinent and you will never find outside the circle of theatrical politicians an Indian dressed like Pundit Nehru. For a start, most couldn't afford the laundry bills for such highly starched *khadi* cloth. Nehru was aware that he was consciously striving to set a standard of national dress in the absence of any such external uniform. India exists and operates on the inner strength of her vibrant cultural diversity, reconciled in the tolerant interchange of equals.

Unlike in politics, where appeals to work together are constantly being made to different regions over water or border rights, the Railways have soared clear of these regional rivalries. This is a tribute to the professionalism of the service as well as to the common sense of the travelling public who wish to preserve a system that can take them with equal ease to the furthest parts of the country. The fact that the Railways have stayed together as a family is one of the great transport miracles and gives the lie to the often heard despondency of the ordinary citizen that Indians need a big stick before they accept discipline. No system as overwhelmingly complicated as IR could run for a day without considerable self-discipline at its myriad levels. Alone of civilian activities, during prolonged agitations it is the functioning of the Railways that keeps public morale from plummeting. The service is always considered to be bigger than the individual. In a rural nation of primitive passions and maverick dependence on the feudal axiom that might (or money) is right, the Railways prove an exception to the widespread acceptance of the colonial assessment of the second-rate status of all things Indian.

For the stranger aboard trains, every country announces its different concerns. In few countries, however, will you find the twin faults of an Indian journey where passengers either thirst only for flattery of their nation, or indulge recklessly at the other pole of decrying everything Indian. Here is evidence of the bewildering extremes that testify to India's ability to reconcile opposites, surely the secret of Hinduism's survival kit.

The railways enable people from all parts to know their country better and to arm themselves against the political untruths that stress the incompatibility of different cultures. The lines smoothly cut through all kinds of terrain, nor does the change from metre to broad gauge cause the passenger to falter even slightly. The system is emphatically, triumphantly, one. Against all the odds India has a truly national railway.

Stray Memories from India's Four Railway Corners

What after a marathon covering of the rail map does the Indian experience teach; what are the lessons to be drawn from an entire traverse of the system? Stray notes may tell more than considered formulations for, made off the cuff, they carry the essential perfume of the moment. We can start in the westernmost station with the profligate stupidity of bureaucrats. At Dwarka India receives the last rays of the setting sun. To catch them properly a local civil servant has erected 'Sunset Point of India, Scarcity Relief Work'. Festooned with marble plaques they tell us, among other things, that this shoddy and derelict eyesore was built in 1974 and cost Rs 14,000 which seems a lot when there is so much sand and so little cement in a visibly crumbling structure. 'Somras creeper has unpleasant taste and is not intoxicating', reads another marble notice, and having thrown away the nation's money this administrative entertainer now proceeds to waste the public's time with his carefully tillered account of ancient Aryan customs to try and make that hard-drinking race of gamblers measure up to modern Gujarati Gandhian ideals. 'Somras is not hated liquor but a pious drink almost craze of the holy men of the day.'

As one travels by train, one picks up other odd scraps of information. Regional timetables include random statistics—Rajasthan has the third largest metre gauge system (over 5500 km); Indian Railways own a lakh of bridges 10,000 of which are of major dimensions (by any reckoning that is a lot of big bridges). Level crossings number 42,000. Each year the number of tickets printed runs to 135 crore. You learn that the tractive effort of the broad gauge is almost double that of the metre gauge and that Indian Railways has a 6 to 1 advantage over road transport in terms of fuel consumption. Some 37 per cent of the railway staff are housed by IR and 100 railway hospitals succour their families, as do 750 educational institutions. The Railways employ a medical staff of 50,000 and in sports every fourth winner of the national Arjuna Awards is a Railway person (IR provides national champions in 10 disciplines).

Still in the west zone, on a metre gauge platform I spoke to a group of women rag pickers from Jodhpur. Plainly dressed but animated in inverse proportion to their appearance they mockingly declined a group photograph on the grounds that the poor should not be exposed to further embarrassment. This led to some erotic banter and a fishing for further compliments, one of which I recorded: 'What has poverty to do with beauty, O Bewitchers of the declining day where the Sun hath ceded the play to more effulgent competition?' The ladies laughed not at the irony of their situation but with pleasure at the gallant doggerel.

In the Western Railway timetables I read, 'A baby boom is nation's doom', whereas in the South Central's a more ambiguous comment on the demographic curve read, 'Not before twenty never after thirty'. Surprisingly, in view of its crucial position as untramelled begetter, the North Eastern timetable makes no reference whatsoever to family planning.

'Any complaints about her performance?', I asked the driver of the YP engine from Udaipur which was to climb the Aravallis for the great leap down to Marwar over Khambli Ghat. 'I am a sportsman', said the driver 'and get the best out of any class of engine entrusted to my care.' He was fairly knowledgeable about the YP which had been developed from a special order of Jodhpur to Baldwin of Philadelphia back in 1948. These locomotives are actually two-thirds full size models of American Pacifics and it seems likely the last sounds of steam in India will emerge from US profiles rather than UK ones. These handsome engines are the nearest any of us will see to the ultimate steamers—the Niagara class.

On the train to Jodhpur after descending the thrilling *ghat* (where a YG specialized in the careful braking required) my empty compartment filled up with a bevy of young lady doctors going home from Marwar for the weekend. After eliciting a cure for my slightly flushed condition (two tablets of Crocin a day for five days), the 'doc-ettes' (as I christened them) assured me that for a woman in modern India they had got themselves the best possible job, with money, status and individuality. That they hadn't got freedom from petty worldly rivalry I noted when the girl sitting opposite me rather pointedly stuck her foot out to try and delimit any physical contact between my corner position and the shapely spread of the tightly wedged maiden immediately alongside. Nature proved more compulsive in its flow of flesh than the divisive mind and to the chagrin of the unfriendly warning toes, the warmth of overlapping layers (with their own language of urgent contact) were not so easily prised asunder. Where two makes one, that is real. (It probably also accounted for my flushed state.)

Parables in Jodhpur; Miracles in Jaisalmer

If the railways are a total metaphor of our journey through life, the behaviour of some tiny shoeshine boys on the platform at Jodhpur was a parable of the nation. These particularly persistent followers of the tourist camp are easier to give in to than argue with. Having taken my Delhi-made pirated Nike boots for minor surgery before cleaning, the urchin contracted out the job to an equally diminutive colleague. As the agreed rate had been a rupee they fell to bickering about the division of spoils. To quell their tiresome aggression I offered to pay them each a rupee, thinking this would spur them on to finish the job and leave me in peace. Instead, they came to blows and in their earnest trading of punches one could see the history of the subcontinent as it sought to come to terms with an equitable distribution of any bounty. While they fought I put my unpolished imitation boots back on. The contestants were clearly more interested in fighting each other than in doing an honest day's work.

Jodhpur, with its terrific Mehrangarh Fort (with flanged cannons on rooftop rails commanding the town) ought to have been every monarch's dream of style and status but, alas, the rich find contentment only at the end of expensive rainbows and the town has another extraordinary modern palace unsurpassed for architectural pointlessness. The Umaid Bhavan Palace, like the Dwarka sunset platform, claims to be a 'drought relief work'. Never has so much stone been put together with so little feeling. Too boring to be oppressive and too bland to be ugly, this dollop of masonry is too phoney even to be pompous. It might just pass muster as a *terminale* for Mussolini's Abyssian Empire. By contrast, at the end of the modern metre gauge branch line I stood atop the Jaisalmer fort in its luxurious ochre authenticity. The wind carried away from my flapping notebook a print of Lord Srinathji which I had bought a day or two earlier, following the metre gauge from the pilgrim town of Nathdwara. The rasping wind flung the paper high, then let it spin down sycamore-like to land at the foot of a woman who entered the palace wicket exactly at that moment. She picked up the coloured postcard and clutched it to her heart as though her day had been blessed. As the humble instrument of her miracle I could share her delight at this windfall from God.

Random Memories Culled in the East

Diary notes made on an eastward run are equally random, but their crude concerns speak of the indignity of crushed humanity in the Gangetic heartland. '*Kiul.* Why do people screw so much? Crowded, steaming, jammed bodies squeeze you like a tube of toothpaste. What is all this copulation in aid of? My kind-hearted companions give food and coins to the regular column of cadgers who come and poke skinny fingers or pudgy fists through the window. Such geniality marks genuine goodness. These passengers—equally poor—exude decency, concern and the sense of simple sharing that gives meaning to the baffling extremes of human relationship. Is unbridled breeding pleasure, compulsion or plain stupidity? Does God "give" babies? Is God as big a fool as the poor man claims he is?'

More sex as we clack drowsily past the foothills of minor Himalayan states when a government servant from one of them hopes to shock me by alleging that the ruler has illicit relations with his sister-in-law. I remind him there is no point in being the ruler if you can't make the rules but he is incensed at such unfairness. (Apparently there are three sisters-in-law.)

The ordinary passenger delights in things outside himself—children, bright clothes, bangles, anything colourful and sensuous. The appeal is enhanced by the non-utilitarian nature of the object which should have an exciting shape and admit of glittering associations. Outside the window, wheeling white egrets peel down to the loud green paddies and skim the strips of water along the line choked with purple hyacinth music which the train snatches up in her stride. As the timetable claims, the metre gauge—being small—is a happy family. The line doesn't slash through the countryside (like the political bulldozer funded by the World Bank) but follows contours, obeying the advice of nature and getting unseated when natural forces throw up resistance—as they do regularly in this earthquake-prone region.

India's largest river, the Brahmaputra, looks more like a sea than a stream. When the line first started one hundred years ago it ran from the port of Dibrugarh inland for coal, tea and timber. The river was the highway, the land entirely jungle. The beauty of the valley is in the mist marching up the hills, one range imposed delicately upon the other, blue merging into subtler shades until azure is achieved, like the play of individual souls against the overarching hue of the divine. At hand are green flats touched by the gold of ripening paddy, timber-framed dwellings, clean and elegant like simplified mini-Tudor manors in a land that is subdued by the life of the river. This small line has become part of the sinuous landscape, not striding headlong to conquer but deftly leaning to the curve of the valley's shapeliness.

In matriarchal Assam you must accept the railway as mother and respect the maternal possessiveness of the coach attendant as he jealously guards his clutch of reserved passengers. Here, everyone is found to be friendly. A man gets on and plonks his outsize kettle in the middle of the compartment to indicate his monopoly in the plying of tea. No words are needed, just a finger raised or a nod, like at the best of auctions where men of their word foregather. Food is also served with flair.

A vendor gets on with a wooden tray strapped round his neck. On to this have been nailed tins of various sizes all painted a bright colour and filled with a miscellany of tasty items—chick peas, grated onion, peanuts, and puffed rice. When you give the order the vendor removes the central tin and spoons in the various items to meet your request. Then putting the lid back on he does a brisk cocktailing of the contents, ending up with a drum solo just to show you how far his talents run. Then, with a final flourish he draws out a six-inch square of old newspaper, twists it expertly into a cone and pours the contents of the cocktail into the paper cup. Not only have you been fed but entertained. As he works his way through the coach and his supply of food dwindles you hear the slappity-slap of his drum each time he reaches the climax of his show.

Against the flooded marshlands, the raised enbankment is a sign of hope that keeps the wheels of trade turning. Crammed on to the train roof locals have no fear on this stretch of tunnels or high tension wires. The metre is yet too modest to aspire to electrification. There is a peculiar monotheistic pleasure in watching a plethora of junction lines interchange, switch points, then merge back to the main one, now no longer temporarily distracted, grabs back all into its sweep, like a whale opening its mighty jaws to draw in all manner of fish.

Civilized Southern Impressions

Going south, among my souvenirs is the remains of a reservation list once pasted up on the door. After two nights of traversing the cool plateau of the Deccan its faded type announces the typical mix of a passenger complement: 'Lalu Ram, D.S. Reddy, R.C. Sharma, Mohd Ahmad and Party, Master Pankaj, Bill Aitken (M.56)'. Age and sex forewarn the passenger of his expected company. In Dharmavaram as the *ekka* clops away you sway to its motion puzzled by the driver's nods. When he signifies 'No' he means 'Yes'. To complicate matters he does not mean 'Yes' when he signifies 'No'. In short, a nod is as good as a shake of the head. A notice at the bus stand (the only sign in English in the whole town it seems with not a single Hindi syllable in sight) might be applicable to our problem: 'Staff found guilty of violating these rules will be dealt with in accordance with standing instructions existing in this regard'. As I climb out of the high-wheeled horse-drawn tub I muse on how instructions manage to stand if they do not exist.

At Tirupati station further south while having *idli* I noticed on the menu sandwiched between the rice pudding and fruit salad an intriguing onomatopaeic dish called *tom-tom*. I was about to order it when the boy serving me identified it by clutching his stomach and uttering the dread formula—'black motion'. At Rameshwaram, the final stop, the train pulls in empty and is greeted by a swarm of waiting crows who fly into the compartments to look for scraps. After checking in to a pleasant budget hotel right next to the temple I sampled the local food. *Dosa* making is the art of eating out of thin air—being the next best thing to materialization from the psychic realm. Coffee making is another involved ritual with jugs and strainers and the compulsive backwards and forwards pouring without which the south Indian day would not be made. There is thunderous music at the bus stand, 'Tamil rock' according to a driver. It requires three forms to change reservations for a later bus and the company—named after an ancient Tamil poet-saint—has a marvellous effect on public memory. We all swear we will avoid this bus company (and its patron's poetry) for the rest of our lives.

In Kerala the black railway flags are out, telling the then current prime minister to 'Go back'. Lurid film posters (since the south does everything better than the north) astound the eye with their bumptious uplift. 'She was a rebel. She was a sensation. She was Pamela', screams a hoarding that shows a hefty wench in an evening gown which makes up for its lack of cover in the upper portions by bustles around the base line. At the bus stand in Kovalam I am accosted by a Kashmiri shopkeeper who gives me his card overprinted ominously with a family name that has come into its English version from the Urdu via a Malayalam speaker. It read '*Macdoom*'. I queried a German hippy buying fruit on the beach why he asked for 'condom bananas'. 'Because they are flesh-coloured and limp', he said, with Prussian precision. This enterprising young man has worked out an extraordinary itinerary by train that took him to see most of the south Indian temple towns within a week. 'You cannot do this in the North,' he added. 'Nothing is ever on time there.'

Return to Northern Decadence

To prove him right, the journey back from Kerala was one of the most delightful train passages I can remember, with charming company, intelligent conversation and exchanges of genuine regard. But the moment we hit the Devanagari script of north India the cultural buoyancy of the south dipped and became progressively more submerged. As we neared Delhi, the compartment became crowed with interlopers, loud and nasally aggressive to prove that Hindi at least on the score of noise can claim to be one of the leading languages of the world. From being a spotlessly clean compartment the litter and mess of Aryan culture soon asserted itself. The conductor had made himself scarce and the level of verbal abuse rose. Better dressed, better educated but pigmented to no advantage, the Kerala company went into its shell.

The last of the passing scenes that goes to make up an India no one has seen all of, is of a little girl's doodles on my note pad. Harshini has drawn a drooping camel and a tree that is all trunk—which taken together add up to the dismal environmental scene we have passed on to her generation. But she has drawn the railway quite accurately, with rows of passengers evenly spaced (behind their reading matter), being hauled by a box-like diesel. The vision is hardly poetic but, at least, with its stress on justice and the absence of overt privilege, it suggests the railways are seen as heading in the right direction. As further confirmation of hope she had drawn her classroom window that opens out on to the world. On the wall above it is a magical date: 'This school will reopen on 26th January' (Republic Day).

CHAPTER NINETEEN

'No Mention Please'

The subject of railway accidents always appears at the end of annual reports (unless there has been a dramatic decrease in their number) and invariably come to our notice under the heading of 'safety'. From the very first day of passenger involvement when Mr Huskisson got out of the wrong side of the carriage in 1830, the less fortunate fall-out of the permanent way has never failed to fascinate the public mind. The definition of an accident perhaps derived from the pragmatic Victorian belief in self-help. Samuel Smiles, who spread this conviction, used the life of the first railwayman—George Stephenson—as his exemplar. 'A hurt that causes the sufferer to be during the space of twenty days in severe bodily pain' remains a legal definition that makes no allowance for mental anguish, psychic dislocation or spiritual disillusionment. Indian Railways mundanely contracts to transport your body, leaving your soul to travel on the theologically sound assumption of its indestructability. Unlike road transport, where the grip of rubber on a yielding surface can burn to a halt swiftly in spite of a following load, the polished metal between the track and engine wheel offers little resistance. Any rider on a locomotive footplate knows the numbing sensation when little happens no matter how hard you apply the brakes. In India especially, where straying on to the lineside is an accepted countryside norm, the prospects of disaster are enormous as traffic speeds up. The Shatabdi at 140 km.p.h. requires more than a kilometre to come to a dead halt. The very permanence of the steel rails makes this in-built danger of slow braking a constant worry dangling over the head of the operations superintendent. Because of the pending danger at every crossing, Indian railwaymen have grown

unusually alert and even though the dangers can never entirely disappear, at least the tradition of a conscientious running staff and a
methodical maintenance routine remains high. As a South Central
notice puts it: 'The only effective safety device is a careful employee'.

A detail of the Ooty rack railway that often gets overlooked is the
efficient roster of brakemen who stand woodenly, one to each carriage.
As the train runs blind to the advancing corners, with the engine at the
rear, they are ready to semaphore back to the driver for the instant
cutting off of steam. The clockwork precision of these signalmen makes
a fine study in the demands of duty for they cannot take their eye off the
track or off one another for a moment. Similarly, the engine crew,
faced with the extra responsibility of the rack mechanism on top of their
steam commitment, labour under extreme pressure as they too have
to keep a nimble eye on the flagmen ahead. The Ooty line (with the
actual rack section terminating before the level crossing at Coonoor
station) has had only one bad accident in its history when in 1982 a
coal special rolled back killing eight people. The cause of the accident
was put down to casual maintenance of both line and rolling stock.

Transport Safety Not Inborn But Thrust Upon Reluctant Operators

Aging assets are a real threat to railway safety and it is often forgotten
that the greater length of the IR system was inherited from the British.
While Indian skill to improvise is brilliantly original and enables
minor miracles of movement to occur, such makeshift solutions are
no final answer to the assault of decrepitude. The only solution to the
years of neglect of the metre gauge was resurrection, and this was to
come about by the decision to include its modernization in a short-list of
technological missions (a decision now reversed).

In 1984 a terrible accident befell the narrow gauge line between
Nainpur and Jabalpur during the rains when the 'monsoon works',
like almost every other detail of the supposedly strict maintenance
schedules, had been allowed to lapse on this unpaying line. As always
after the enquiry, guilt spurred the Railways to make amends and the

Satpura lines, thanks to the death of more than 100 passengers, has now been given a new lease of life.

One of the most brutal facts of transport history (as true of the railway track as of the TT motorbike circuit on the Isle of Man where helmets were made compulsory only seven years after the races had been in vogue) is that improvements in public safety do not arise from any sentimental concern of the directors for our health but from the public outrage that follows accident reports highlighting the company's carelessness. You only had to be a third class passenger on any early line to know how casually the company treated your comforts. In India, the poor were herded in and when no more would fit, the door was locked to prevent them getting out—for all the world more like the Gestapo shipping Jews than the passage of fare-paying rustic pilgrims.

Public opinion as early as 1840 forced the British Parliament to set up an Inspectorate to investigate accidents. The reports of these inspectors' findings invariably discomfited the pockets of the railway companies who were forced to go in for expensive technology (like continuous automatic brakes) that financial prudence dictated should be postponed until their price had dropped. (Exactly the same sort of industrial attitude greets our modern gaze in the reluctance of polluting, giant companies to own up to their environmental responsibility.) As a result of accidents many advances were made, though the famous block system of signalling was enforced only in 1889—some twenty-eight years after the notorious Clayton Tunnel disaster.

Irrational Reactions to Disasters.

All over the world train disasters make for headlines because of their spectacular potential to stir up the metabolism of sluggish commuters at the breakfast table. In transport history the Tay Bridge disaster, like the sinking of the Titanic, acquired a kind of sacerdotal status productive of the awe that enables insurance companies to wriggle out of their commitments on the strength of the small print that welcomes 'Acts of God' as face (and money) saving devices. As the world grows more sophisticated, enquiry commissions resort to the 'hand of God' explanation of accidents which infuriates the public, especially its better educated sections. A recent rail crash on a new broad gauge line in Kerala which resulted in the familiar but now suspicious excuse of 'unseasonally high winds' for capsizing a speeding diesel over a bridge has led to unprecedented disgust at official reluctance to detail the cause of such a shocking lapse of Railway efficiency. In this instance, almost as a reflex action, the rail minister, having been pulled up by his employer—the public of India—gave the sack in turn to the Member (Traffic) of the Railway Board to try and appease his howling detractors. This gratuitous gesture only made the minister more culpable in the eyes of intelligent railway observers. If the cause of a train flying off a bridge had been due to high winds why should a member of the Railway Board be dumped in this unscientific gesture of sacrifice?

Human fascination with carnage and the primeval desire for the violent eruption of atoning blood guarantees that any book of rail accidents will be a best seller. L. T. C. Rolt's classic *Red for Danger* was published in 1955 and is now, thirty years later, in its fourth edition (updated by Geoffrey Kichenside). As the blurb declares 'Blizzard Blinds Flying Scotsman', 'Troop Train Tragedy at Gretna Green', 'Boiler Blow up on the Irish Mail'—these accident stories refer only to major British disasters. Of some 150 accidents listed only two come anywhere near the 'Act of God' category. All the others are chillingly the work of human complacency, distraction or inattention to detail. A more recent work by a professional railway signaller (*Obstruction Danger* by Adrian Vaughan) fills in the details by looking at the less spectacular derailments in Britain. While Rolt addressed himself to the general public and was careful not to lower the esteem of the Railway Establishment in its eyes, Vaughan caters to a more specialized railway audience and pulls no punches in describing how it is always simpler to blame the driver or the person least likely to articulate his defence.

Sometimes the cause is as grim as the punishment. The Scots servant girl who placed a large stone on the line before the wheels of the very first train out of Glasgow on the West Highland line 'to see what would happen' was rewarded with some bitter findings to her experiment.

She was sentenced to be transported for life. Other train wreckers have escaped more lightly and few can emulate the fluctuating career of George Fernandes who ended up as rail minister. Another incumbent, L. N. Misra was blown up while on railway duty, it is suspected by followers of a railway clerk turned Mahatma. Fernandes's last act as minister was to get those of his colleagues suspended for acts of railway sabotage reinstated. But it must be borne in mind that at the time of his disruptive activities India was clamped under a disgraceful Emergency that invited guerilla-like reprisals from any self-respecting citizen. Those who condemn Fernandes glibly for his actions then are guilty of an even worse sin, that of transvestite convenience, changing their coats every time the government is replaced.

The public is not urged to enquire into accidents too thoroughly while Press interest is as sensational as it is unsustained. A damaged length of line will be held up in the newspaper for the public to examine one day, with the accusation that the investigators did not give it the respect such evidence was due. This will be followed by a stiff rejoinder in formal language and at great length from the Railway authorities pointing out that the surmised length of line—had it been exhibited—must surely have been examined thoroughly. The debate then dwindles to the 'Letters to the editor' column where the mysterious length of line shrinks to the contours of a red herring, according to one point of view or expands to the dimensions of a smoking pistol in another. Rare is it to find any serious follow-up and the student of railways is forced to conclude that the daily newspaper only finds the subject interesting when matters go wrong, preferably with a body on the line.

Though railway officers may have to soften the blow of 'safety performance', when they retire they can safely call a spade a spade. (For example, R. P. Matta's exhaustive *Railway Accidents, Causes and Preventions* is a privately printed distillation of his experience as a safety officer on Indian Railways.)

Statistical Jockeyings

In a remarkable divergence from precedent, G. S. Khosla (whose eminence as a journalist added to his managerial experience perhaps taught him the advisability of facing the facts) uses the dread word 'accident' in the index of his history. He also quotes from *Secret Doings on Indian Railways*, an expose written by a disgruntled Englishman in 1911, who listed the sort of goings-on the Railways were at pains to keep away from public knowledge. But such courage does not outrun the colonial era and no inside stories are forthcoming about the current suppression of information which is not deemed to be in the public interest. We are asked to believe that the sum of accidents have come down drastically with Independence but this reassuring assertion forgets to inform us that the number of accidents only dived steeply in 1972, the year it was decided to reclassify what constitutes a report-worthy accident.

The Year Book for 1988 records an all time low figure of 604 'consequential train accidents'. It blames 62 per cent of the damages on 'failures of the railway staff' and records the deaths of 103 passengers. The Railways paid out nearly a crore and a half rupees in compensation and suffered more than a 10 crore loss in rolling stock and permanent way. To dismay the reader who likes to get his teeth into the subject but has to be content with the silky summary of bureaucratic evasions, the trend in recent years is for the official statistics to make up in appearance for what they lack in content. For example, my copy of the *Annual Report* for 1984–5 gives a remarkably vivid precis of nine 'mishaps involving heavy casualties'. One of these was the narrow gauge disaster already referred to on the Satpura lines: 'On 16.8.1984 the tender of the train, engine and four coaches of 4GJ Jabalpur-Gondia Passenger fell into a breach caused by the swirling waters of Manpur Nullah on Jabalpur NG section of South Eastern Railway. As a result of this accident 112 passengers lost their lives [300 according to some press reports since this section prior to the accident was low in checking priorities] and 76 others were injured. The accident occurred due to the sudden convulsion of nature combined with the failure of railway staff.' There is both truth and poetry in this resume of the preliminary findings.

Since then the *Annual Reports* have carefully omitted any mention of individual accidents but changed the paper of these selective reports from the workmanlike to the extra glossy. It seems only when some international mileage is to be extracted that such reports are comparative. For an example one could go back to the 1971 comments in the children's publication *The Story of our Railways*. To show how cheap and safe it is to travel on Indian Railways the author sets out statistics to prove that it is four times cheaper to travel on IR than British Railways . . . and twice as dangerous!

Any reader who keeps a scrapbook of newspaper railway clippings needs no reminder that a large part of his transport crop relates to the unproductive weed of calamity. 'Rail safety record better', declares the headline of a national daily, stating that the figure of 604 consequential collisions in 1990 shows that the trend continues to diminish. However, the very same day the Dehra Dun-Bombay Express met with an accident involving the death of six passengers. A month later 100 passengers on a local train were burnt alive when an oxygen cylinder blew up in a compartment near Patna. Shortly afterwards a new Act was passed to enforce the law against inflammable material being carried in a passenger compartment. Having been on a train near the site of the tragedy I recall how a passenger in front of me had bribed the railway policeman to allow him to put his inflammable cargo aboard. My instinct was to retreat to a safely distant part of the train rather than place hope in any well-meaning law being complied with.

Recent Railway Calamities

The year 1990 must have been one of the most traumatic in the history of Indian Railway finances and if Mr Fernandes had hoped his own incendiary past might have been forgotten, the ferocious student agitation against implementation of the Mandal Commission Report (to reserve jobs for the low castes) heaped up memorable losses of hundreds of crores of rupees against the minister's short tenure. The irony of this situation was that the inspiration for destruction arose not from the Luddite rural sector but from the urban offspring of educated government employees. In their frustration the 'haves' also decimated Delhi's bus fleet. These despairing remedies, of making one's own transport problems impossible to solve, could only arise in those castes so conditioned as to think that others are born to perform the menial callings and to replace the fleet. (No greater justification for the Mandal Report could be publicly demonstrated.)

Official statistics are all things to all men and in a layman's introduction to the working of Indian Railways published by the National Book Trust, the well known engineering figure M. A. Rao lays out the accident pattern since 1951. We see the decline in the number of consequential accidents, from nearly 2000 in 1951 to under 1000 in 1980 (which means if present trends continue there will be no accidents to record by the year 2000). Unfortunately for this ideal scenario, the statistics for accidents other than those considered consequential are not so encouraging. For those who infer by the absence of any reference to them in current reports that these figures must be too painful to recount, there are the earlier projections to point to for confirmation of their suspicions. In 1952 the total number of accidents was over 16,000. Mysteriously, it dropped at a steady rate of 2000 each year until a very satisfactory under-5000 figure was arrived at in 1971. Perhaps Justice Wanchoo, whose committee was set up specifically to look into railway accidents—itself rather odd when their number was crashing down with an almost mathematical predictability—smelt a rat, as the public is disposed to, on seeing a much too spectacular nose-dive on the accidents graph.

In a footnote, Mr Rao feels constrained to add that 'the apparently sharp rise in the total number of accidents from 1972–3 onwards is not due to any serious deterioration in operation but is due to a change in the statistical norms, as recommended by the Wanchoo Committee.' Thus the 2000 per year drop went into reverse and by 1980 the total number of accidents had leapt back to 12,000, with the end of the century possibilities alarmingly at odds with the 'consequential' nil! Since most of us regard doctored figures as the proper sphere for some unbargained official light relief, we can only pray that the accident figures now set on a collision course will be suitably redefined by yet another committee before their year of impact. To be fair to both Messrs Rao and Wanchoo, they stress the huge increase in traffic against which the Railway staff has had to exert extra effort in order to achieve its safety targets.

As for the willingness to be ready for emergency calls it may have been noticed by the observant traveller that at every divisional HQ station a rake is kept ready and waiting in the sidings with medical vans, a crane and mechanical backing ready to rush to the site of an accident. These emergency trains are allowed fifteen minutes to make themselves battle-ready and their crews have been taught to scramble as smartly as a fighter squadron. Though you may not get this impression in the north, in the South Central and Southern zones the relief train is kept beautifully trim and its freshly painted crane is usually a work of art, probably the nearest thing to a well-maintained life-boat you will find in India.

Dr Lardner's Original Prescriptions

For the last laugh we inevitably have to turn to Dr Lardner whose original remedies to avoid accidents have earlier been explored. Some of his statistical research could result in death by seizure: 'Three-eighths of the accidents ought to be assigned to the goods business.' '732,073,847 is the number of passengers who must travel one mile to cause the death of a railway servant.' 'Before a collision takes place the engine driver ... ought to have the means of observing the object ... with which the collision is about to take place.' It is clear therefore that ... the number of brakes provided should have reference to the magnitude and speed of the train.' 'There could be no difficulty in providing means by which any passenger could at his pleasure sound the whistle of the engine so as to give the engine driver notice to stop.' (The Indian variant of this facility is to pull the communication cord.)

Lardner comes in for some withering fire from L. T. C. Rolt who displays all the professional's contempt for the enthusiastic amateur. It is difficult to find any virtue in Lardner's pompous inexactitudes but while he was wildly wrong in detail, some of his instincts were sound. He has been scorned for suggesting that long tunnels would risk asphyxiating passengers and laughed at for suggesting a gradient out of a tunnel would increase the risks and render the passengers unconscious from a lack of oxygen. And yet two of the worst railway accidents have contained precisely the ingredients of Lardner's fears, both involving European tunnels. In one case the gradient caused the train to stall and 530 passengers were asphyxiated. In the other, the gradient was too steep to brake the train and it eventually derailed at 90 m.p.h. killing 543 troops. Neither of these accidents was the fault of railwaymen and in both instances the drivers had protested against the loads they were ordered to pull. Military miscalculations led to the carnage—and gained some respect for Dr Lardner's hysterical caution.

Sociologists and psychologists concerned for recording suicide statistics also might not think Dr Lardner's 'irresistible impulse to throw oneself in the path of an oncoming train' is so far-fetched when you consider the number of times the information is suppressed. Dozens of films have this theme as the most effective remedy to human misery and according to a recent newspaper, 'In Delhi hardly a day passes without a suicide on the track, mostly of unidentified persons'. There is a scope for crime here where murder can be made to look like suicide by rearranging the corpse in the path of a train. In this regard, during the Emergency the non-political brother of George Fernandes, Laurence, was arrested and tortured by the police to try and extort the whereabouts of his wanted relation. In an affidavit sworn before the High Court, Laurence Fernandes alleged that the police threatened to throw him on the railway track in front of a moving goods train.

The Illusion of the Emergency Claims to Efficiency

Mention of the Emergency revives in some people the notion that during that time the Railways overnight improved their efficiency. India's Rail Minister earned the country ridicule all round the world when he made the same claims as Mussolini about the test of a nation's health being reflected in the trains running on time. But a glance at the statistics will show that faster timings were achieved at greater risks. Before the Emergency the total number of accidents was around 8000 but this figure leapt up to nearer 12,000 in 1976. The column of 'consequential' accidents speaks its own story of how the Emergency achieved its illusory image of a nation safely on the move. From 782 serious accidents in 1974 the figure went up to 925 in 1975 and increased to 964 in 1976. In the following year, when the Emergency was withdrawn, the number of accidents dropped dramatically to 780 (the tables do not specify which were caused by sabotage).

The Emergency's iron fist did have one positive effect on anti-social railway users. The cases of 'alarm chain pulling', which stood at 35,000 in 1955, rose to a lakh in 1966 and had moved to Guinness Book proportions in 1971 with over 350,000 false alarms. The Emergency brought a 50 per cent drop in improper use of the chain and the bite of fear led to an astonishing further drop in 1976 to bring the level to under 70,000 on a par with the more modest anti-social statistics of 1961 when Nehru was alive.

To give us a peep into an official reading of what causes accidents, Mr Khosla appends a report dating back to 1857 in which a station master was held responsible for not locking his points, leading to the derailment of the Down mail. The station master was let off lightly with a fine that cost him two months wages. Proper punishment was reserved since he had a blameless record and (perhaps more to the point) the other station masters might have resigned *en masse* in protest against any more severe a penalty.

From a second-hand book list, I managed to acquire a Railway Board accident report which refers to an accident that befell the Tuticorin Express in November 1956 when some 154 metre gauge passengers lost their lives. This *Report on the Judicial Enquiry into the causes of the Accident to Train no. 603 Tuticorin Express between Ariyalur and Kallagam stations on the Southern Railway on 23rd November 1956* by Shri Himansu Kumar Bose, Judge, High Court Calcutta, runs to 53 pages, the last twelve of which constitute the report of the technical assessors appointed to assist the judge.

Examination of an Accident Report

The chief impression of this document is the fairness of the judge and his refusal to be budged by anything but the actual evidence at the site of the crash. The train was running an hour and a half late pulled by

YP 2069; the bridge on which it came to grief had been built in 1928. Neither the judge nor the assessors found any fault in the bridge. The assessors discovered 'minor lapses here and there' in the performance of the staff responsible for the safety of the permanent way in freakish weather conditions. The river had a reputation for producing flash floods and it seems the engineering attitude towards it was too complacent. Also, the reaction of the inspector of the track was sluggish in that he did not anticipate danger to the bridge from scouring. The engine driver, being late, ran the engine at full speed over the weakened foundation and had he been warned of the need to proceed cautiously the accident might have been averted. The patrolman passed a formal caution notice to the assistant station master but as the former's lantern did not light up the piers of the bridge (where the storm water was wreaking its havoc), he concluded that the raging river level—just two foot under the spans—was nothing unusual for this temporarily furious stream.

'After giving certain evasive answers', an engineering witness was forced to admit that the Marudayar bridge was 'important yet it was classified as unimportant'. Further evasions led the judge to conclude that 'the attitude on the part of the Engineering department of the Railway cannot be described as anything but an attitude of utter indifference and carelessness.' However, he also deplored the attempt by the more senior staff to narrow down the responsibility to the illiterate patrolman. 'The poor patrolman has been made a tool in the hands of others and has been induced to make all sorts of contradictory statements. The assistant station master when the patrolman did not report on time—owing to the weather conditions—failed to inform either the driver of the fated train or the permanent way inspector of possible danger . . . I feel constrained to observe,' says the judge, 'that the Permanent Way Inspector's and his Assistant's conduct shows an utter lack of responsibility which attaches to the offices they were holding at the time.'

The judge exonerated the driver for taking the bridge at full speed since he had not been warned of the rising river. Also, because of the design of the YP cab the driver had no real sense of the devastating downpour his train was heading into. As a result of the enquiry,

'Good glass should be fitted to YP engines to make it possible for the drivers to see through the glass at a distance especially during rains.' The other crucial recommendation was that 'Night patrolmen should have as part of their equipment a strong electric torch to enable them to observe the level of water and strength of current flowing through the bridges or along the abutments.' Possibly the whole story would have been different had the patrolman been provided with a torch instead of a lantern. Therein lies the stark findings of penny-pinching in an expensive judicial exercise about an accident which cost the Railways dearly in terms of public esteem.

What irony that the world's greatest industrial disaster in Bhopal in 1984 occurred in a company that produced the life-saving batteries for the common man's torch. There too, the compulsions of cutting down on safety measures and the lack of any generous outlay to offset the lethal leak of gas resulted in appalling human suffering worsened by the callous indifference of a whole hierarchy of supposedly responsible officials publicly and privately employed. The gruesome industrial slaughter of the innocent only needed the remark of a local politician—asked to move the factory outside the town—to make the accident inevitable: 'It is not a stone that you can pick it up and place it elsewhere', the local leader is reported to have said of the noisome chemical plant placed suicidally next to the railway station. This disregard of people only makes the likelihood of accidents far greater. Giving pride and individuality to humble employees—as Corbett did—is the best guarantee of the loyal and safe performance of duty.

That is why it is always encouraging to read such small news items as follows: 'Train mishap averted by an alert employee: Mandsor (M.P.) October 5th. Mr Vishwanath, a railway *jemadar* on track inspection duty, found that a rail between Nandsaur and Neemuch was cut at two places minutes before a train was due to pass over it. By detecting sabotage he averted a major accident as he stopped the train just before a bridge. If the train had derailed it would have fallen into a stream.'

Not so encouraging is the example of the astute passenger who reported to the railway police at New Delhi that there was a bomb on the Shatabdi Express. The train was held up for two hours in Aligarh but a search revealed nothing. Intrigued by the agitated informant, who had expected the train to return to Delhi, an alert railway constable asked for the young man's name and then quietly compared it with the reservation list. There his name appeared next to that of a young lady it transpired he was passionately in love with. On being arrested the lovesick bomber confessed that having missed the Shatabdi the only way to restore 'absence of body' was to use presence of mind.

CHAPTER TWENTY

The Real Thing

We have argued that the permanent way was a great deliverer from society's stagnant rootedness. In India, particularly, the railways shook up the conventional idea that caste could never be circumvented. The early fears that the railroad would set all the world a-gadding and result in 'grave plodding people ... becoming the most immeasurable liars' (as predicted in 1836) have—outside the economic embarrassment of ticketless travelling—not proved true. Most road users in contemporary traffic snarl ups, whether in Delhi or London, remember nostalgically the gritty journeys by steam which got them into the heart of the city smoothly and free of the pollution and despair that the internal combustion engine now so wastefully stalls our day with.

The motor car, like the horse before it, speaks to elitist tastes, and its dependence on imported petrol encouraged colonial attitudes towards the producing countries. The railways, on the other hand, addressed themselves to the liberalizing movement of nineteenth century republicanism and happened to come to their most dynamic fruition in Chapelon's locomotive no. 242A1 (which the French National Railways were forced to scrap in the middle of the twentieth because its steam performance distressingly showed up the limitations of electric traction).

The Urgent Relevance of Railed Transport

Both road and air travel frustrate by their terminal delays. No matter how broad the motorway or how fast the Concorde, the passenger is made to fret, on the one hand, or is reduced to a passive item of luggage on the other—all scope for meaningful interaction with the passing landscape stilled by inappropriate responses to the needs of the soul as well as the body. 'I go for beasts of burden, it is more primitive and scriptural', boasted the critic of 1836, but today his vote would go for the railway over the strangled promises of alternative transport systems.

We have tried to suggest that the primitive import of foreign devils has been brilliantly adapted by India and that which had been the prime mover of imperialism switched convincingly to a line in consonance with the best directions of India's development. The steam engine arose in Britain and gave her the right to rule the less industrial of outlooks. Steam was the motive power of imperialism, and the hissing piston was both the symbol and anthem of empire, its smooth stroke epitomizing the efficiency and thrust of a nation confident of its own mastery. Indian Railways now displays this virtue of mastery over the tracks, being the only government undertaking open to public scrutiny which is seen to work efficiently. In the history of socialist collectives, IR is perhaps the only organization that has proved size is not incompatible with profits.

From the beginning, the railways 'gave us wings'—as a character of Nathaniel Hawthorn put it—'they spiritualized travel'. They overcame the inertia and prejudice of the past and after Independence they easily outgrew any stigma of their Anglo-Indian content. One reads of five priests from Udipi who have filed an appeal with the Supreme Court, alleging that their pilgrimage to Ayodhya by rail has been interfered with by the deliberate governmental cancellation of their train. Today, those of even the most orthodox persuasion no longer find any imported stain in the lines that stretch from Karnataka to the confines of Nepal. Hinduism is the great naturalizing force and within its six systems of philosophy might be found some rationale for the efficient existence, side by side, of the six gauges of lines at the Delhi museum.

Analogies from Hindu Philosophical Schools

The broad gauge obviously represents the official line of *Advaita*

Vedanta where the hidden *atman* underpins the system and also overrides it in the pantograph of electric traction, proof that the Railways are plugged in to the source of real energy. The metre gauge came with lesser minds than Dalhousie's, unconcerned with the oneness of his transport vision. Mayo was into the numbers game and might be compared to the *Samkhya darshan* which like so many other schools of academic theology was averse neither to counting the number of angels able to take off vertically from a pinhead nor as to how many properly fed cavalry horses one could stand alongside each other to further imperial military compulsions. Possibly we can derive some traffic classifications from these ancient numerary systems. The three *gunas* (qualities), those strands of transport wisdom that combine together to make the whole, may be unravelled in the titles of classical IR numbers. Thus the Toofan Express agitates likely comparison with the quality of *rajas* (passion) while the trundling Bhojipur Shuttle epitomized the sluggard pace of *tamas* (sloth). For the *sattvic* (pure) principle we need look no further than the frenzied prohibition announcements that furnish the Rajdhani with its futile airs of self-righteousness.

The mechanically disposed might also find symbolic applications in the trio of broad gauge alternatives to Calcutta—and there is undoubted music in the ring of 'Grand Chord, Main Line and Loop Line' from Mughal Sarai. It is noticeable that many of the recently introduced Expresses are of Hindu nomenclature and hark back to Sanskritic models—*Kashi-Vishwanath Express, Prayag Raj Express*, and *Ganga-Kaveri Express*. However, to prove its evenhandedness IR also runs the Islamic titled *Gharib Nawaz Express* and *Minar Express*.

The narrow gauge lines might be deemed to possess the reduced theological standing of *Dwaita*, the lowly regarded school of dualistic thought. As with the little lines, unpopular with all pundits, the recognition of God and His creation as separate is a popular creed only with the poor man. Conveniently the narrow gauge is divided into two systems (the Z and the Q) and so too are the perceptions of those saints wedded to the doctrine of *Dwaita*. The smallest (2 ft.) gauge might qualify as grace in the image of the kitten being carried in its mother's mouth, where the devotee entirely surrenders his welfare

to the care of God. The more hardy 2 ft. 6 ins. gauge views grace more
vigorously and insists that the proper perspective is that of a young
monkey clinging to its mother's back, grace no doubt abounding but
requiring some effort from the passenger.

Paul Theroux remarked how easily the Buddhist wheel on the
national flag could be interpreted as a railway object. What he does
not mention is that in the golden age of steam the different classes of
travellers were guided to their seat by the shades of the carriage that
make up the Indian tricolour. White distinguished the first class, green
the second, and brick red, the third. The reason the latter survived when
the more colourful touches went out of vogue was due to the sooty
quality of coal used for the engines which in turn derived from the
directors concern to cut costs. The same applies today and the scruffy
YPs you see around Tinsukia in Assam, for example, are a sign of a
loss-making company while the immaculate YPs of the South Central
sheds speak of a viable line.

The constant extraction of virtue from the ore of one's travels con-
vinces the Indian rail traveller that here is a prodigious undertaking
that discharges itself, if not brilliantly, then certainly adequately and
sufficiently well to qualify as a monstrously unlikely success story.
The effective management of 62,000 kilometres of track, with all the
paraphernalia of life and property strung along its length, makes IR
the proper subject for an epic. Its heroism is not in the speed nor in the
punctuality but in the sheer accomplishment of simple duty by millions
of forgotten hands. In its research apparatus and design institutes, IR
houses many fine minds that influence and penetrate all levels of the
system. For example, in recent years India has produced a modern
Edmundson in Mr Lakshman Prasad of Aligarh. In 1984, 134 years
after Edmundson's invention, he invented the 'Numex' self-inking
railway ticket dating and timing machine (however, this inventor is
not a railwayman).

The Unique Indianness of Indian Railways

Every rail system has its own character and speaks its own national language. IR may have developed from a British model and borrowed from the Americas but it is just as pointless to look for a 'Chatanooga Choo-choo' scene in India as it would be to expect gentlemen in thirsty tropical settings to refrain from relieving themselves while the train is standing in the station on the line. The genius of Indian Railways lies in its adaptation of a foreign and potentially dangerous mode of transport to suit local conditions, making a success of a vast public enterprise by fashioning it to the unique requirements of a rambling subcontinent. It is the Indianness of the IR experience that makes for its easy running and provides positive examples of the bigness of character of the Indian railwayman. Meticulous, reliable and scientific, he is everything the tourist is taught to believe the Indian is not.

Naipaul, whose early Indian encounters caused his ancestral twice-born fantasies to plummet, still manages to find amidst all the darkness of his self-imposed blinkers a railway that seemed too good for the rest of that tumbledown nation his prejudices had weighed overnight and found instantly wanting. Dalhousie from the very beginning had predicted, 'A government always works at greater expense than anybody else', and by all capitalist theories Indian Railways should have collapsed, if not from the weight of its enormous work force, then certainly from the hundreds of unrecognized unions vying in suicidal rivalry. No amount of petty criticism of the system can shake the astounding unlikelihood of India having overcome the odds to allow her railways to flourish after the British departed. As well as manage its own rail destiny, IR has won laurels abroad for the professional way in which it set up railway lines in several disparate situations.

Theroux goes so far as to claim that India functions primarily because of her railways, which is a compliment compared to the usual American complaint that the subcontinent only yields that despairing offspring of a match between Hell and Utopia—'functioning anarchy'. In view of her colossal contradictions and cultural impasses, for India the railways are a vital symbol of functioning order. The achievement of IR has been to overcome the greatest single problem facing the nation—the negative inertia of the past. If the grisly Partition exchange of population was not even more bestial, thanks must go the functioning of the railway staff who, against impossible deprivations, managed to maintain a semblance of order and continuity. Many British officers withdrew gloating from India in the belief that efficiency and the practical challenge of running a railroad would be beyond the skills of its inheritors.

An Unlikely Tantric Anecdote

The Railways are an enduring organ of self-support entirely adapted to the Indian gait. Our attempt at teasing out some of their poetry call for their acceptance as a major *dharmic* force in the land. No doubt the only reference to rails in ancient Indian history is in the Buddhist balustrades of the Sanchi stupa but the symbol of the spoked wheel of righteousness turning in its appointed path is easily susceptible to the idea of a moral track along which the concept of *dharma*, the sustainer of human actions, runs to gather momentum. We have seen how the strict *pujaris* of Udipi invoke the Railways as part of their creed, and at the opposite end of the spectrum can be detailed similar evidence of unorthodox adoption of the iron way. Step down from the rural and formerly princely platform of Sangrur in Punjab and you enter the sweepers' lines. Railway colony architecture is robustly inegalitarian, and those of the staff not twice-born in the pages of the gazette dwell in brick huts as constricted as the accommodation of the rail pundits is rambling. A common feature of these quarters is their cement barrel roofs which march away in graceful progression, presumably easier to sketch and behold than to live in under the grilling heat. Ventilation for these grim lowly habitations at the foot of the IR pyramid is often indicated by a curved earthen pipe stuck up like a glazed periscope to announce some form of life below. Unlikely as it must sound, here is buried an English ADC to the Maharaja of Jind, who elected to have his ashes placed at the feet of his sweeper-guru. Captain Boult, though attached to a Sikh ruler, found his solace in the tantric teachings of a master whose congregation was made up of Railway *jemadars*. The tantric association is not inappropriate for the engineering marvel that Indian Railways represents. Lost for a new symbol that will soon leave behind' the plume of steam in the effective but obsolete logo,

IR's secular creed may not allow it to borrow what might seem made for the job, the *Sri-Yantra* symbol that contains within it mechanically appropriate wisdom and psychological wholeness, plus the hint of the miraculous in its squaring of the alchemic circle. The *Sri-Yantra* is a formalized rendering of the Mother Goddess and what it may lack in the absence of maternal tenderness it makes up for in the extraordinary balance of composite forces and the reconciliation of conflicting angles. It is a sign of beauty to both engineer and aesthete, a truly sacred design that rises above any sectarian marking. The idea of the Railways appearing as a feminine force is not so novel when we consider the many-handedness of the goddess and the wide array of weapons she has to bring to bear on the problems besetting our world. It is true that Hinduism has not yet promoted any particular deity to the stature of Railway god, though Vishvakarma is invoked as the patron of all skilled mechanics. This omission must be the best evidence of the secular credentials of the Railways, which in spite of many attempts to sanctify its proceedings (the early locomotives were garlanded and worshipped as minor deities) has managed to achieve a balance in the external display of regard for its working parts. Nameplates for engines, a peculiar token of British affection for the more visible steam engines, were eschewed in the Indian setting except for special occasions. A few still linger, bestowed, it seems, according to the whim of the driver.

Modern profiles of diesel 'Bo-Bos' and the slightly more personalized cabs of electric 'Co-Cos' are hardly likely to stimulate any spotting rage now that that the athletic appearance of steam has faded. India's rail affections will always remain the property of intellectual aficionados until an effort is made by IR to advertise its doings with a more human face and view its fleet as something better than mere vehicular objects. In Britain, the land of the most enthusiastic railway spotter, the sport flourished from the lighter touch of private enterprise. The leaden feet of the Railway companies refused to issue their own book of lists and caused Ian Allen to become a transport publishing giant when he began to furnish 'reference' books of trains on duty. The ominous word 'board' used to designate Indian Railway's management portal from which policy emerges, gives the unfortunate suggestion of something dense and uncomprehending. Wedded to a government culture, the top IR officials view initiative in sharing information almost as fearfully as they shun the hint of not being seen as absolutely up-to-date, irrespective of whether this fixation to be *avant-garde* is relevant to India's transport needs.

The Current Up-beat Mood

'A dirty, vile malodorous business', was how one foreign visitor remembered the railways in India century ago. But most visitors have been more than impressed by the comforts and innovations that made a long journey (at least in the upper class) seem memorable. (It happens that India was years ahead of the West in providing bathroom facilities.) If the charge of herding the poor into 'Native IIIrd' was considered the chief vice of the early days, the accusation has been satisfactorily overcome in the finely sprung second class sleeper coaches produced at Perambur and Kapurthala. The charge of promoting luxurious travel that attended the early trains still applies in the air-conditioned first class which rivals the airline companies in its fare and outdoes them in its ambience of travelling in style. (The hysterical warnings about the mental and moral fall-out from fermented spirits are mercifully absent from these compartments.) A 'national passion' was how one newspaper described the poor man's reaction to the railways as early as the 1850s, and internationally the subcontinental mail trains earned for themselves a niche in transport history by the elegance of their service and their pampering to individual tastes in toiletry. Everyone agreed that Indian station masters were a splendid body of men wielding their authority with charm and tempering difficult decisions with originality. Mark Twain records how when he was left standing on the platform after the unusually precipitate departure of his train, the station master waved his flag peremptorily and had it brought back.

By keeping abreast of the changing mood of democracy the Railways have long ceased to be the callous carrier contemptuous of the poorly-dressed passenger. Today, the roles have been reversed and too many well-dressed passengers feel they are entitled not just to

travel ticketless but comfortably in reserved and upholstered accommodation. The system that outlasted British exploitation of India's
disunited state is now approaching its severest test when the theory
of a strong centre—which the Railways have been blessed with since
Independence—is under stress. The holding up of traffic (from regional compulsions to twist the arm of New Delhi) leads not just to
loss of revenue but to the weakening of national integrity since it must,
in the long run, end with a collapse of India's fragile unity. If this
sounds alarmist, it is better to face the possibility now and to apply
weed-killer immediately rather than let disruption grow which will
eventually uproot the track and destroy the oneness of the system.

The Strength of the System

Commentators as far apart as the poet Edwin Arnold and the media
figure James Cameron have remarked how the Railways bind India
together. The author of the *Light of Asia* believed, 'Railways may do
for India what the genius of Akbar could not affect by government.
They may make India a nation.' Cameron describes the coming of the
Railways as the most important social development India has ever
experienced. By allowing family reunions, the most sacred of Indian
ties was honoured by the Railways, but just as the pole that stirs the
funeral pyre gets consumed from its exercising, so the Railways
homoeopathically delivered blows to the caste system. In appearing
to strengthen familial tradition, the inexorable lines opened up traditional minds to new ideas and made possible the ingress of both science
and adventure.

The radiant beauty of the passing countryside from a train window,
with its honest round of steady labour and the constancy of industry
rewarded amidst drought or floods by the green spread of sustained
effort, reminds us—thanks to the Railways—that India is not the
land of work-shy aspiring babus of foreign perception. Whatever the
explosive divisions that arise from disgruntled northerners forced to
face the mounds of rice that constitute the rail 'meals' of the south (or
of the southerner's distaste for wheat *chapatties*), the gap is overcome

and, as with language, where a commodity special to a region is not sought to be thrust down the throat of those from other provinces, a working compromise is arrived at. Without pushing from either quarter it is common now to find on railway stalls in the south *rumali rotis*, just as *dosas* and *idlis* have become trendy items in the north. The language promoters might take a lesson on how to encourage Hindi from the spontaneous interchange of subcontinental diets. If it does not happen naturally it can never be forced. Human attitudes when soft can absorb any possibility, but once hardened they do not allow reconsideration.

In a railway classic, Pierre Berton has described the forging of the Canadian Pacific line across a reluctant continent as 'the national dream'. The coming of this seemingly impossible line cemented an uncertain nation with a bond of self-confidence. Prior to its construction, Canada was but a conglomeration of immigrant colonies loosely bound by their loyalty to the British monarch. In India, the lines underwrote the traditional oneness that Shankaracharya had formalized in the creation of the *char dham* (the cardinal points) of orthodox Hinduism. Possibly no other living religion has been so comprehensively served by the railways and three of the four pilgrim temples of the great *Advaitin*—Puri, Dwarka, and Rameshwaram—have lines to their door. (The Himalayan outrider of Badrinath is now but a day from the railhead at Rishikesh.) Buddhist pilgrims are likewise served with convenient routes and a special train is run to cater for foreign tourists who wish to see the auspicious sites of the Enlightened One in the style of the prince of Kapilvastu. Islam similarly has some trains convenient to pilgrim traffic such as the wonderful cross-Deccan express from Ajmer to Hyderabad and, for Christians, the train from Goa to Velankani.

With greater environmental awareness and the increasingly obvious stupidity of large empty motor cars clogging city streets, the case for railed traffic grows stronger by the year. Jokes about the lateness of the trains have always been a staple of the railways, but at least the delays have not been intensified by pollution, nor does a train give rise to the special frustration that attends the driver of a Lambhorgini. (In Assam, a soldier newly arrived from Delhi heard a Japanese wartime bulletin during Christmas of 1944 which boasted of the Imperial Army being at the gates of India's capital in time for the New Year. Everyone looked towards the new arrival for his verdict on this prognostication. He shook his head gloomily and said, 'Not if they go by train'.)

Recipe for Growth

The experience of Dhiren Bhagat, a young journalist friend who died tragically in a road accident in Delhi (a victim to the absence of a railed transport system that any self-respecting metropolis should possess) illustrates the problems the Rail administration has to face. On an assignment to cover the 'Palace on Wheels' he had incorporated in his blurb the observation that 'the feudal age whatever else its shortcomings was certainly colourful'. The Rail Bhavan authorities shied away from accepting the idea that anything at any time in Indian history could have been less than perfect. They eventually forced him to agree that the only stricture on the feudal set-up acceptable to Indian Railways (which has to answer to Parliament) was that it was colourful! Such cringing postures of government servants are matched by the duplicity of their socialist ministers who try to pass off newly constructed saloons as belonging to the princely era in order to attract the dollars of foreign tourists. In his brochure, Dhiren Bhagat dared not mention the fact that the bar stools of the modern imitation coaches were covered in rexine. In the Delhi house where I write this, is the real furniture and fixtures of a royal saloon. The sofa runs for nearly eight feet and is almost three in width. The cupboards, slim by contrast, are magnificently contrived with silver door catches. Also in my possession is the railway file that goes with this saloon... The first letter from its royal owner, demanding that the Railways make a bid for it, is dated January 1958. (The saloon had been built in the NWR Workshop at Moghalpura in 1914 and cost a lakh in those days.) 100 letters, telegrams, estimates and offers later, in January 1964, the file closes with no end in sight to the negotiations over this piece of railway history. Countless appointments were made—then cancelled—for the Railway engineer to inspect the saloon, just as incessant demands were received by the ruler for demurrage and his saloon's use of railway sidings. To be fair to the Railways, it appears that many of the appointments had been cancelled owing to the Maharaja's habit of keeping a shine on the leather of his bar stool. Similar escape routes were not unknown to the Railway staff and a senior employee who had the chance of promotion to officer rank was advised by his divisional superintendent to give up the bottle if he wanted to reach a more exalted station. The employee refused the advice with the argument that after a couple of drinks he already felt like a full member of the Railway Board.

To survive the lickspittle service of officers on deputy to their own convenience; to withstand the fissiparous demands of hundreds of would-be unions in search of recognition; to outlast the procession of khadi-clad ministers and their flunkeys who are dedicated more to perks and pensions than to tracks and traction; to overcome the demoralizing behaviour of Board chairmen eager to appear grovelling when called upon to stand up for IR honour; to put up with subsidized commuters, ticketless travellers, pilferers and loss-making lines; to face endlessly the carping woes of middle-class fastidiousness and the penchant of the Press to highlight only the disasters; to bravely front the elements of flood and drought and contain a variety of human agitations —all these gauntlets the Railways have to run. That they continue to run smoothly is the best evidence of a vigorously resilient system.

A Final Recollection of In-Train Pleasures

When we weigh Wordsworth's reference to the railways as 'mischief with the promised gain', the answer is all around us in the ease of soul that rail travel still brings. 'Nor should we forget the benefit to rural genetics brought about by the railway. With less intermarrying the village idiot has disappeared.' This optimism of an early defender of the new transport mode seems belied by our current urban idiocy with stalled traffic and increasing health hazards. Rail seems to be the only answer to mass transit and the future lies with sound investment in a faster and safer permanent way. The Calcutta Metro is a splendid sign of an upswing in Railway thinking and a confident assertion that India can rise to the challenge of modern transport needs. Meanwhile the long distance pleasures continue as before. 'We rushed through a barren thirsty land and saw the peasants watering their fields and the blue jays sitting on the telegraph wires and the mud-walled villages and the buffaloes going out to the water.' Against this sunny scene witnessed by a Bengal civilian's wife from the window of a train rattling across the Plains, compare the gloomy outlook of her husband's master, Lord Curzon, as he rode the Trans-Caspian Railway a hundred years ago, as the dawn 'scarcely dissipates the impression of sadness, of desolate and hopeless decay, of a continent and life sunk in a mortal swoon.' Both are valid for the rail traveller who can never complain that he does not get his money's worth in scenic variety or food for rumination.

Whether we view life as an exciting railway journey with open access to the ends of the earth, or as a siding where we shunt away our idle hours till the scrapyard auctioneer returns us to the round-house above, the lines lie there before us, inviting the adventurous soul to sally forth and discover its destiny.

Recently, I had a letter from a friend who travelled by the T. G. V. (one of the world's fastest trains) in France. He concluded by saying he could not wait to get back to India and experience our 'filthy, ancient and reliable steam locomotives—more like the real thing'.

My own transport high that outsoared both gliding and the thrill of a Tiger Moth was to ride aboard the footplate of a WP Pacific over the Talaghat uplands to Salem in Tamil Nadu. The engine driver was an Anglo-Indian and his surname painted on the side of the cab suggested he was a relation of Lady Chatterley's gamekeeper. That run was a musical bedlam of unbridled delight, a marriage of heaven and hell, with eros and angelic hosannas rolled into one. It is true that the mere sight of a WP arouses in its admirers the most classic of penis envy symptoms, but the actual experience of many tons of metal flying flat-out controlled only by voluntary sweat, made this trip sail far beyond the notions of any physical transport. It caught the very metre of primordial poetry, it was the music of the spheres spread out in a cosmic opera: frightening, exhilarating and utterly transcendental.

'You can't imagine how strange it seemed to be journeying on thus, without any visible cause of progress than the magical machine with its flying white breath and rhythmical unvarying pace.' This was written by the first woman, Fanny Kemble, to travel on the footplate of the *Rocket* in 1830. How lucky those of us domiciled in India are, to be able to record the wonder of the last days of steam, experiencing (as the first advertisement put it)—'The benefits of railways—or the virtues of Boiling Hot Water'.

Bibliography

Historical

Allen, Charles, ed., *A Glimpse of the Burning Plains: Leaves from the Indian Journal of Charlotte Canning* (London, 1986).

Allen, G. F. and Whitehouse, P. eds., *The Illustrated History of British Railways* (London, 1981).

Berton, Pierre, *The National Dream—The Great Railway 1871–81* (Toronto, 1970).

Bhandari, R. R., *Jodhpur Railway* (New Delhi, 1982).

————, *Kalka Simla and Kangra Valley Railways* (New Delhi, 1983).

————, *Western Railway Metre Gauge System* (Baroda, 1987).

————, *The Blue Chip Railway 1887–1987* (Madras, 1987).

Chakrabarty, Nrisingha, *History of Railway Trade Union Movement*, Delhi, 1981).

Crooke, William, *Things Indian; Being Discursive Notes on Various Subjects Connected with India* (London, 1906).

Davidson, G., *The Railways of India with an Account of their Rise, Progress and Construction, Written with the Aid of the Records of the India Office* (London, 1868).

Jones, Howard, *Steam Engines, An International History* (London, 1973).

Khosla, G. S., *A History of Indian Railways* (New Delhi, 1988).

Millar, Charles, *The Lunatic Express, An Entertainment in Imperialism* (New York, 1971).

Sahni, J. N., *Indian Railways: One hundred Years* (New Delhi, 1953).

Sharma, S. N., *History of the Great Indian Peninsula Railway Part 1 (1863–69); Part 2 (1870–1900)* (Bombay, 1990).

Simmons, Jack, *The Railways of Britain* (Bristol, 1986).

Smithison, Alsion and Smithison, Peter, *The Euston Arch* (London, 1968).

Rao, M. A., *Indian Railways* (New Delhi, 1975).

Rolt, L. T. C., *Red For Danger: A History of Railway Accidents and Railway Safety, Revised by Geoffrey Kichenside* (London, 1986).

Mechanical

Ahrons, E. L., *Locomotive and Train Working in the Latter Part of the Nineteenth Century*, 6 vols. (Cambridge, 1949 et seq.).

Antia, K. F., *Railway Track: Design, Construction, Maintenance and Renewal of Permanent Way* (Bombay, 1960).

Bhandari, R. R., *Locomotives in Steam* (New Delhi, 1981).

Harrison, M. A., *Indian Locos of Yesteryear* (London, 1972).

Hollingsworth, Brian, *An Illustrated Guide to Modern Trains* (London, 1983).

————, *How to Drive a Steam Locomotive* (London, 1983).

Hughes, Hugh, Steam in India (London, 1986).

————, *Indian Locomotives, part 1, Broad guage 1851–1940* (London, 1990).

————, *Indian Locomotives, part 2, Metre Gauge 1872–1940* (London, 1992).

————, *Indian Locomotives, part 3, Narrow Gauge up to 1940* (London, 1993).

————, *Indian Locomotives, part 4, Miscellaneous Locomotives from 1940* (forthcoming).

Mackay, J. C., *Light Railways for UK, India and the Colonies. A Practical Handbook Setting Forth the Principles on Which Light Railways Should be Constructed, Worked and Financed* (London, 1896).

Railway Board, *Important Tunnels on Indian Railways* (New Delhi, 1959).

————, *Important Bridges on Indian Railways* (New Delhi, 1965).

Rolt, L. T. C., *A Hunslet Hundred* (Exeter, 1964).

Administrative

Atal, Yogesh, *Daulat Darbar; The Life Story of a Retired Railway Station Master* (New Delhi, 1988).

Cooper, B. K., *Modern Railway Working* (London, 1957).

Da Costa, Francis, *Introduction to Railway Operation* (Saharanpur, 1991).

Ghose, S. K., *Railway Pension Rules and Retirement Benefits* (Saharanpur, 1991).

Khosla, G. S., *Railway Management in India* (Bombay, 1972).

Matta, R. P., *Railway Accidents: Causes and Preventions* (Saharanpur, 1992).

Natesan, L. A., *Regrouping of Railways* (New Delhi, 1951).

Nock, O. S., *Railways of Asia and the Far East* (New Delhi, 1980).

Saxsena, K. K., *Indian Railways; Problems and Prospects* (Bombay, 1962).

Official Publications

Directorate of Safety, *Safety Performance 1991–92* (New Delhi, 1992).

Ministry of Law and Justice, *The Railway Act 1989* (New Delhi 1989).
Ministry of Railways, *Indian Railways Year Book* (New Delhi, annual).
————, *Annual Report and Accounts* (New Delhi, annual).
————, *Status Paper on Indian Railways: Some Issues and Options* (New Delhi, 1990).
————, *Report on the Judicial Inquiry into the Cause of the Accident to Train No. 603 Tuticorin Express between Ariyalur and Kallagam stations on the Southern Railway on 23rd November 1956 by Shri Himsu Kumar Bose, Judge, High Court Calcutta* (New Delhi, 1958).
Railway Board, *All India Railway Timetable* (New Delhi, now discontinued).
————, *Trains at a Glance; Abstract of Mail and Express Timings* (New Delhi, biannual).
————, *Indian Railways* (New Delhi, monthly).
————, *Facts and Figures* (New Delhi, 1987).
————, *Rail Travel Concession Guide*; illustrated (New Delhi, 1989).
————, *Passenger Handbook*; illustrated (New Delhi, 1989).
————, *Mini-timetable*, fold-out (New Delhi, 1989).
Regional Railway Headquarters, *Zonal Timetables* (biannual).
Survey of India, *Railway Map of India*, eleventh edition (Dehra Dun, 1981).

Background Reading

Anderson, R. G. W., *Science in India*, catalogue (London, 1982).
Arora, A. K. and Misra, B. S., *Nehru and Indian Railways* (New Delhi, 1989).
BBC, *Great Railway Journeys of the World* (London, 1981).
————, *Great Little Railways* (London, 1984).
Betjeman, John, *London's Historic Railway Stations* (London, 1972).
Birdwood, G. C., *The Arts of India* (New Delhi, 1988).
Dethier, Jean, *All Stations: A Journey Through 150 Years* (London, 1981).
Ellis, Royston, *India By Rail* (London, 1989).
Garratt, Colin, *Around The World in Search of Steam* (London, 1987).
Hollingsworth, Brian, *The Pleasures of Railways: A Journey By Train Through the Delectable Country of Enthusiasm for Railways* (London, 1993).
Kennedy, Ludovic, *A Book of Railway Journeys* (London, 1981).
Lardner, Dionysius, *Railway Economy; a Treatise on the New Art of Transport. Its management, Prospects and Relations–Commercial, Financial and Social, with an exposition of the practical results of the railways in operation in the United Kingdom, on the Continent and in America.* (London, 1850).
————, *Dr Lardner on the Steam Engine* (London, 1850).
Marshall, John, ed., *The Guinness Railway Book* (London, 1989).

Nock, O. S., *Pocket Encyclopaedia of British Steam Railways and Locomotives* (London, 1986).
Northern Railways, *Rail Transport Museum*, catalogue (New Delhi, 1980).
Religious Tract Society, *Every Boy's Book of Railways and Steamships* (London, c. 1914).
Rolt, L. T. C., *George and Robert Stephenson* (Harmondsworth, 1978).
Satow, Michael, and Desmond, Ray, *Railways of the Raj* (London, 1980).
Simmons, Jack, *Dandy Cart to Diesel: The National Railway Museum York*, catalogue (London, 1981).
Southern Railways, *Mysore Rail Museum*, catalogue (Mysore, 1980).
Theroux, Paul, *The Great Railway Bazaar. By Train Through Asia* (London, 1977).
————, *Riding The Iron Rooster. By Train Through China* (Harmondsworth, 1989).
Theroux, Paul and McCurry, Steve, *The Imperial Way: Making Tracks from Peshawar to Chittagong* (London, 1985).
Vaughan, Adrian, *Obstruction Danger: Signficicant British Railway Accidents 1890–1986.* (London, 1989).
Westood, J. N., *Railways of India* (Newton Abbot, 1973).
Williams, Alan, ed., *Purnell's Pictorial Encyclopaedia of Trains and Railways* (London, 1978).
Wood, Heather, *Third-Class Ticket* (Harmondsworth, 1984).

Literary References

(non-fiction)

Corbett, Jim, *My India* (London, 1989).
Gandhi, Mahatma, *An Autobiography or The Story of My Experiments With Truth* (Ahmedabad, 1927).
————, *Hind Swaraj* (Ahmedabad, 1938).
Devi, Maharani Gayatri, with Rao, Santha Rama, *A Princess Remembers: The Memoirs of the Maharani of Jaipur* (Delhi, 1976).
Nehru, Jawaharlal, *The Discovery of India* (Delhi, 1981).
Newby, Eric, *A Book of Travellers Tales* (London, 1985).
Palling, Bruce, *India; A Literary Companion* (Delhi, 1992).
Panter-Downes, Mollie, *Ooty Preserved: A Victorian Hill Station in India* (London, 1967).
Naipaul, V. S., *An Area of Darkness* (London, 1964).
————, *A Wounded Civilisation* (London, 1979).
Wolpert, Stanley, *An Introduction to India* (Delhi, 1991).

(fiction)

Bond, Ruskin, *The Night Train at Deoli and Other Stories* (New Delhi, 1988).
Bond, Ruskin, *Anthology of Railway Stories* (New Delhi, forthcoming).

Brooks, J. A., *Railway Ghosts* (London, 1985).
Dickens, Charles, *Dombey and Son* (London, 1898).
————, *Hard Times* (London, 1854).
Forster, E. M., *A Passage to India* (London, 1926).
Hubbard, Freeman, *Railroad Avenue* (Golden West, USA, 1945).
Lever, Charles, *Tales of the Trains: Some Chapters of Railroad Romance* (London, 1882).
Masters, John, *Bhowani Junction* (London, 1954).
Milligan, Spike, *Transports of Delight* (London, 1975).
Rudyard Kipling, *Kim* (London, 1901).
Singh, Khushwant, *Train to Pakistan* (New Delhi, 1988).

Miscellaneous Railwayana

Alphabetical List of Indian Railway Stations or All India Railway Distance Table (Saharanpur, annual).
Bahri's Handbook for Railwaymen (New Delhi, annual).
Calculated Fare Table: Supplement to Distance Ready Reckoner (Delhi, annual).
Chandra, Jag Parvesh, *Delhi is Doomed Without Metro* (New Delhi, 1993).
Granada, *The Making of 'Jewel in The Crown'* (New York, 1983).
India: A Travel Survival Guide (South Yarra, Victoria, 1981).
Indian Railways, *Rail Yatri*; in-train magazine (discontinued).
Manorama Year Book (Trivandrum, annual).
Mitra, Mrinal, *My First Railway Journey* (New Delhi, 1986).
Newman's Indian Bradshaw (Calcutta, monthly).
New Revised Railway Rules Handbook (Saharanpur, annual).
Railway Board, '*Rel Pari Ki Kahani*' (Rail Fairy), (New Delhi, 1989).
Rao, Amiya, and Rao, B. G., *The Press She Could Not Whip: Emergency in India As Reported by the Foreign Press* (Bombay, 1977).
Singh, Jagjit, *The Story of Our Railways* (New Delhi, 1971).
Vaidyanathan, K. R., *A Train Load of Jokes and Anecdotes* (Delhi, 1992).

Index